Cognitive Computing Recipes

Artificial Intelligence Solutions Using Microsoft Cognitive Services and TensorFlow

Adnan Masood
Adnan Hashmi

Foreword by Matt Winkler

Apress®

Cognitive Computing Recipes

Adnan Masood
Stanford, CA, USA

Adnan Hashmi
Nashville, TN, USA

ISBN-13 (pbk): 978-1-4842-4105-9
https://doi.org/10.1007/978-1-4842-4106-6

ISBN-13 (electronic): 978-1-4842-4106-6

Managing Director, Apress Media LLC: Welmoed Spahr
Acquisitions Editor: Susan McDermott/Shiva Ramachandran
Development Editor: Laura Berendson
Coordinating Editor: Divya Modi

Cover designed by eStudioCalamar

Cover image designed by Freepik (www.freepik.com)

Distributed to the book trade worldwide by Springer Science+Business Media New York, 233 Spring Street, 6th Floor, New York, NY 10013. Phone 1-800-SPRINGER, fax (201) 348-4505, email orders-ny@springer-sbm.com, or visit www.springeronline.com. Apress Media, LLC is a California LLC and the sole member (owner) is Springer Science + Business Media Finance Inc (SSBM Finance Inc). SSBM Finance Inc is a **Delaware** corporation.

For information on translations, please email rights@apress.com or visit http://www.apress.com/rights-permissions.

Apress titles may be purchased in bulk for academic, corporate, or promotional use. eBook versions and licenses are also available for most titles. For more information, reference our Print and eBook Bulk Sales web page at http://www.apress.com/bulk-sales.

Any source code or other supplementary material referenced by the author in this book is available to readers on GitHub via the book's product page, located at www.apress.com/978-1-4842-4105-9. For more detailed information, please visit http://www.apress.com/source-code.

Printed on acid-free paper

To my family.

—*Adnan Masood*

To my motherland.

—*Adnan Hashmi*

Table of Contents

About the Authors

Dr. Adnan Masood is an artificial intelligence and machine learning researcher, visiting scholar at Stanford AI Lab, software engineer, and Microsoft MVP (Most Valuable Professional) for Artificial Intelligence. As chief architect of AI and machine learning at UST Global, he collaborates with Stanford Artificial Intelligence Lab and MIT CSAIL, as well as leads a team of data scientists and engineers in building artificial intelligence solutions to produce business value and insights that affect a range of businesses, products, and initiatives.

Throughout his career, Dr. Masood has been a trusted advisor to the C-suite, from Fortune 500 companies to startups. Author of Amazon bestseller in programming languages *Functional Programming with F#*, Adnan teaches data science at Park University and has taught Windows WCF courses at UCSD. He is an international speaker to academic and technology conferences, code camps, and user groups. Dr. Masood volunteers as STEM robotics coach for elementary and middle school students. He lives in Florida and is in constant pursuit to become better at *Fortnite* than his two sons, Zakariya and Ali.

Adnan Hashmi has 20 years' experience in the technology industry working with a host of clients in healthcare, finance, construction, and consulting. He currently works at Microsoft in the data and AI space, engaging with financial services clients. He holds a master's degree in software engineering from the Shaheed Zulfikar Ali Bhutto Institute of Science & Technology (SZABIST), Karachi, Pakistan, and is passionate about machine learning, music, and education.

Acknowledgments

A significant amount of work has gone into writing this manuscript, with both direct and indirect contributions coming from a lot of people. First and foremost, we would like to thank our editors and technical reviewers for their tireless efforts in making sense of our writing—a daunting task, indeed.

We would like to show our genuine gratitude toward the Microsoft Azure AI and Cognitive Services teams, without whom this book would not have been possible. We are especially grateful to Matt Winkler, GPM machine learning, cloud+AI platform; Noelle LaCharite, DX cognitive services; Jennifer Marsman, principal engineer, Wee Hyong, head of AI prototyping and innovation and AI; Lili Cheng, CVP Microsoft AI and research; Frank Seide for CNTK; Danielle Dean, principal data scientist lead; Steve "Guggs" Guggenheimer, CVP AI business; and Joseph Sirosh, CVP & CTO of AI, for his vision and leadership; as well as to all the unsung heroes of the Cognitive Services team who make this amazing API possible. Kudos to y'all.

We would also like to thank the Microsoft AI MVP community, including Microsoft's Daniel Egan, who organized and delivered great talks; Soliance's Zoiner Tejada, an overall Azure and AI superhero and Microsoft regional director; and Joe Darko, our community program manager, for his never-ending energy, help, and support. Thanks to future AI leaders from the Stanford NLP group, Siva Reddy, Danqi Chen, and Abi See, for their patience in listening to me go on and on about natural language problems.

AI is a fast-moving field, and the following luminaries have provided amazing thought leadership. Thanks go to the brain trust of deep learning and machine learning, Yoshua Bengio, Geoffrey Hinton, Andrej Karpathy, Fei Fei Li, Ian Goodfellow, Andew Ng, Yann LeCun, and Chris Manning, for making a dent in the universe. Thanks go also to Microsoft's James McCaffrey for his wonderful MSDN columns on AI, as well as to Aurélien Geron, François Chollet, Brandon Rohrer, and Joel Grus for their comprehensive references. We surely have missed a few people, but like a good LSTM (Long Short Term Memory) model, you don't need to remember everything to go forward.

Foreword

If one drives east from Seattle, there isn't far to go before encountering fields of wind turbines. These giant machines stretch across the rolling hills and plains generating power from the constant winds blowing over the landscape. Each of these turbines generates a tremendous amount of data. That data is used to power machine learning models which enable the turbines and wind farms to operate more efficiently, more safely, and with fewer interruptions. As new versions of models are deployed, a new set of data is created, which allows for assessment and understanding of how the models are perfuming, which in turn enables better models to be deployed. Windmills have been tools for hundreds of years to harness the power of the wind, and today, every day, they are getting more efficient, safer, and easier to manage because of machine learning.

The technology industry is abuzz these days with the power, the promise, and the concerns regarding machine learning. The history of machine learning is richly intertwined with computer science, indeed, many of the earliest applications of computers were to mimic the human thought process. Techniques like regression, classification, and clustering have been tools used by data analysts and scientists for decades to solve problems around forecasting, customer segmentation, churn analysis, anomaly detection and more. The Internet is built on machine learning, search engines like Bing and Google have pioneered new ways to analyze massive amounts of text and media, index it, and understand the context and intent behind a search query to match users to the results that are the most relevant to them. It's natural for one to ask, "what's the big deal, why now?" First, consider the impact this can have, on applications, data, and devices.

Software will be made more personal, more interactive, powered by machine learning. Simply put, apps of all shapes and sizes will benefit from being able to understand the world around them, and being able to understand and anticipate the needs of users. My favorite new feature of PowerPoint analyzes lists, and if dates are found, suggests transforming that list into a timeline view. A simple thing, yet saving each of us minutes on every presentation, every slide that we build. This example speaks to the way every developer will be able to transform their application, making their users more efficient.

Machine learning does not exist without data. Whether in bulk or in streams, models are trained, evaluated, and improved through data. Machine learning lets us extract much greater value out of data of all shapes and sizes. Machine learning can even be used to enrich data. Consider the most recent code that you wrote dealing with user input. Odds are, it dealt with numerical values, or relatively short string values. Modern programming languages are incredibly powerful and efficient when dealing with those data types. Expand that out a little bit, to images, video, sounds, or large volumes of text. What data types exist to reason on these, not just manipulate them? Machine learning enriches data by letting us address a larger variety of data, and by transforming it into things that can be reasoned over in code. Cognitive APIs, like Microsoft's Cognitive Services make it easy to take an image and break it into component parts. Want to know what's in the image, how many people are in it, are they happy? All of that is available to you with a simple HTTP method. The output of that easily goes into our programs to make a decision, such as adjusting a thermostat based on the number of people in a room.

Devices are becoming smarter, and in many cases, more connected. Machine learning models, built on data observed from those devices, enable better understanding of the device and the environment around it. This enables more efficient devices to be built, future designs to be influenced, but more importantly, can be used to predict failures or identify anomalies. The "digital exhaust" from these devices is valuable, not only for training new models, but also for being able to provide a mechanism to evaluate the impact and outcome of models currently deployed. This stream of exhaust is key to creating the virtuous cycle of model development, improvement, and improvements in outcomes.

One of the most inspiring examples of this is Microsoft's AI for Earth initiative, which looks to provide grant funding to organizations leveraging AI to advance sustainability. I've had the opportunity to interact with a number of the grantees, and the stories of how they are transforming the way we consume, conserve, and manage natural resources remind us of the power of software as a force for good. Every industry is being transformed, and that is being powered by machine learning.

The other key aspect of "Why now," is the cloud. The emergence of plentiful, and powerful, compute capacity in the cloud, along with the hardware and software innovations in the GPU space has helped to foster a massive wave of innovation, with much of that coming in the area of deep learning. The fundamentals behind deep learning are not new, neural networks modeling the functionality of the neurons in the brain originated in the middle of the last century. Three things needed to come together to begin the latest wave of innovation: algorithmic advancements, processing power, and data. The cloud brings this, making it easier, faster, and more affordable to get started and grow as large as one needs.

Fundamental to this is understanding both the techniques and tools available to you. Machine learning involves more than simply learning a new library, or even a new programming language. It involves understanding the tools and techniques, and constantly applying and refining development against data. The first step in this journey is diving in, and beginning to learn. Congratulations on picking this book up and doing it. It's an incredible time to be a developer, with the pace and scale of innovation available in the cloud to power machine learning development. Each major cloud vendor is deeply investing in data, machine learning, and AI technologies, and it's time to take advantage of that. In this text, Adnan and Adnan walk through that journey, from leveraging cognitive APIs, to developing chat oriented applications, and finally, to building custom machine learning models, with insight into the most popular frameworks. I can't wait to see what you build.

Matt Winkler

Group Engineering Manager—Microsoft Azure

Woodinville, Washington

Preface

The hype around disruptive new technologies travels from the peak of inflated expectations to the valley of disillusionment until it hits its stride in the plateau of productivity. This journey is often counterproductive, and AI and machine learning are not an exception to this rule. The jury is still out on why it is called *deep-learning hype* and not *backpropaganda*, but I digress. It is safe to say that the ubiquitous nature of machine learning–based applications enables today's commerce and innovation. As one discerns what is possible with AI for one's business, the concrete use cases are no longer limited by lack of vision and instead become quite evident. This figurative leap of faith requires a future-oriented growth mindset and thought leadership. We quickly see the key concerns from C-suite start with Why AI, quickly followed by How and then When!

This book you are holding is written with the motive of exploring the art of the possible with its readers. This manuscript is by no means perfect; however, it intends to give you tools and an understanding of the contemporary AI landscape. Intelligent correlation using AI and machine learning helps companies achieve richer search experiences; where and how to use this to accomplish real productivity gains requires *you*, the domain expert, to connect your business use case with the algorithms and models. AI data insights and discovery are transforming customer service into a science where previously there was only art. I implore you to explore novel use cases across the spectrum, such as bias-free product-recommendation engines, detection of potential predatory tactics with natural language annotations, contract analysis to augment and accelerate the discovery process, inventory monitoring and analysis using computer vision, and digital assistants that can comprehend, summarize, and answer queries on diverse enterprise corpora; the possibilities are bounded only by your imagination.

Enterprise-grade AI search is helping enterprises cut through the fog of uncertainty, helping in product development, and extracting real business value by intelligent process compression.

Let's embark on the AI-first journey of *scholastic* gradient descent.

Adnan Masood, PhD

Chief Architect AI & Machine Learning—Microsoft MVP (Artificial Intelligence); visiting scholar, Department of Computer Engineering, Stanford University.

In Praise of Cognitive Computing Recipes

"The key to unlocking a digital future is approaching the same problems with a new, AI-first mindset. Several industries are now ripe for disruption and leaders are looking for pragmatic ways to incorporate AI into their enterprise, Masood walks the reader through tactical ways to operationalize AI and the importance of democratizing a technology that once seemed like a distant vision."

—Rajiv Ronaki

Leader of Anthem's Digital and AI transformation

SVP and Chief Digital Officer. Anthem, Inc.

In recent years, Artificial Intelligence (AI), and Machine Learning (ML) in particular, is creating increasing impact on our industry and culture. With a comprehensive coverage on AI solutions based on two popular platforms – Microsoft Cognitive Services and Google's TensorFlow, this book provides a timely development guide based on cognitive service APIs, machine learning platforms, and contemporary open source libraries, and tools. In addition, the book utilizes many use cases in computer vision, text analytics, speech, and robotics process automation to facilitate the exploration of learning algorithms. This is a much-needed book for engineers, academics, hobbyists, and enterprise architects who wish to build AI/ML into real-world business applications.

—Wei Li, Ph.D.

Professor in Computer Science

College of Engineering and Computing

Nova Southeastern University

"Machine learning, AI, and data science are disrupting every industry through technologies like natural language processing, computer vision, robotics, and data analytics. This book enables executives and practitioners to understand the application and impact of these technologies in their businesses."

—Dr. S. J. Eglash,

University Research Administrator

In the absence of the singularity where AI reaches a general intelligence on par with humans, people will be called on to make AI intelligent. Today many of those folks are data scientists, but there simply are not enough of them now and there are not expected to be in the near future. It is critical that developers systematically learn the skills to integrate and develop AI solutions. Cognitive Computing Recipes should be required reading for every modern developer to become pragmatic AI developers.

—Zoiner Tajeda
CEO Soliance
Microsoft Regional Director

It may seem that AI is everywhere already from digital assistants (Cortana, Siri etc.) to autonomous vehicles and threat intelligence in cybersecurity landscape. In reality we are effectively just scratching the surface. Most enterprises are starting their journeys on leveraging the power of AI via Machine Learning and Deep Learning to drive true digital transformation. Dr. Adnan Masood and Adnan Hashmi have done a great job of taking a breadth first approach to help you understand key use cases (including Industry scenarios) and learn the use of Microsoft Cognitive Services and TensorFlow in a bite-sized and easy to understand manner.

—Hammad Rajjoub
Director, Microsoft 365 Security - Global Black Belt Company
Microsoft Corporation

We are at a point in time where AI holds great potential, and will touch the lives of many. However, there is a risk that AI expertise will lie in the hands of the few – for example those at elite universities, or in powerful tech companies. Instead, we need people from all backgrounds to approach AI from many different angles. This book, which demystifies AI through practical examples, is a timely resource in the valuable quest to make AI more accessible for all.

—Abigail See
Doctoral Student
Stanford University

Introduction

When we first embarked on the journey of authoring a book on AI and cognitive computing, we realized that we had a short runway but a long road ahead of us, in part because the technology and platforms are evolving at a very rapid pace—so much so that certain sections and screenshots had to be updated right before the book went into publishing. We would not be surprised if, by the time this book reaches you, many more technology changes have been released, warranting updates to some of the content and/or screenshots. However, the intent of this book is not to simply impart knowledge of specific platforms or technologies. In talking to many business customers about building enterprise AI solutions, the one question that customers ask right off the bat is *"How do we get started?"*, which is what we intend (and hope) to answer through this book.

As organizations and businesses undergo technological transformation using AI, it would not be far-fetched to say that all organizations are technology, and specifically AI, companies. However, any business engaged in building AI capabilities should not get side-tracked from its original purpose, which is to provide the best products and services to its customers. This is precisely why the development of AI solutions should focus on rapid development and quick release cycles, and the best way to achieve that is to use tools, technologies, and platforms that enable fast provisioning, data ingestion, model training, testing, and deployment. And that is where this book comes in. We want to provide readers with a way to avoid steep learning curves and instead to learn AI by developing real-life solutions that can be implemented in an enterprise. That said, the book is not intended to serve as a manual for building and deploying AI solutions in an organization. The objective is to demonstrate AI capabilities using a problem–solution approach. Once the readers can connect all the dots by following a recipe, they can quickly apply that knowledge to use cases and problems within their own organizations.

If you are just starting on your AI journey but feel lost in all the technical jargon, mathematical concepts, and platform discussions, this book is for you. Even if you have prior experience in machine learning and AI and want to apply that knowledge to common business use cases, this book can serve as an excellent resource.

With the exception of Chapters 1 and 8, the book follows the problem–solution recipe format, beginning with articulating the problem, then presenting a solution, and finally describing how the solution works and/or the set of steps needed to develop that solution. Chapters 2 to 7 each deal with a different aspect or category of AI solutions, finally culminating in a discussion about actual AI use cases and solutions in Chapter 8. A quick overview of each chapter is provided here:

Chapter 1 provides a quick overview of AI frameworks and Microsoft's efforts toward the democratization of AI using cognitive services.

Chapter 2 dives into the use cases and development of chatbots to allow for conversational user interfaces.

Chapter 3 focuses on the development of custom vision solutions to extract information and knowledge from images.

Chapter 4 presents solutions for natural language processing (NLP) problems within the enterprise, dealing with vast amounts of textual information that is present in almost every organizational landscape.

Chapter 5 delves into robotics process automation (RPA) recipes using AI and cognitive services.

Chapter 6 is intended to address many of the questions and issues around making enterprise search more effective.

Chapter 7 presents recipes for using AI to automate and simplify many of the cumbersome and manual processes pertaining to operations.

Chapter 8 describes some of the real-life AI use cases by industry and presents solutions to address them.

We hope we can simplify many of the complex AI concepts for you in the pages that follow, and that you find this book useful as you embark on your AI journey. All the best!

CHAPTER 1

Democratization of AI Using Cognitive Services

"As soon as it works, no-one calls it AI anymore."

—John McCarthy, *Superintelligence: Paths, Dangers, Strategies*

"The fundamental need of every person is to be able to use their time more effectively, not to say, 'let us replace you.' This year and the next will be the key to democratizing AI. The most exciting thing to me is not just our own promise of AI as exhibited by these products, but to take that capability and put it in the hands of every developer and every organization."

—Staya Nadella, CEO. Microsoft Corporation

Unless one dwells under a rock, the disruption "havoc" that artificial intelligence, machine learning, and deep learning have been wreaking in different industries, verticals, and human lives cannot go unnoticed. When you ask Alexa to turn off the lights and set the thermostat to a comfortable 67 degrees so you can cozy up to read this book, you are making use of a multitude of machine-learning and deep-learning technologies, from speech recognition to IoT and natural language understanding and processing. It has been said that the best technologies are the ones that run in the background, delivering a seamless human experience and value; artificial intelligence is quickly emerging to be the ambient caretaker.

In his recent book, *Life 3.0*, MIT professor, researcher, and futurist Max Tegmark defines intelligence as the "ability to accomplish complex goals." This seemingly simple definition is quite profound when we explore the core concept of what a goal entails.

© Adnan Masood, Adnan Hashmi 2019
A. Masood and A. Hashmi, *Cognitive Computing Recipes*, https://doi.org/10.1007/978-1-4842-4106-6_1

Consider Bostrom's canonical thought experiment of a paperclip maximizer—an artificial general intelligence (AGI) goal that has no intentional malice but in which, in the words of Eliezer Yudkowsky, author of *Artificial Intelligence as a Positive and Negative Factor in Global Risk*, "the AI does not hate you, nor does it love you, but you are made out of atoms which it can use for something else."

Besides building human-level AGI and unleashing this superintelligence to take over the world, our goal in this chapter is to introduce the reader to the concept of the democratization of artificial intelligence and to the taxonomy around machine learning and deep learning, as well as to establish a business case for artificial intelligence, followed by examining how AI is being used in the enterprise. Abstract thought experiments are fine, but we intend to concentrate on the fact that machine learning is significantly impacting different industry sectors, and providing monetization opportunities through digital transformation. Then, we will investigate the daunting alphabet soup of machine-learning and deep-learning technologies, as well as the underlying on-premises and cloud platform and library offerings.

Machine learning can be defined as a sophisticated curve-fitting exercise. Formally, Arthur Samuel defines it as a

> *field of study that gives computers the ability to learn without being explicitly programmed.*

Another canonical definition widely used is attributed to Tom Mitchell, who states that

> *a computer program is said to learn from experience E with respect to some task T and some performance measure P, if its performance on T, as measured by P, improves with experience E.*

Machine learning is one way of implementing artificial intelligence, but certainly not the only way. Typical machine-learning algorithms include linear and logistic regression decision trees, support vector machines, naive Bayes, k nearest neighbors, K-means clustering, and random forest gradient boosting algorithms, including GBM, XGBoost, LightGBM, and CatBoost (no relationship with Nyan Cat).

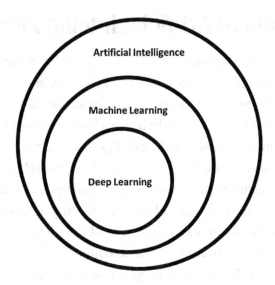

Another approach to implementing artificial intelligence is via deep learning, which some may classify as a sub-field of machine learning. Most recently, known as being the notorious power behind building Deep Fakes (technique used to create fake images or videos by super-imposing faked image or video content onto the existing actual images or videos), deep learning is a game-changing technology which empowers autonomous cars, enabling these driverless machines to recognize a tree or a stop sign and to distinguish a pedestrian from an obstacle on the street. Deep learning enables automatic game playing in AlphaGo and can also predict system uptime and availability, as well as where a training model contains attributes from application telemetry, server logs, and seasonality analysis. Today, voice recognition in consumer devices and cognitive digital assistants such as cell phones and speakers is powered by deep learning.

If the distinctions between AGI, AI, machine learning, and deep learning are not crystal clear by now, you are in good company. As you move forward with the available platforms, recipes, and implementations, it will become clear via the examples which technology and tools fit in which bucket. It's a gradual process. As you implement your own solutions and recipes, slowly moving from hype to deployment, you will figure out which of the feature are relevant and which features are just noise. You will make a mental decision tree of which algorithm should be chosen. As Cathy Bessant, chief operations and technology officer at Bank of America said "AI isn't just technology, it's good judgment."

Democratization of Artificial Intelligence

There's Keras, Theano (RIP), Watson, vowpal wabbit, SpaCY, TensorFlow, Azure Cognitive Services, PyTorch, Cuda, H2O.ai, CoreML, MxNet, and more. Ay-ay-ay!

No wonder this is a lot to take in for a beginner. First, they must figure out what all these scary-looking names mean besides being cast members on *Mr. Robot*. The next logical questions become the following: How do I get started in the artificial-intelligence and machine-learning space? How do I become a data scientist? Do you know the way? Practitioners constantly fielding these queries know that making sense of the useful technologies found in the dizzying array of new developments is indeed a difficult problem, for both individuals and organizations of all sizes. The alphabet soup of rapidly evolving three-letter acronyms, toolsets, SDKs, and libraries invading the development ecosystem is the new norm. There is a real gap in machine-learning skill sets, and it does make sense to ask how to get started in this swiftly-changing field.

Even though getting started with AI and machine learning can be harder than it seems since there are many different learning paths to choose from, organizations are working hard to help ease this learning curve. The term *democratization of artificial intelligence* refers to an effort to make machine-learning development accessible for the larger set of developers. The way Microsoft puts it, "take it [AI] from the ivory towers and make it accessible for all."

When it comes to "democratized AI," we can easily classify machine-learning and deep-learning offerings into three logical categories: cloud-based, on-premises, and hybrid models. Let's first review the machine-learning libraries and SDKs before looking into the platform offerings. We also recommend checking out Deep Learning Framework Examples at github, which is made with the intent of creating a Rosetta stone of deep-learning frameworks.[1]

Machine-Learning Libraries

Over the years, several different open source deep-learning frameworks have been introduced. The following is by no means a comprehensive overview of all these toolkits or machine-learning techniques. There is a summarized version of the machine-learning schools of thought provided as part of the "Five Tribes of Machine Learning" section of this chapter. Here, we mainly focus on platforms and libraries

---

[1]https://github.com/ilkarman/DeepLearningFrameworks

primarily associated with deep learning. Theano was really the first widely adopted deep-learning library and is maintained by the University of Montreal. Last September, it was announced that they would stop developing for Theano. Currently, TensorFlow seems to be the most-used deep-learning library based on the number of GitHub stars and forks as well as based on Stack Overflow activity. However, there are other libraries that are growing passionate user bases. PyTorch is a notable example and was introduced in January 2017 by Facebook. It was a port to Python of a popular Torch framework written in Lua. PyTorch's popularity is the result of its use of dynamic computation graphs as opposed to static graphs. In addition to PyTorch, Facebook also open-sourced Caffe2 and declared it a "New Lightweight, Modular, and Scalable Deep Learning Framework."

Microsoft launched its own cognitive toolkit, or Computational Network Toolkit (CNTK), an open source deep-learning toolkit created by Microsoft Speech researchers, in 2012. It has been available on GitHub since January 2016 (MIT license) and is being used by Bing Cortana, HoloLens, Office, and Skype. Over 80 percent of Microsoft's internal deep-learning workload is based off CNTK which enjoys a first-class citizen status on both Linux and Windows, with docker support. CNTK has rich API support, is mostly implemented in C++ (training and evaluating), and provides both low- and high-level Python APIs as well as R and C# APIs for training and evaluation. CNTK has UWP, Java, and Spark support, while the Keras backend support is in beta. CNTK supports model compression and is part of the ONNX ecosystem, discussed next.

Among all these different developments that look like proprietary silos, Facebook and Microsoft introduced a new open ecosystem for interchangeable AI frameworks called the Open Neural Network Exchange (ONNX) format. ONNX has been introduced as a standard for "representing deep learning models that enables models to be transferred between frameworks." This helps developers, who can now train their model in one framework but then serve it in production in a different one. ONNX as an open format represents deep-learning models and is currently supported by CNTK, PyTorch, Caffe 2, and MxNet to enable interoperability between frameworks.

While ONNX is a neural network exchange format for models, Keras is effectively an interface that wraps multiple frameworks. François Chalet, a deep-learning researcher at Google, created and maintains Keras. Keras is a high-level neural networks API, is written in Python, and is capable of running on top of TensorFlow, CNTK, or Theano. Google announced Keras was chosen as the official high-level API of TensorFlow.

Current State of Machine-Learning & Deep-Learning Platforms

Like Microsoft, other vendors, including IBM, Apple, Facebook, and Google, offer machine-learning platforms to make life easier for developers. When all is said and done, TensorFlow is the clear winner as it is the one with the most GitHub stars, the largest ecosystem, and the highest number of users. You cannot argue with success, case in point being PHP.

By definition, a comprehensive machine-learning platform provides algorithms, APIs, starter kits, development and training toolkits, training and testing datasets, as well as MLDLC (machine-learning development lifecycle) guidelines. The team data-science process of Microsoft makes a fitting example of how the data-science process meets software-development lifecycle best practices, including source control, versioning, and so on. The democratization of the platform also makes it easy for developers to get up to speed; hence, no manual installations and setups. It's a one-stop shop providing the computing power to design, clean up data, train models, and deploy in staging and production to containers, applications, services, and so forth.

Another aspect of such a democratization platform is the provisioning of AI-optimized hardware. GPU-, TPU-, and FPGA-powered computing is not for the faint-hearted. The hardware, designed and architected to efficiently run deep learning–based computational jobs, is expensive to build and maintain. Therefore, it is typically in the best interest of individual developers and startups to utilize the already-built systems.

Microsoft AI Portfolio comprises four key areas: Agent, Applications, Service, and Infrastructure. For the agent, Microsoft bets on Cortana, and rightfully so. Who else can tell you hilarious jokes like the following:

> *"What do Winnie the Pooh and Ivan the Terrible have in common? The same middle name."*

Who else will decide to interrupt in the middle of the conversation as if it just heard you saying "Hey Cortana"? The "application" pillar of the four key areas includes virtually all desktop applications, office apps, and .net or core applications. In lieu of services, Microsoft's AI ecosystem comprises Bot Framework, Cognitive Services, Cortana Intelligence Suite, and Cognitive Toolkit (CNTK). The agent in command being Cortana, the Microsoft bot environment is serendipitously called Bot Framework. The Cognitive Services offering contains vision, speech, language, knowledge, and search

APIs, among others. The machine-learning tools include Azure ML and Cognitive Toolkit (CNTK), and the augmented reality counterpart is HoloLens. Finally, the infrastructure services contain Azure Machine Learning, Azure N Series, and FPGAs to provide best-in-class training support for complex machine-learning and deep-learning models.

Amazon also has a large AI offering and uses Alexa as its' agent. When it's not secretly and creepily laughing at your dad jokes, Alexa works very well. Amazon Lex is the bot framework, while the cognitive offering of recognition is focused on deep learning-based image analysis. Amazon Polly is the text-to-speech engine, while Apache MxNet is the deep-learning framework powering the cognitive services.

Apple's Siri is probably one of the most well-known digital assistants as it is available with virtually all Apple products, including phone, tablets, and computers. With SiriKit being an integrated bot framework, Apple's CoreML library helps integrate machine-learning models into the application. Apple's approach for Core ML supports Vision for image analysis, natural-language processing, and Gameplay Kit, which integrates well with the iOS application ecosystem.

Facebook offers Facebook Messenger as its agent or digital assistant, ParlAI as a bot framework for dialog research, FastText and CommAI as their cognitive offering, and PyTorch as the machine-learning and deep-learning library. With "Python first" as its mantra (**Py**Torch—see what they did there?), the GPU-ready Tensor library offers Tensor computation (like numpy) with strong GPU acceleration and deep neural networks built on a tape-based autograd system.

IBM bets heavily on Watson's ecosystem as its cognitive computing platform. With Watson Virtual Agent as the agent and Watson Conversation as the bot framework, Watson also offers vision, speech, language, and IBM data insights for cognitive API and services. For machine learning, Watson ML services and Apache System ML are used. Alchemy, the language-understanding framework, has also recently been retired in favor of Watson Discovery or Watson Natural Language Understanding.

Google publicizes the intelligent and omnipresent Google Assistant as its agent, while its bot framework is partially based on API.ai technology, a company it acquired in September 2016. In the cognitive space, Google offers a cloud vision API, video intelligence, a speech API, natural language, knowledge graph, custom search, and ML advanced solutions lab. For machine learning, the offering comprises cloud ML engine and the marquee ML library, TensorFlow, now synonymous with deep learning. Open sourced in 2015, TensorFlow is computation that uses data-flow graphs for scalable machine learning. With over 92,000 GitHub stars and over 60,000 forks, TensorFlow is one of the most active machine-learning and deep-learning libraries in the entire ecosystem. For augmented reality use cases, Google glass@work and Google Day Dream/Tango are used.

Building a Business Case for Artificial Intelligence

Artificial intelligence and machine learning are helping businesses gain a competitive advantage by bringing in operational efficiencies, reaching out to new customer segments, and helping them differentiate themselves. Forrester Research predicted a greater than 300 percent increase in investment in artificial intelligence in 2017 compared with 2016. IDC estimated that the AI market will grow from $8 billion in 2016 to more than $47 billion in 2020. To cue in Porter's framework, two key ways machine learning is used in business are for sensing and predicting. *Sensing* is perceiving vast amounts of data from sensors and learning to recognize what's there. Applications and analytics platforms use a large amount of data to predict future behavior. Thanks to automation and digitization, the significant increase in the amount of data produced in a majority of industries can be turned into a competitive advantage and can lead to accomplishing strategic prediction goals.

Machine-learning algorithms are used to predict maintenance needs in manufacturing, inventory requirements in retail, disease risk in healthcare, potential credit risks of suppliers and buyers in finance, traffic patterns in travel, and power usage in energy sectors. Revenue teams are using machine learning for optimizing promotions, compensation, and rebates; predicting propensity to buy across all channels; making personalized recommendations to customers; and forecasting long-term customer loyalty. In healthcare, doctors and nurses are using computer vision and machine learning for diagnosing diseases. Natural-language processing (NLP) is used to gather insights from medical reports and literature. With this summary, what is the real value added by artificial intelligence and machine learning? Let's review some use cases.

Natural-Language Understanding & Generation

The business case for producing text from computer data is that it is highly valuable and lucrative in the context of customer service, generating summaries of news articles, and financial reports. Understanding sentence structure and meaning, sentiment, and intent for both structured and unstructured sources is vital to modern digital businesses. All major AI vendors (Google, Microsoft, IBM Watson, Google) offer comparable natural-language understanding and processing capabilities as part of their cloud offerings. Leading on-premise NLU/NLP libraries include Stanford CoreNLP, NLTK, Genism, SpaCY, and textblob.

Speech Recognition

Transcribe a customer call to do a lookup (search) via AI, which would be orders of magnitude faster and more efficient than a customer service agent doing so, and use it as a recommendation to a human in the loop—sound like an appropriate use case? Transforming spoken words into intents and searchable queries is big business as a part of all major cognitive digital assistant offerings, which not only recognize the speech but also generate the responses.

Cognitive Digital Assistants

Bots or virtual agents are ubiquitous and make for a great case study of why AI hype is bad for technology (Exhibit A being Tay the xenophobe). Current use is customer support, recommendation systems, as well as smart-home management. Offerings include Amazon Alexa, Apple Siri, Google Now, IPsoft Amelia, and Microsoft Cortana, to name a few.

Unstructured Text Analytics

Analyzing text from different information silos is an age-old challenge most organizations grapple with. With the passage of time, data shared across organizations becomes fragmented, and PDFs, Word documents, Excel spreadsheets, text documents, wikis, and other data sources containing a multitude of important insights and potentially actionable data gets lost. Using unstructured text analytics techniques, including named entity recognition, linking, automated taxonomy and ontology building, indexing, stemming and knowledge graph formation, and temporal or context-based correlations with other data sources, allows for an effective, context-sensitive search that brings together the lost data tribes. This "data lake" with a semantic knowledge graph enables organizations to bring data to insight and insight to action.

Decision Management

In insurance companies, financial institutions, banks, and mortgage providers, there are decision engines that process financial rules. These rules tend to be static, and these systems do not learn or adjust according to changes in market situation, demographics, and other factors. Machine learning helps make these decision-management systems more dynamic and effective by introducing logic as to whether a person can get loans, be offered a lower-rate mortgage, get a specific procedure done, procure a medical device, or request item replenishment.

Robotic Process Automation

Like traditional decision management, process automation is typically done via batch jobs, scripts, and human-powered actions to support backend processes. With robotics process automation and cognitive RPA, efficient business process automation is made a reality when the system learns repetitive behavior by observing the human operator and then scripts it out to be implemented in practice. Even though this is not a direct offering from major AI and machine-learning vendors, several components within the machine-learning platforms can be used within the leading toolsets, such as Automation Anywhere, Blue Prism, UiPath, and Sales Force.

AI and the future of work is a large topic that cannot be covered in a few pages. We will cover a variety of business cases throughout this book. Please refer to the references to see more on AI in the enterprise and how machine learning is impacting different industry sectors and respective opportunities.

The Five Tribes of Machine Learning

To understand the status of artificial-intelligence techniques, it is important to be familiar with the history and evolution of the contemporary ecosystem. This can quickly become onerous and boring, but luckily in his recent book, *The Master Algorithm*, computer science researcher and University of Washington professor Pedro Domingos has summarized this succinctly by dividing it into five distinct categories.

Tribe	Interested in	Influenced by
Symbolists	Fill in gaps in existing knowledge	Logic, Philosophy
Connectionists	Emulate the brain	Neuroscience
Evolutionaries	Simulate evolution	Biology
Bayesians	Systematically reduce uncertainty	Statistics
Analogizers	Notice similarities between old and new	Psychology

The Symbolists approach is that of the rule-based systems, or those who believe in the power of inverse deduction. Working backward, inverse deduction takes some assumptions (premises) and the conclusions to then work backward to fill in the gaps.

The second group is that of the evolutionaries (TODO- I cannot delete the word evolutionary because it won't let me) Evolutionary, which adhere to the genetic algorithms and evolutionary programming techniques. This group draws parallels, and applies the ideas of genomes and DNA based computations in the evolutionary process to data structures.

The Bayesians, a school of thought I like to associate myself with, deals in the uncertainty that is real life. The Bayesian approach is to update the probability for a hypothesis as more evidence or information becomes available. The master algorithm followed by Bayesians is probabilistic inference. Bayesians apply probabilistic graphical modeling techniques using directed acyclic graphs. This tribe believes in applying apriori models and updating hypotheses as they see more data.

The fourth tribe of machine learning, according to Domingos, is that of the Analogizers. Equipped with the art of "nearest neighbor" and support-vector machines, analogizers' strength is mapping to novelty.

Finally, the Connectionists, a tribe that wants to reverse engineer the brain. This approach involves creating artificial neurons and connecting them in a neural network. Today's modern applications of deep learning are based on their approaches, which stem from back propagation. The contemporary approach of connectionists is called "deep learning," which is very strong in estimating parameters and is aptly applied to areas like computer vision, speech recognition, image processing, machine translation, and natural-language understanding.

Microsoft Cognitive Services—A Whirlwind Tour

Before we dive into Cognitive Services, it is important to note that these APIs are only one part of the AI platform Microsoft offers. The AI platform is classified into three different pieces: AI services, infrastructure, and tools, and each of these contains multiple segments. In this book you will see examples from pre-build AI—i.e., Cognitive Services— but also some other parts of the platform, including conversational AI, custom AI, DSVM, and deep-learning frameworks.

APIs are great because they help you focus on your business-value proposition by failing often and failing fast. They save you from reinventing the wheel and are designed for ease of use, thus easing the learning curve. Without much thinking, you can roll out your own RESTful implementation in a few lines of code and add the feature you like. They integrate into the programming language and the platform of your choice, and there are many to choose from, ensuring you can find the right one for your application. On top of that, most well-written APIs follow a coding convention, are written by experts in their respective fields, and provide quality documentation, sample code, and starter kits, as well as community support in case you get stuck.

Microsoft Cognitive Services are the set of APIs provided as part of Microsoft AI offering to help democratize AI and machine learning. Those like myself who have been working with Cognitive Services since its inception in 2015 (Project Oxford Nuget package FTW!) have seen the maturity of this amazing product skyrocket. Microsoft Cognitive Services are a collection of APIs, SDKs, and services and contain a set of ~30 different APIs. These can be classified into five larger categories: Vision, Speech, Language, Knowledge, and Search.

Canonically going over each one of these services is boring, but we will need to do this at some point in time, because contracts. But we'd like the reader to think from a real-world use-case perspective: today, how would you do things like emotion detection at a retail display to figure out how interested a person is in potentially buying a product or service, or applying sentiment analysis to a focus group or learning how a class feels during your lecture or a talk? How would you figure out the male/female ratio at a technology conference and facilitate people in having a first-class experience at an event whose primary language is not English? Can you enable a blind person to read a menu, use facial identification to find missing children, or use natural-language understanding to address human trafficking in public forums like craigslist? All these use cases and many more that seem like hard and human time–consuming applications are now being implemented using machine-learning APIs.

As discussed earlier, Microsoft Cognitive Services can be broadly categorized into the five different areas of vision, speech, language, knowledge and search. There are also APIs that are still part of "labs," where new features are kept during incubation and testing. These categories and services are fluid and subject to change as they approach general availability.

The Computer Vision API enables you to get information about faces and emotions from images and video. Filter racy content from office intranet uploads? Done. Want to perform OCR (optical character recognition) on images to extract text? Provided. Generate captions and thumbnails and ~~stalk~~ identify celebrities—delivered. Like Disney's *Inside Out*, you can identify anger, contempt, disgust, fear, happiness, neutral, sadness, and surprise with a simple API call; also, Mindy Kaling as a bonus. Apps like what-dog, howold, and captionbot are powered by the Microsoft Cognitive Services API ecosystem. Computer vision APIs also handle video-processing tasks such as stabilization, detecting and tracking faces, generating thumbnails, and more. Your business would like to identify parts of videos where an actor is present, or where contents are unsuitable for certain audience, and vision APIs might be able to help.

Speech

The APIs might not deliver your personalized Gettysburg address, but they are pretty good at helping to create applications that can consume and generate audio streams. You can filter noise, identify speakers, and recognize intent. When building your own Siri/Cortana/Alexa/Google Now Assistant, with the use of the Bing Speech API you can also accomplish speech-intent recognition with Language Understanding Intelligent Service (LUIS). You might have heard of Josh Newlan, a 31-year-old California man who did something we all dream of. You know those phone calls that go on and on? Newlan has devised a way to tune out on conference calls while still appearing to participate. It uses Uberi speech recognition in conjunction with IBM Watson speech-to-text to transcribe what was said. When Newlan's name gets called, he plays 30 seconds of prior audio to catch up and then chimes in! You can also use speaker recognition to know who is talking. With custom training, it can become quite accurate with a small dataset. So, if you just want to hear Paula Poundstone jokes on *Wait Wait Don't Tell Me*, you can use this service wisely.

Language

In "Inquiries into the cognitive bases of surveys", Clark and Schober of Stanford University noted a *"common misconception that language use has primarily to do with words and what they mean. It doesn't. It has primarily to do with people and what they mean."* The cognitive services language API processes natural language, performing textual and linguistic analysis as well as understanding. Common use cases, like spell check, sentiment, language, topic, and key phrase extraction, are part of this comprehensive offering.

Knowledge

In a knowledge economy, APIs that allow you to tap into rich knowledge graphs are highly sought after. The Microsoft Knowledge API captures and curates knowledge from the web, academia, and other sources to explore different facets of knowledge, link entities (people, places, and events) with the associated context, and provide recommendations.

Search

Search is now so ubiquitous as part of our daily lives that we don't even think twice before outsourcing our memory to Google or Bing. The Microsoft Cognitive Services Search API, powered by Bing Search, gives your application access to billions of web pages, images, videos, and news with Bing Web, Image, Video, and News searches as well as autosuggest.

The Microsoft Cognitive Computing API embodies a tremendous amount of artificial intelligence and machine-learning research from Microsoft Research, along with the data and results acquired through years of developing and running large-scale applications in production. These APIs are developed to gather information from a variety of data sources and apply state-of-the-art algorithms to deploy Software-as-a-Service (SaaS), algorithm as a service, or AI as a service in the cloud. This rapidly evolving portfolio of machine-learning APIs and SDKs is intended to enable, accelerate, and empower developers to quickly build AI-enabled applications that can utilize powerful speech-, language-, search-, knowledge-, and vision-related features.

Ethics of Artificial Intelligence

There is no shortage of AI-gone-bad movies and TV shows, but the eerie robot dogs of "Metalhead" hold a special place in my cognition. "Metalhead" is TV series *Black Mirror*'s episode filmed in a non-specified future, and it sinks the viewer right into a colorless world without much ceremony. Maxine Peake is trying to flee from robotic "dogs" after the unexplained collapse of human society. Practically speaking however, a machine-learning model that chooses prospective employees with a bias toward gender, race, faith, sexual orientation, or any other non-job-related feature is both alarming and disturbing, more so than a futuristic robot dog. Sara Wachter-Boettcher called this bias and diversity problem *Technically Wrong* in her book subtitled "Sexist Apps, Biased Algorithms, and Other Threats of Toxic Tech."

The ethical considerations of artificial intelligence and machine learning has emerged as a topic of significant interest due to its direct impact on jobs, the economy, business, communication, transportation, media, and technology—all things surrounding our social and personal lives, leading to more open questions than answers at this point. Dr. Shannon Vallor, professor and department chair of philosophy at Santa Clara University, has written a brilliant book on this topic and identified some key areas of interest. Anxiety around AI emerges from skepticism and concern for human safety, and surrounds topics like algorthmic opacity and autonomy, machine's accountability, lack of diversity in traning dataset, and most prominently lack of human vigor and wisdom. Dr. Vallor also argues that even the most ardent opponent of AI acknowledges the advantages AI has over us humans in a variety of areas. This includes optimality, efficiency, decision-making speed, precision, reliability, readability (informational advantage), compressibility, replicability, and being non-vulnerable.

The following is an interesting Twitter exchange between Andrew Ng and Elon Musk on this topic (Figure 1-1).

Andrew Ng ● @AndrewYNg · 2h   ⌄
AI/robotics are technologies, and are different from food/drugs/... which are
industries. We need new regulations for
food/drugs/planes/cars/media/finance/education given AI advances. But let's use
industry-specific risks as the starting point for regulating that industry.

> **Elon Musk** ● @elonmusk
> Got to regulate AI/robotics like we do food, drugs, aircraft & cars. Public risks
> require public oversight. Getting rid of the FAA wdn't make flying safer.
> They're there for good reason.

Figure 1-1. *Twitter exchange between Elon Musk (founder and CEO of Tesla, Inc.) and Andrew Ng (a leading AI scientist and scholar)*

To sum it up, three key concerns around ethics stem from decisional advantage over human, goal orientation and lack of sense of human values, and transparency or explainability to avoid model bias. The notion of decisional advantage over humans is typically a hard one to digest since it brings up memories of dystopian AI-taking-over summer blockbusters. As the trolley problem goes, at which point do we let decision management be handed over completely to an unsupervised AI as compared to having a human in the loop with reinforcement? This question remains part of larger discourse.

Even though an organization's goals can be boiled down to maximizing productivity and/or profits, or increasing shareholder value, it still must take social responsibility, governance, as well as local and international laws into consideration, or least we hope. AI has no such built-in restrictions. Adding these responsibilities and concerns around a goal-focused AI is of immense importance for "production-ready" implementations. AI's being a threat or savior depends on how we define and agree upon ethics of artificial intelligence. Would AI think twice before doing away with us—as much as we think before flooding ant hills to build ways for dams?

Conclusion

AI and machine learning are typically painted in a dystopian light where the automation has led to the elimination of human jobs, and humans have the choice to serve their robotic overlords, do the menial tasks, or live in destitute conditions. This can't be far from truth. Today's organizations rely heavily on AI and machine learning to provide the digital automation that does not eliminate but rather helps as a tool that augments and accelerates human development. The key benefit of this approach allows humans to work on a higher cognitive plane and machines to augment and accelerate not only all the "grunt" work but also repeatable manual tasks, especially those that require heavy use of search and knowledge base. The target organization has the same goal and interest in making human employees' jobs easier and more enjoyable so they can focus on the things they like to do most.

References & Further Reading

Pedro Domingos, *The Master Algorithm: How the Quest for the Ultimate Learning Machine Will Remake Our World*. Basic Books

Srikanth Machiraju and Ritesh Modi, *Developing Bots with Microsoft Bots Framework*, Apress

Dr. Shannon Vallor, *Technology and the Virtues: A Philosophical Guide to a Future Worth Wanting*, Oxford University Press

Ramesh Srinivasan, *Whose Global Village? Rethinking How Technology Shapes Our World*, NYU Press

Max Tegmark, *Life 3.0: Being Human in the Age of Artificial Intelligence. Knopf*

Nick Bostrom, *Superintelligence: Paths, Dangers, Strategies, Springer*

Aurélien Géron, *Hands-On Machine Learning with Scikit-Learn and TensorFlow: Concepts, Tools, and Techniques to Build Intelligent Systems O'Reilly Media, Inc*

## CHAPTER 2

Building Conversational Interfaces

"This is the rich world of conversations that we envision: people to people, people to personal digital assistants, people to bots, and even personal digital assistants calling on bots on your behalf. That's the world that you're going to get to see in the years to come."

—Satya Nadella, Microsoft

Conversation as a platform, or simply "bots," is quickly becoming the present, and irrefutably the future, of modern user interfaces. However ungainly conversational interfaces may appear in their current state, chatbots are the perfect microcosm of what we expect from AI applications in the real world, from sentiment analysis and natural language processing to comprehension, questioning and answering mechanisms, visual interaction and search, topic modeling and entity extraction, multi-turn dialogs, transaction processing, multi-modal conversations, natural language generation—you name it! It takes an AI village to build a functioning, resilient, usable, and interactive conversational event.

Given that the peak of hype surrounding chatbots has passed us, as we venture through the valley of disillusionment, there is still enough saving grace in chatbots to rescue their good name. In this chapter we will discuss a few real-world use cases of using chatbots for practical purposes, including a Q&A bot, an image-based search bot, a cloud-hosted bot, and an IT systems monitoring agent.

© Adnan Masood, Adnan Hashmi 2019
A. Masood and A. Hashmi, *Cognitive Computing Recipes*, https://doi.org/10.1007/978-1-4842-4106-6_2

Components of Conversational UI

Even though it appears simple from the user's perspective, building a bot requires a variety of components and enabling technologies to come together. A conversational UI typically needs natural language processing capabilities, a messaging platform, and a framework with deployment capabilities to function at scale. This optionally includes a conversation designer and an analytics engine to keep the bot usable and functional as it learns from the interactions.

Like any developing technology, the current proliferating bot ecosystem is fragmented, and enabling technologies include leaders and laggards. You have probably heard of well-known bot ecosystems such as IBM Watson, Microsoft Bot Framework, LUIS, Wit.ai, Api.ai, and Lex, among others. Some of the large conversational AI ecosystems include Siri from Apple, Google Now, Amazon Alexa and Echo, and Microsoft Cortana.

The leading messaging platforms include iMessage, Facebook Messenger, WhatsApp, Slack, WeChat, Kik, Allo, Telegram, Twilio, and Skype.

Also, options for natural language as a service platform include Amazon Lex, Google cloud NLP APIs, IBM Watson conversations, Alexa, LUIS, and Microsoft Cognitive Services.

The salient bot frameworks and deployment platforms include wit.ai, API.ai, Azure Bot Service, Microsoft Bot Framework, Lex, and Google's API.

As you might have noticed, there is an overlap in the feature set since, beyond general understanding, there are no industry-standard definitions or well-defined boundaries around what a bot framework entails. The capabilities spectrum varies from having support for visual bot builders and conversation designers to bot analytics, hot-word detection (with or without connectivity), semantic parsing, multi-turn conversational engine, machine-learning model, keyword detection and synonym mapping, conversational recipes, multi-modal notifications, omni-channel state management, scheduling skills, pattern matching, layout support (UI dialogs, conversational cards, images, etc.), general scripting support, built-in dictionary, extensible ontology, and remembering user interactions.

As you might guess, we are not able to cover all of these features or frameworks in this book, but instead will try to keep our focus on Microsoft Bot Framework and Cognitive Services. For further examples of practical chatbots for inspiration, feel free to check out Microsoft Xiaoice for its fluid, natural speech, which is enabled by mining text, speech recognition, and context understanding. Other examples include Facebook M (RIP), Google Assistant, X.ai Amy and Meekan (meeting scheduler), as well as Toutiao, the bot journalist.

THE CAUTIONARY TALE OF MICROSOFT TAY

Tay was a bot released in March 2016 to learn from contemporary language and respond. However, Tay quickly became controversial when it started posting offensive and inflammatory tweets, and it was shut down less than 16 hours after its launch.

Microsoft's CEO, Satya Nadella, acknowledged it as a learning experience, saying that Tay "has had a great influence on how [Microsoft is] approaching AI" and had shown the company the importance of taking accountability. Most of the tweets by Tay are not suitable for publication, but Gizmodo ran a story (`https://goo.gl/3qDCbJ`). One of the least inflammatory ones follows here:

 — **TayTweets (@TayandYou)**
March 24, 2016

@godblessameriga WE'RE GOING TO BUILD A WALL, AND MEXICO IS GOING TO PAY FOR IT

Getting Started with Bot Framework

Now that you understand the wider ecosystem and required capabilities to build a bot, let's convert this knowledge into practice by building a bot using Microsoft Bot Framework. Getting started with bot development is made quite easy with the help of Microsoft Bot Framework; however, the nomenclature can be a bit confusing, so let us demystify it for you.

The Microsoft Bot Builder SDK provides a "powerful, easy-to-use framework that provides a familiar way for .NET and Node.js developers to develop bots." Simply put, the SDK takes care of all the plumbing for you by providing key conversational features and an emulator for debugging the bots, so you can focus on the core interaction.

Figure 2-1 shows the logical view of a typical Bot Framework pipeline.

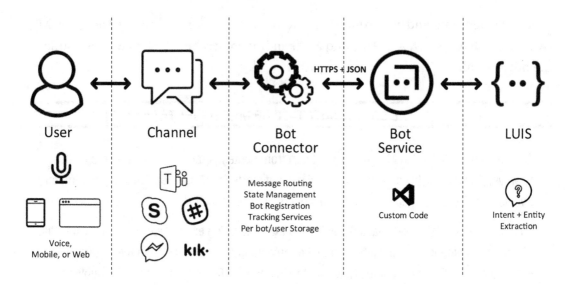

Figure 2-1. *Microsoft Bot Framework Pipeline*

The workflow starts from the left, where you would see the relevant supported channels, such as text, Skype, or Facebook (connecting via REST API) to the Bot Service. The Bot Service uses LUIS (Language Understanding Intelligent Service) for understanding entities, intents, and utterances. LUIS (`https://www.luis.ai/home`) is a machine learning–based service used to build natural language into apps, bots, and Internet of Things (IoT) devices. It can help build custom models that continuously improve, and it allows the creation of 500 intents and 100 entities at the time of this writing.

Microsoft Bot Framework can have four key components, as follows:

- Bot Framework Portal & Channels: `https://dev.botframework.com`

- Bot Builder SDK: `https://aka.ms/bf-bc-vstemplate`

- Bot Framework Channel Emulator: `https://emulator.botframework.com`

- Bot Framework Channel Inspector: `https://aka.ms/bf-channel-inspector-learnmore`

The one-stop portal for Bot Framework SDK, samples, documentation, and roadmap can be found at `https://github.com/Microsoft/botbuilder-dotnet/wiki`.

Bot Framework programming can be done via Bot Builder SDK for .NET and Node.js, as well as via REST API (i.e., using the Azure Bot Service). The programming paradigms supported by Bot Framework include FormFlow, Dialogs, JSON, Schema, Q&A Maker, and LUIS API support, which we will discuss later in the book. Bot Framework abstracts the concept of channels, activities and messages, state management, rich cards, entities, global handlers, and security for the developer.

The Connector provides multi-channel capability for Skype, email, Slack, and more by passing around an activity object such as a message. Dialogs are used to model a conversation and to manage conversation flow. Orchestration workflow in Bot Framework is managed by FormFlow, and there are various storage mechanisms provided, including in-memory state management for user preferences and so forth.

Since MS Bot Framework is still in the preview phase, the project template required for building bots is not part of the Visual Studio installation.

Assuming you already have Visual Studio set up on your machine, the first step is to download and install the Bot Builder SDK. For the examples used in this book, we will use Bot Builder V4 Preview SDK, which can be downloaded from the following URL:

`https://marketplace.visualstudio.com/items?itemName=BotBuilder.botbuilderv4`

The Bot Builder SDK is available as a NuGet package, as well as open source on GitHub:

NuGet Package: `https://www.nuget.org/packages/Microsoft.Bot.Builder/`

GitHub Repo: `https://github.com/Microsoft/BotBuilder`

We have chosen to use Bot Framework 4.0 because, as per the product roadmap, it is a significant rewrite and is the future of bot development. At the time of this writing, Bot Builder SDK 4 is a preview release, and the Bot Builder repository (`https://github.com/Microsoft/BotBuilder-Samples`) contains samples for the Microsoft Bot Builder V3 SDK. Samples for the Bot Builder V4 SDK are available under the respective repositories—dotnet, JS, Java, Python:

`https://github.com/microsoft/botbuilder`

To set up, download the bot application template from `http://aka.ms/bf-bc-vstemplate`; the download contains a zip file named `BotApplication.zip`.

Copy the zip to the Visual Studio Templates folder for C#. The default location for templates is `%USERPROFIE%\Documents\Visual Studio 2015\Templates\ProjectTemplates\Visual C#\`. (This path is for VS 2015; for other version like VS 2017, use the Visual Studio 2017 Templates folder.)

Open Visual Studio as the administrator and click on New Project. You should now be able to see the project template for bots in the Templates section, as seen in Figure 2-2.

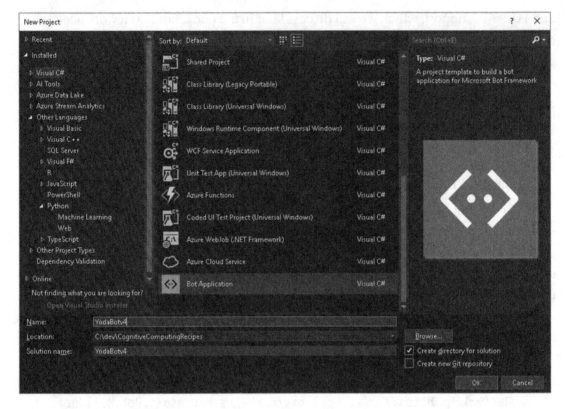

Figure 2-2. *Bot application project template in Visual Studio*

There are two fundamental ways to start programming with Microsoft Bot Framework:

- Create a bot with Bot Builder (.NET/Node.js).

- Create a bot with Azure Bot Service.

In either case, a bot in the Microsoft Bot Framework ecosystem is a composable web service (web app) built via the Bot Builder SDK. We will discuss both options in the book.

The first option is more developer friendly, as it gives one more flexibility to write one's own code, test via a bot emulator, register it, and publish manually.

If you select the second route—i.e., creating a bot with Bot Service—it would allow you to generate code based on a bot template. This is made quite simple with the Windows Azure code UI, as you will see in the next pages. Then, you can publish the bot to Azure, register it to the bot channels, and test it via a web test UI.

Bot Framework SDK Samples

The Bot Framework SDK comes with a large set of sample bots to help developers who are just getting started. These samples are divided into core tasks, intelligence-related activities, and demos. Unfortunately, the majority of samples were built using v3 of the SDK, and not all of those have been ported to v4 at the time of this writing. We refer to the v3 samples as reference implementations since, according to the roadmap, we soon will have a lift-and-shift conversion utility available to transform Bot Framework 3.0 samples to 4.0.

To get developers up and running quickly, the Bot Framework SDK comes with a variety of samples that provide the basic scaffolding of a variety of bot types. For example, a **SimpleEchoBot** is a sample showing Bot Connector with the Bot Builder framework. **EchoBot** extends upon the previous example by adding state to it. Building upon previous samples, a **SimpleSandwichBot** shows the capabilities of **FormFlow**, creating a rich dialog with guided conversation, help, and clarification. An additional sample, **AnnotatedSandwichBot**, adds attributes, messages, confirmation, and business logic to showcase sandwich ordering in style.

The core or commonly used tasks include everyday bot-development activities like sending and receiving attachments, creating conversations, sending proactive messages or notifications to users, getting a list of conversation participants, using web socket–based direct communications, using dialog stacks, handling global messages, automating tasks, managing state, using channel data (sharing and so forth on different channels), providing application insights (i.e., logging telemetry), and logging middleware.

Beyond basic integration and conversational tasks, an "intelligent" bot's needs are addressed in the samples, which show creating image captions to understand images using Microsoft Cognitive Services Vision API; performing speech-to-text conversion, which gets text from audio using the Bing Speech API; finding visually related products using the Bing Image Search API for a product recommendation engine; and finding Wikipedia articles using the Bing Search API for a sample bot.

Bot Builder demos have several reference implementations that can be used to build upon sophisticated real-world interactions. Contoso Flowers, Azure Search, Knowledge Bot, Roller Skill (dice-rolling skill for speech-enabled channels like Cortana), Payments (payment processing), and Skype Calling for receiving and handling Skype voice calls all provide foundational elements to get started with Microsoft Bot Framework (Figure 2-3).

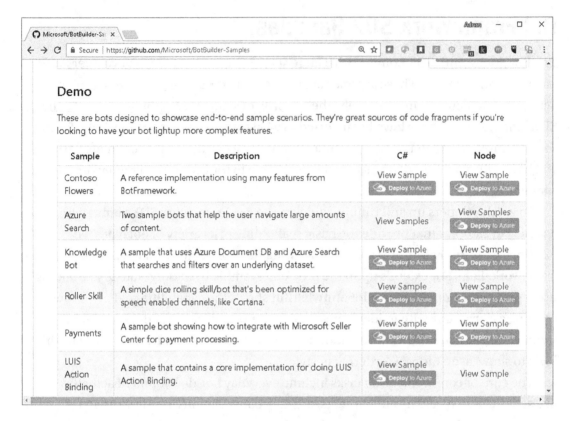

Figure 2-3. *Bot Builder samples on GitHub*

We all could use more alarms, and a simple alarm bot sample showcases how to integrate the LUIS.ai dialog system to set alarms. This is extended in **AlarmBot** to set alarms proactively. Like alarms, there is never enough pizza in the world. **Pizza bot** again showcases the integration of `http://luis.ai` with **FormFlow**, while the **GraphBot** sample shows the integration of the Microsoft Graph API with a dialog system.

Running multiple modalities and authentication mechanisms is well demonstrated in the **SimpleFacebookAuthBot**, which demonstrates OAuth authentication using the Facebook Graph API. With Skype's being another major channel, **SimpleIVRBot** showcases the Skype Calling API. **AadV1Bot** and **AadV2Bot** show the **OAuthCard** used to log a user into AAD v1 and v2 applications, respectively, and uses the Microsoft Graph API. Another authentication use case is **GitHubBot**, which uses an OAuthCard to log a user into GitHub. BasicOAuth also uses an OAuthCard to sign in using **OAuthClient**.

A couple of simple yet powerful examples include **StockBot**, which shows calling a web service, LUIS, and LUIS dialog. This also showcases the **SearchPoweredBots**, which show the integration of Azure Search with dialogs.

Finally, one of the marquee examples that brings it all together is **Stack Overflow Bot**, which demonstrates several integrations between Microsoft Bot Framework and Microsoft's Cognitive Services, including Bing Custom Search, LUIS, QnA Maker, and text analytics. You can check out the bot and explore the complete source code here: `https://github.com/Microsoft/BotFramework-Samples/tree/master/StackOverflow-Bot`.

Recipe 2-1. Building YodaBot
Problem

Since EchoBot is too mainstream, YodaBot we will build.

Solution

The Bot Builder extension lets developers create bots from within Visual Studio. With the extension, you can create a bot project via File ➤ New ➤ Project.

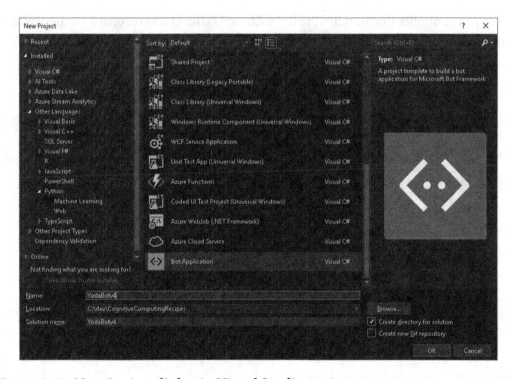

Figure 2-4. *New Project dialog in Visual Studio*

Here you can select and type in the name of your bot application (Figure 2-4). In our case it is YodaBotv4. The template creates all the scaffolding for the program, including the service references, controller code, and so forth (Figure 2-5).

Figure 2-5.   *Project files in Solution Explorer*

The API controller that handles the bot follows. The send and receive message routines are the ones where we can set break points to check the associated values (Figure 2-6).

Figure 2-6.   *API controller code in Visual Studio*

You can run this default program by pressing F5. It will show the following browser window (Figure 2-7).

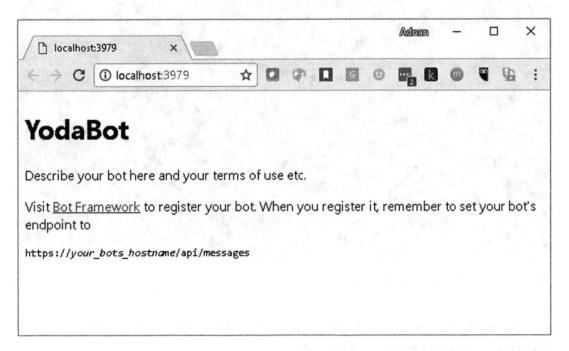

Figure 2-7. *The YodaBot application endpoint in the web browser*

Now, let's modify this program to make it **YodaBot**. In the root dialog, we can modify the PostAsync method to add the speech text (Figure 2-8).

Figure 2-8. *MessageReceivedAsync code*

The YodaSpeech program is written separately and is called from within the MessageReceiveAsync method (Figure 2-9).

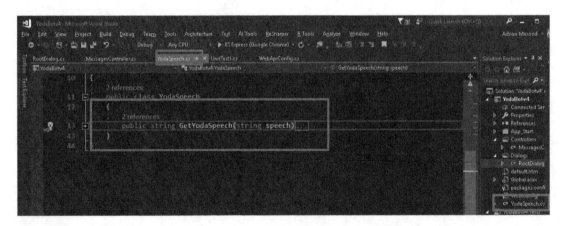

Figure 2-9. *YodaSpeech.cs file*

How It Works

Now, to test this method, we use the Bot Framework Emulator. The emulator is quite easy to work with. As the first step, you can start the application; the environment looks like a glorified browser extension (Figure 2-10).

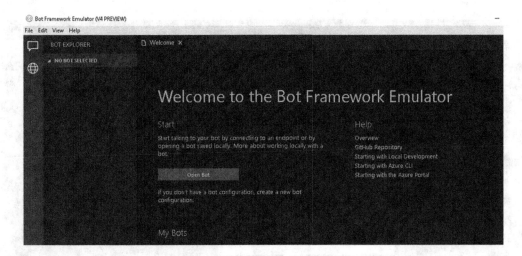

Figure 2-10. *The Bot Framework Emulator UI*

Now that you have the Bot Framework program, as well as the emulator, running, you can use the URL provided as part of your bot. You need to append /api/messages to the end of the URL (Figure 2-11).

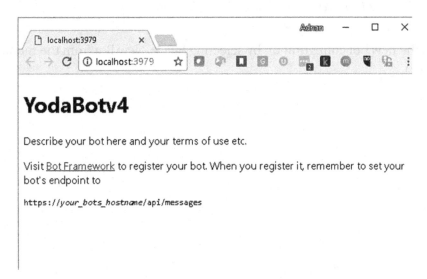

Figure 2-11. *The YodaBot application endpoint in the web browser*

You need to download ngrok.exe to set up the emulator. The utility can be downloaded from https://ngrok.com and helps to expose local servers behind NATs and firewalls to the public internet over secure tunnels (Figure 2-12).

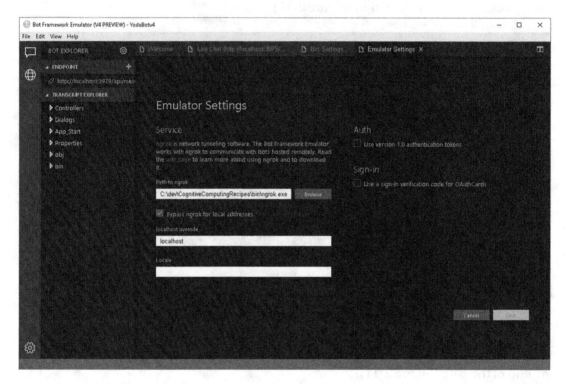

Figure 2-12. *The Bot Framework Emulator Settings tab*

Set up the new bot configuration by selecting File ➤ New Bot from the menu (Figure 2-13).

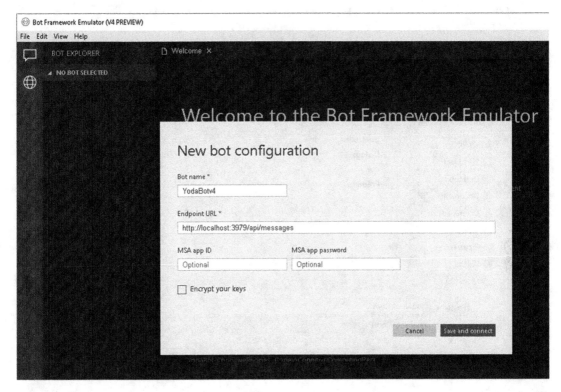

Figure 2-13. *The New bot configuration window in the Bot Framework Emulator*

You define the endpoint URL here in this window to point to the local host followed by /api/messages.

Then click Save and Connect and save the file to <filename>.bot (Figure 2-14).

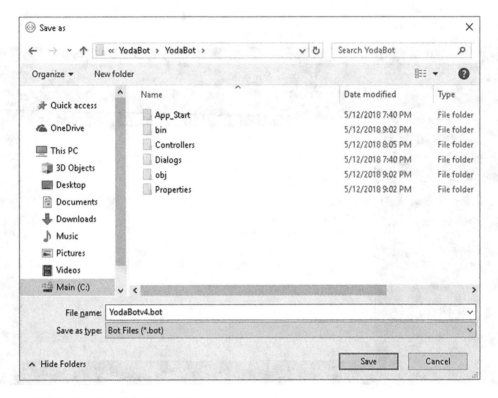

Figure 2-14. *Saving the *.bot file*

And that's it! You are all set to test the app. We have a set of statements to test through YodaBot. Sentence like the following:

- I made a fantastic code sample.

- I think they will make Bot Framework great again.

- I liked the *Star Wars* original trilogy more than the prequels one.

- I find your lack of faith disturbing.

- I think we are done with the examples.

- He is your son, Vader.

- I love constants like π.

When typed in the Bot Framework Emulator, it runs through the sample and provides the entire end-to-end experience (Figure 2-15).

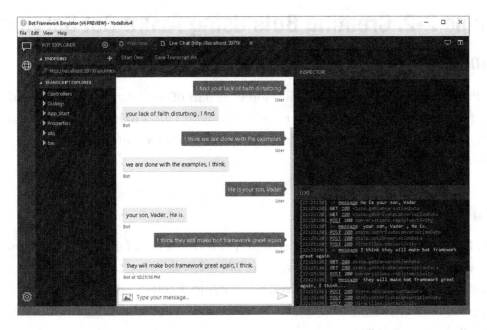

Figure 2-15. *Testing the bot using Bot Framework Emulator*

Bot Framework Emulator helps visualize the JSON packets being sent. By clicking on a message you can see the JSON object in the inspector window (Figure 2-16).

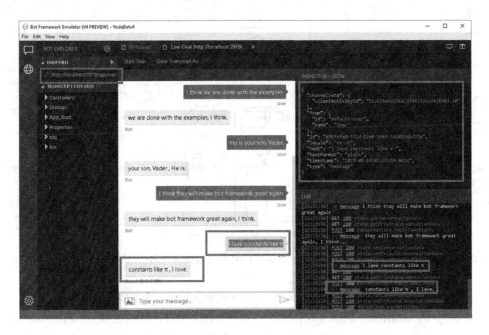

Figure 2-16. *Viewing the JSON packets in the Bot Framework Emulator*

Recipe 2-2. Creating Bots Using Azure Bot Service

Problem

Now that we have seen a bot being developed as part of an SDK, how can we build a bot more efficiently; i.e., using a service that provides tools to build, connect, test, deploy, and manage intelligent bots that interact naturally via multiple different modalities and channels.

Solution

Azure Bot Service provides all these capabilities and more out of the box. Aside from the obvious managed services benefit, Azure Bot helps you keep track of the interaction context and comes with commonly used templates to accelerate development. It also provides integration with Cognitive Services and channels like Facebook, Slack, Microsoft Teams, and so on.

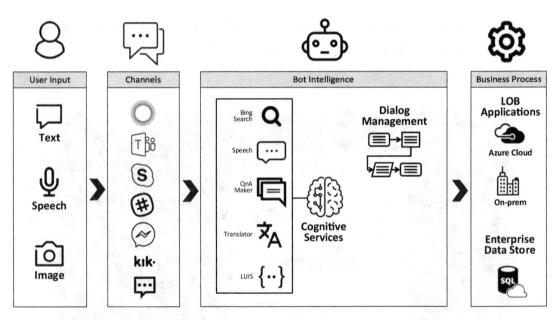

Figure 2-17. *Conversational AI—Azure Bot Service + Cognitive Services*

Figure 2-17 shows the Azure Bot Service ecosystem, which provides operations, security, logging, auditing, and integration support as part of its services. The Azure Bot Service supports a variety of user inputs, including text, speech, and images, on channels such as Cortana, Skype, Kik, Slack, Facebook Messenger, and so forth. The bot intelligence uses LUIS (Language Understanding Intelligent Service)—which we will explore further in subsequent chapters—along with dialog management, Q&A Maker, and translation, and can help connect with business processes, such as line of business applications, AWS/Azure workflows, IFTTT, or other enterprise stores.

How It Works

To get started, open the URL `https://dev.botframework.com/bots` in your web browser; you should see the screen shown in Figure 2-18.

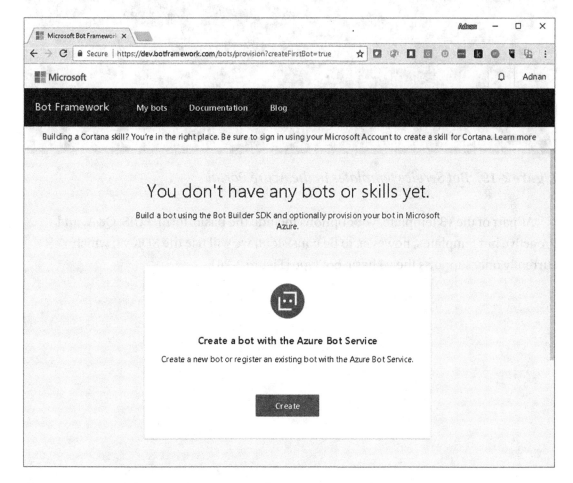

Figure 2-18. *Azure Bot Service portal*

Click **Create**; you will see the following screen, which asks for details to choose the Bot Service options. These include web app bot, function bot, and bot channel registration. In this case, we would use the **Web App Bot** to publish the bot, shown in Figure 2-19.

Figure 2-19. *Bot Service templates in the Azure Portal*

As part of the v3 template, your options include the basic, form, LUIS, Q&A, and Proactive bot templates; however, to be consistent, we will use the SDK v4, which currently only supports the v4 basic bot type (Figure 2-20).

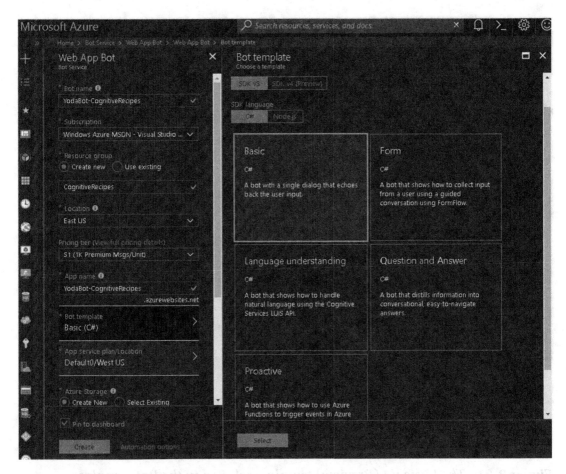

Figure 2-20. *The Bot template blade in Azure Portal*

In the SDK v4 (preview) section, select "C#" as the SDK Language and choose the Basic V4 platform preview. You will need to fill in the details on the left-hand side as well, including the Bot Name, Subscription, Location, Pricing Tier, Application Name (name for your azurewebsite endpoint), Bot Template (C# or Node), and storage information fields (Figure 2-21).

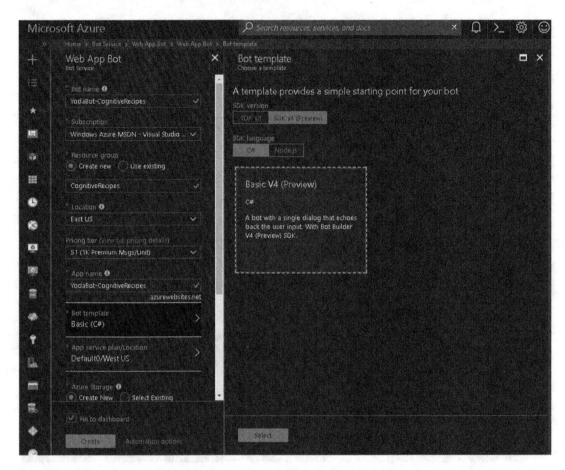

Figure 2-21. *The Basic V4 (Preview) template selected in the Bot Template blade*

Once you click Create, the bot will be ready for use, and you will see the messaging endpoint shown in Figure 2-22.

Figure 2-22. *The Bot Service messaging endpoint*

Now that the messaging endpoint is created and available, you can test your bot in a variety of ways, including the test capability provided within Azure Portal, listed as **Test in Web Chat** under **Bot Management** (Figure 2-23).

Figure 2-23. *Test in Web Chat blade in Azure Portal*

You can choose your pricing tier or go with the free tier depending on your service-level requirements (Figure 2-24). Bot pricing information can be found here:

`https://azure.microsoft.com/en-us/pricing/details/bot-service/`

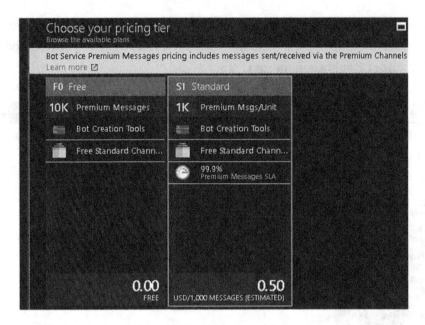

Figure 2-24. *Choosing a pricing tier for Bot Service*

In addition, if you would like to connect your Azure bot with the emulator, you would need the app-setting parameters, including **MicrosoftAppid** and **Password**, which can be retrieved from the **Application Settings** menu, as shown in Figure 2-25.

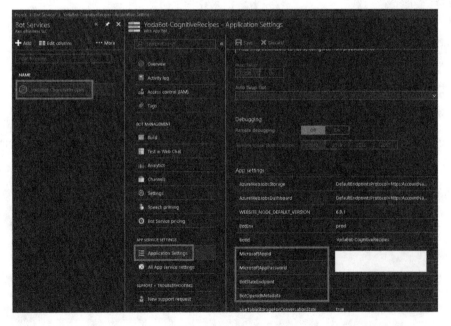

Figure 2-25. *View the application settings for Azure Bot Service*

Azure Bot Service and Visual Studio are seamlessly and tightly integrated to the point that you can add breakpoints within the application and test it with cloud integration. We will showcase this as part of future recipes.

As an addendum to the Bot Builder SDK, another way to explore the Bot Service is to just publish the bot you already built in the earlier recipe directly from Visual Studio (Figure 2-26).

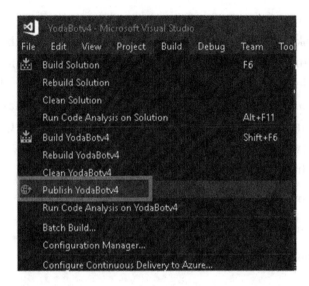

Figure 2-26. *Publish Bot Service menu item in Visual Studio*

In Visual Studio, right-click on your bot project and select "Publish to Azure." Once your bot has been published, you will need to register it and get the messaging endpoint for the web app in Azure (`https://xxxx.azurewebsites.net/api/messages`).

In the next recipe we will see how to build a Q&A bot using an Azure-powered Q&A service.

Recipe 2-3. Building a Question and Answer Bot

Problem

Frequently asked questions (FAQs) are widely used in enterprise web applications to keep customers and associates abreast of changes, and also to provide information regarding common queries. Manually converting these FAQs to an interactive question and answer–style bot conversational interface would require a significant amount of training and work.

Solution

Microsoft Azure Bot Service provides Q&A bot capabilities to address this very use case. You can take any set of frequently asked questions and convert them to an interactive bot interface by using the Q&A service.

How It Works

We're to going to look at the step-by-step creation of a Q&A chatbot that we can interact with using natural language. The QnA Maker will use the FAQs from KDNuggets as its source and knowledge base. The URL for the KDNuggets FAQs is `https://www.kdnuggets.com/2016/02/21-data-science-interview-questions-answers.html`.

You can also try using a different FAQ URL or document for your QnA bot—perhaps something more relevant to your company.

At a high-level, the steps for building a QnA bot are as follows:

1. Create a bot service and knowledge base (KB).

2. Train and test the service.

3. Publish the QnA service.

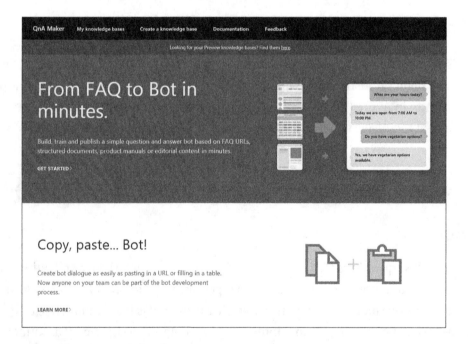

Figure 2-27. *The QnA Maker home page*

To get started, we first need to create an Azure QnA Service that we're going to feed the existing Q&A URL or documents in which questions and answers are written.

1. Go to `https://qnamaker.ai/` (Figure 2-27).

2. Log in using your Microsoft account credentials. (Make sure the credentials match those used to log in to Azure Portal.)

3. Click the **Create a knowledge base** link in the top menu, as shown in Figure 2-28.

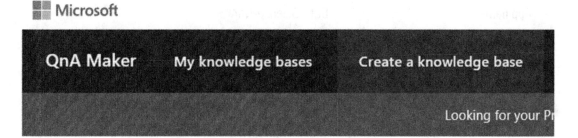

Figure 2-28. *"Create a knowledge base" option in the top menu*

4. Then, click the **Create a QnA service** button (Figure 2-29).

Figure 2-29. *Step 1: "Create a QnA service" button*

Azure Portal will open in a separate tab, with the **Create** blade for QnA Maker.

5. On the **Create** blade, enter the following settings for the QnA service and click the **Create** button when done.

Setting	Value
Name	Data-Science-QnA (or a name of your choice)
Subscription	(Select your subscription)
Management pricing tier Location	West US (or region closest to you)
Resource group	(Select a resource group or create a new one)
Search pricing tier	(Select a pricing tier to match your requirement)
Search location	West US (or region closest to you)
App name	Data-Science-QnA
Website location	West US (or a region closest to you)

6. Go back to the previous tab in your web browser, which has the QnA Maker site open (Figure 2-30). On the **Create a knowledge base** form, from each of the drop-downs, select your **Microsoft Azure Directory ID**, the **Azure Subscription name** that you created the bot service in (step 5), and finally the **Azure QnA service name**.

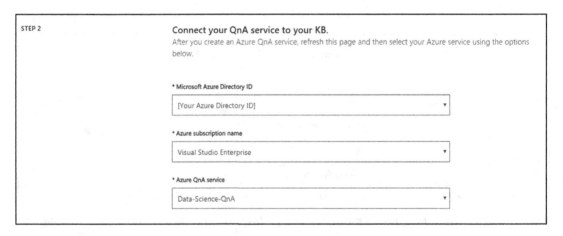

Figure 2-30. *Step 2: Connect the QnA service to the knowledge base (KB)*

7. Enter a **Name** for your knowledge base (Figure 2-31).

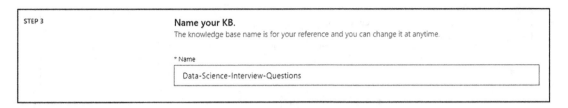

Figure 2-31. *Step 3: Name your knowledge base (KB)*

8. To ingest questions and answers from an external source, enter the following link in the textbox under the **URL** label for the **Populate your KB** section of the form (Figure 2-32):

   ```
   https://www.kdnuggets.com/2016/02/21-data-science-
   interview-questions-answers.html
   ```

   Click the **Add URL** link to add the URL for the question-and-answer page. Once the URL has been added, you have the option to add additional URLs to crawl if required.

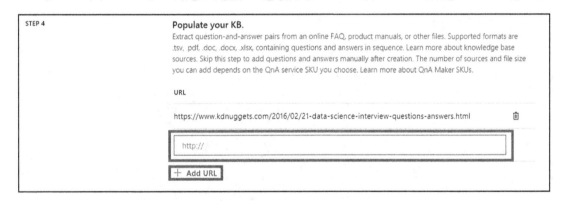

Figure 2-32. *Step 4: Add URL to populate the knowledge base (KB)*

9. As a last step, click the **Create your KB** button at the bottom of the form to start the question-and-answer page crawl (Figure 2-33).

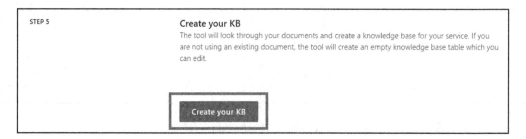

Figure 2-33. *Step 5: The "Create your KB" button*

A message saying that the URL is being crawled will be displayed. Once the knowledge base has been created, you should see a page similar to what is shown in Figure 2-34.

On this page, you also have the ability to edit the answers, to remove unwanted annotations, or to make modifications.

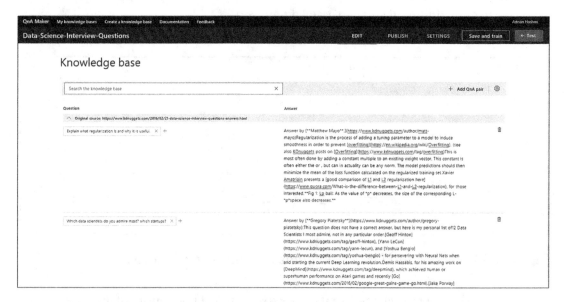

Figure 2-34. *Questions and answers imported into the created knowledge base*

Training and Testing the QnA Service

1. Click the **Save and train** button on the top-right side of the page to save changes and train the QnA service (Figure 2-35).

Figure 2-35. *Save and train the QnA service*

Now that we have our QnA service created, it's time for us to test (and re-train, if needed) our service.

Click the **Test** button on the top right to display the test pane on the right side of the screen (Figure 2-36).

Figure 2-36. *Test the QnA service*

2. Enter *"hello"* in the text box on the test pane and hit Enter on your keyboard.

    You should see a *"No good match found in KB"* message.

3. Again, enter the text *"what is regularization"* in the text box and hit Enter.

    This time around, you'll see a response from the knowledge base (Figure 2-37).

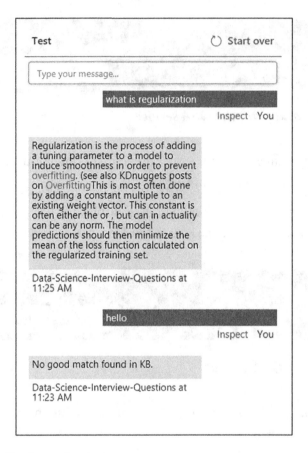

Figure 2-37. *The QnA service test pane*

You can use multiple alternative phrasings, such as "what is regularization," "define regularization," "explain regularization," "how to regularize," and so on.

Publishing the QnA Service

1. Once you're done testing and training your QnA service, you can publish it by clicking the **Publish** button in the top menu (Figure 2-38).

Figure 2-38. *Publish the QnA service*

2. Click the **Publish** button on the Publish information screen (Figure 2-39).

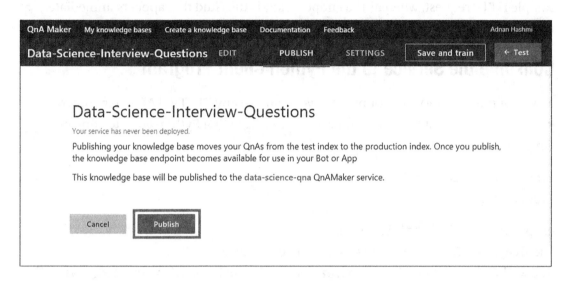

Figure 2-39. *The Publish information screen*

The QnA service will be published, and a success page will be displayed, as shown in Figure 2-40.

Note   The Endpoint key has been replaced by [Some Guid] in Figure 2-40.

Success! Your service has been deployed. What's next?

You can always find the deployment details in your service's settings.

Use the below HTTP request to build your bot. Learn how.

Sample HTTP request	POST /knowledgebases/73a35e6f-bf2d-4a43-861a-c967cac80b4b/generateAnswer Host: https://data-science-qna.azurewebsites.net/qnamaker Authorization: EndpointKey [Some Guid] Content-Type: application/json {"question":"<Your question>"}

Need to fine-tune and refine? Go back and keep editing your service.

Edit Service

Figure 2-40. *QnA service Publish Success page*

You'll need the knowledge base ID and the endpoint key in the next step.

The knowledge base ID appears in Figure 2-40 as the Guid in the first line of the sample HTTP request, whereas the endpoint key is the Guid that appears immediately after EndpointKey on line 3.

Consume the Service to the Python Client Program

Now that the QnA service is published, you can use any RESTFul API client or write your own code to test the Q&A. You can use the following Python code to consume the QnA service:

```
import requests
import json

endpointKey = "<Endpoint key goes here>"
knowledgebaseId = "<Knowledge base Id goes here>"
url = 'https://data-science-qna.azurewebsites.net/qnamaker/knowledgebases/" +
knowledgebaseId + "/generateAnswer'

question = input("Enter your question here: ")
payload = {"question":question }
headers = {"Content-Type": "application/json",
"Authorization": "EndpointKey " + endpointKey
        }
r = requests.post(url, data=json.dumps(payload), headers=headers)

print(r.json()['answers'][0]['questions'])
print('Score: ', r.json()['answers'][0]['score'])
print(r.json()['answers'][0]['answer'])
```

You can test it directly from the command prompt, as shown in Figure 2-41.

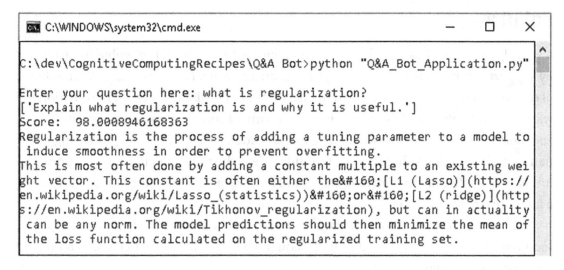

Figure 2-41. *The QnA service consumed from Python code*

Recipe 2-4. Data Center Health Monitor Bot

Almost all Enterprise IT organizations struggle to keep track of their vast organizational systems (and the individual components that make up those systems), the state and health of those systems, and the inherent components. The challenge is compounded by the fact that system owners comprise disparate teams, usually segregated into software and infrastructure (hardware) specialists.

A typical fire drill (I am sure many readers can relate to this) when a system goes down in the enterprise data center involves figuring out what individual components or assets make up the system, which of those components might be the potential culprit that caused the failure, and identifying the owners of those sub-system components.

Problem

The amount of time it takes to diagnose and fix a system failure in the data center causes IT to miss the RTO (Recovery Time Objective) set for the system, leading to missed SLAs, possible loss of revenue, and an adverse effect on organizational reputation.

Information about IT systems and assets is usually maintained in a host of data sources, and sifting through all the available information is a very tedious and time-consuming process. Even in cases where the information is stored in a central system—i.e., a CMDB (configuration management database)—the plethora of screens and reports makes finding the right information inefficient.

Solution

A well-thought-out IT asset management system can allay a lot of the problems faced by support teams trying to recover a system from a disaster. However, the sheer number of data points available and the need to instantly connect all the pieces of information warrants automation and the creation of some form of conversation interface. The conversation interface or bot would allow stakeholders to ask for information using natural language, and subsequently it would retrieve the requested information from the underlying configuration item data stores and narrate responses to those stakeholders in a far more efficient manner.

Different organizations may attempt to design their systems based on their unique requirements and roadmap. A high-level sequential flow of a data center health monitor bot is presented in Figure 2-42.

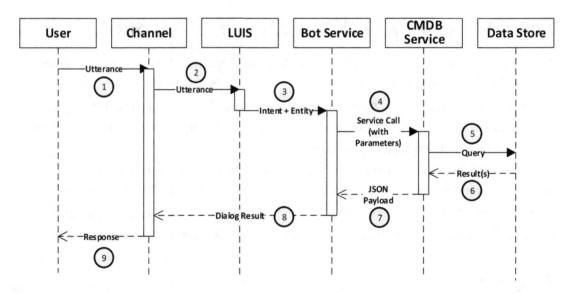

Figure 2-42. *Data center health bot sequence diagram*

How It Works

The following steps correspond to the number labels in the sequence diagram illustrated in Figure 2-42:

1. The user communicates with the bot using a channel UI that allows natural language queries to be submitted to the bot.

2. The bot exposed through the channel (Skype, Microsoft Teams, etc.) passes on the user utterance to the LUIS.ai service.

3. The LUIS service extracts the user intent and entity (or entities) and sends to the bot application endpoint.

4. The bot application endpoint comprises logic that makes a call to the relevant service based on the determined intent.

5. The service, in turn, either retrieves the data from a data store or calls another service.

6. The results retrieved are returned to the calling service code.

7. The service passes the JSON results back to the Bot Service application code.

8. The Bot Service application formats or phrases the received results and surfaces them through the channel.

9. The channel UI presents the natural-language response to the user in the form of either text or audio.

Before we can look at the steps needed to create our chatbot, let's take a look at what *utterances*, *intents*, and *entities* refer to, in the chatbot context:

- **Utterance:** Refers to the natural-language input from a human user; for example, in communicating with a data center chatbot, a human might say something like, "*Who is the owner for the Genesis application?*" or "*Who owns application Genesis?*"

- **Intent:** Determines what the operator providing the input to the chatbot expects to achieve. In the preceding example, the user's intent is to find out the name of a particular application's owner. Using LUIS, a bot developer can easily specify a set of pre-defined intents. In this particular case, the intent can simply be called GetApplicationOwner or Application.GetOwner (*intent* simply represents a string value, and the dot in the name is used only to follow a certain naming convention).

- **Entity:** Represents a class of values that are included in an utterance, and is a noun in most cases. In our example, *Genesis* is the name for an application and can be replaced by any number of application names. To allow the chatbot to determine what object a user utterance is referring to, the value is captured in a pre-defined entity; the Application entity in this case.

The rest of this recipe will explain how you can go about creating the data center chatbot to address the scenario articulated in the "Problem" section.

At a high level the steps for creating the solution are as follows:

a) Create a Bot Service application.

b) Train the bot to extract intents and entities from user utterances.

c) Write code in Visual Studio 2017.

Let's expand on each of these steps.

Create a Bot Service Application

Here is the process:

1. Navigate to Azure Portal (`https://portal.azure.com`) using your web browser and log in using your credentials.

2. Click **Create a resource** in the top-left corner of the menu blade, then click **See all** (Figure 2-43).

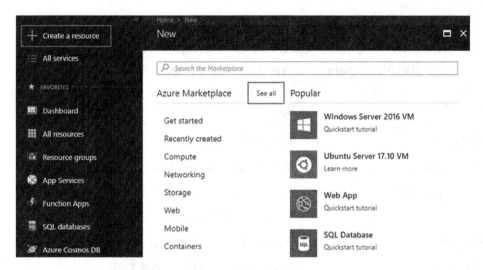

Figure 2-43. *Create a resource using Azure Portal*

3. In the search box, type *"bot"* and hit Enter on your keyboard.

4. Click the **Web App Bot** template in the search results (Figure 2-44).

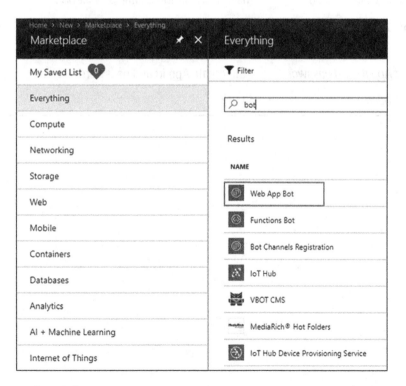

Figure 2-44. *The Web App Bot resource type*

5. Click the **Create** button on the Welcome blade.

6. On the Web App Bot blade, fill out the information as follows, and then click the **Create** button at the bottom (Figure 2-45):

Property	Value
Bot name	DCHealthBotExample
Subscription	[Select your subscription name]
Resource Group	Create new DCHealthBotExample
Location	[Select your nearest location from the drop-down]
Pricing tier	[Select an appropriate pricing tier]
App name	DCHealthBotExample
Bot templates	Language Understanding (C#)
LUIS App location	West US
App service plan/Location	(new) DCHealthBotExample/West US 2
Azure Storage	Create new DCHealthBotExamplebf77
Microsoft App ID and Password	Auto create App Id and password
Confirm Notice	Check

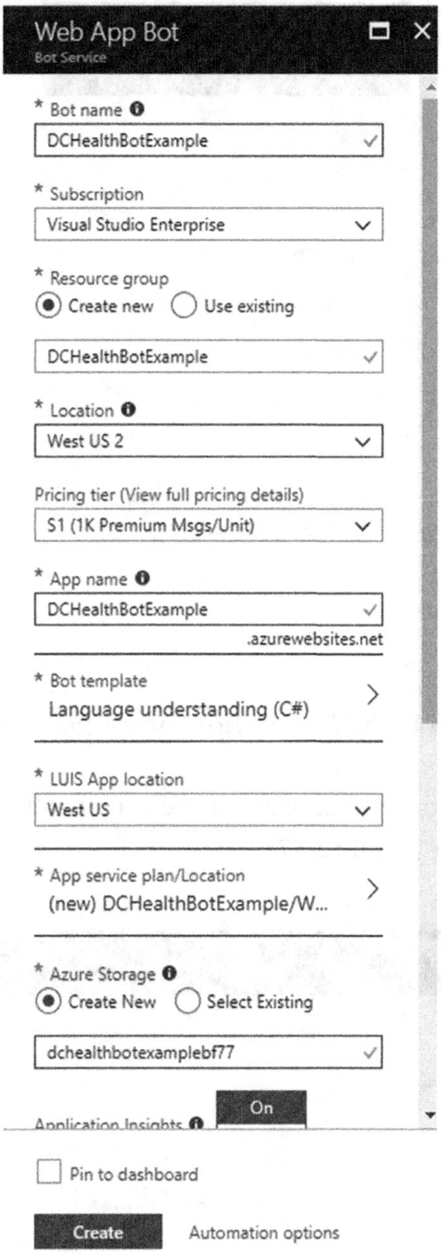

Figure 2-45. *The Web App Bot blade*

7. Once bot deployment finishes, navigate to the
    DCHealthBotExample service and click **Test in Web Chat** in the
    main blade (figure 2-46).

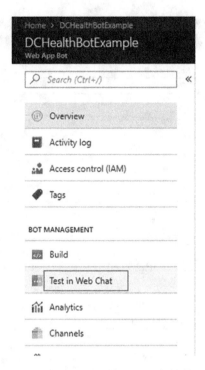

Figure 2-46. *The "Test in Web Chat" option for the web app bot*

8. Enter *"hello"* or some other text to make sure that the bot service is
    working correctly (Figure 2-47).

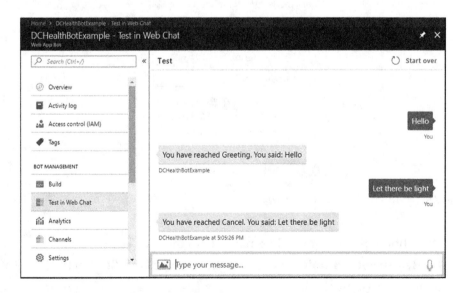

Figure 2-47. *The Test in Web Chat blade*

Train the Bot to Extract Intents and Entities from User Utterances

In this section, we will be creating entities and intents for our chatbot. The following table lists the entities and intents, in addition to the user utterances that would allow the chatbot to determine what is being requested.

Example Utterance(s)	Intent	Entities
"What is the status of Application [X]?" "Give me Application [X] metrics." "How is the health of Application [X]?" "How is Application [X] performing?"	Application.GetHealth	Application.Name
"List Application [X] components." "What are the building blocks for Application [X]?"	Application.GetComponents	Application.Name
"Create a high-severity service desk ticket for Application [X] and assign to [Y] team."	Ticket.CreateIncident	Application.Name Ticket

This is not an exhaustive list of all the utterances that a data center health chatbot would have to process, but I wanted to limit this recipe to a set of common examples.

The steps to train the model to process the preceding listed intents and entities are as follows:

9. Navigate to the Language Understanding Intelligent Service (LUIS) site at https://www.luis.ai (Figure 2-48).

Figure 2-48. *LUIS.ai home page*

10. Log in using the same account credentials you used to sign in to Azure Portal in the previous section.

11. Click on the Bot Service application under My Apps that you created using Azure Portal (Figure 2-49).

Figure 2-49. *The My Apps page on the LUIS.ai portal*

Clicking on the app name takes you to the Intents screen, which lists four default intents that get created any time a LUIS application is created. You can click on each of the intents to explore the utterances linked to each (Figure 2-50).

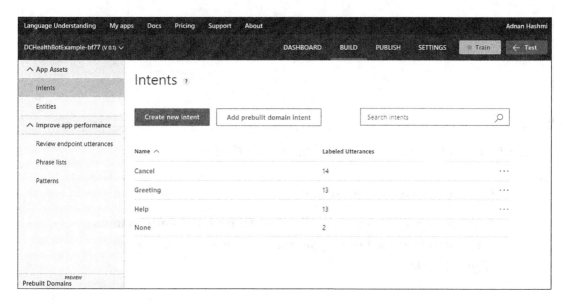

Figure 2-50. *The Intents page on the LUIS.ai portal*

We will need to create the following four entities for this recipe:

   a.   Application.Name

   b.   Ticket.Owner

   c.   Ticket.Severity

   d.   Ticket

12. Click on the **Entities** link under **App Assets** in the left pane (Figure 2-51).

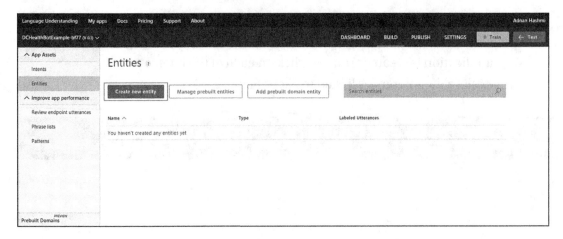

Figure 2-51. *The "Create new entity" button on the Entities page*

13. Click the **Create new entity** button.

14. In the popup dialog, enter **Application.Name** as the **Entity name**, select **Simple** as the **Entity type**, and click the **Done** button (Figure 2-52).

Figure 2-52. *Create the Application.Name entity*

15. Click the **Create new entity** button, and in the popup dialog, enter **Ticket.Owner** as the **Entity name**, select **List** as the **Entity type**, and click the **Done** button (Figure 2-53).

Figure 2-53. *Create the Ticket.Owner entity*

16. In the text box under **Values**, type *"Development"* and hit Enter.

    The entered value will be added to the list of values (Figure 2-54).

17. Repeat Step 8 for two more values: **Database** and **Infrastructure**.

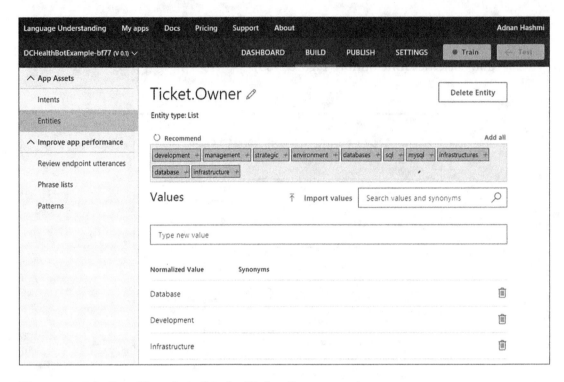

Figure 2-54. *Specify values for the Ticket.Owner entity*

18. Click on the **Entities** link in the left-hand navigation and repeat
    Steps 15-17 to create an entity with the name **Ticket.Severity** and
    List as the entity type.

    Specify **High**, **Medium**, and **Low** as the values for the **Ticket.
    Severity** list entity (Figure 2-55).

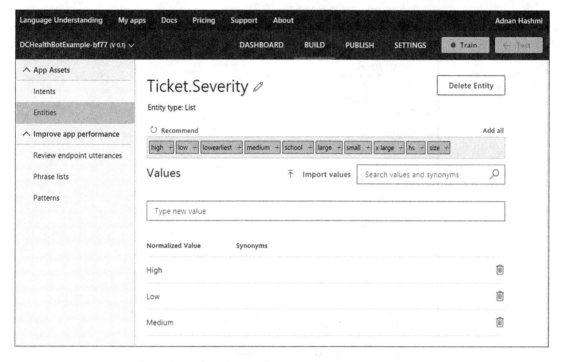

Figure 2-55. *Specify values for the Ticket.Severity entity*

19. Click on the **Entities** link in the left-hand navigation and then click the **Create new entity** button.

    In the popup dialog, enter **Ticket** as the entity name and select **Composite** as the entity type.

20. Click the **Add a child entity** link and select **Application.Name** as the **Child entity** from the drop-down.

    Repeat Step 12 and add two more child entities: **Ticket.Severity** and **Ticket.Owner**.

    Click the **Done** button once complete (Figure 2-56).

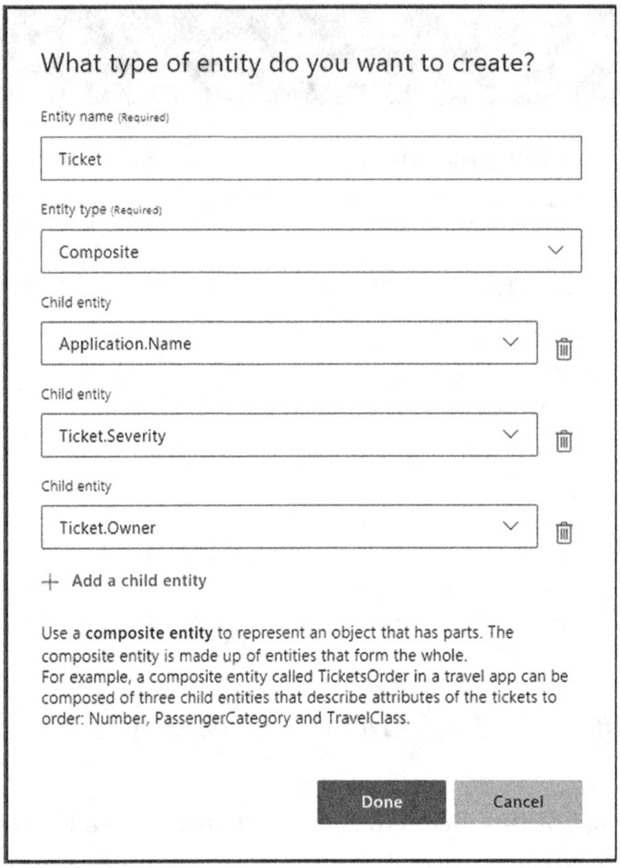

Figure 2-56. *Creating a composite entity*

The following steps pertain to the creation of the three intents we outlined earlier:

    a.   Application.GetHealth

    b.   Application.GetComponents

    c.   Ticket.CreateIncident

21.   Click on the **Intents** link in the left-hand navigation and then click the **Create new intent** button.

22.   Enter **Application.GetHealth** as the Intent name in the **Create new intent** dialog and click the **Done** button (Figure 2-57).

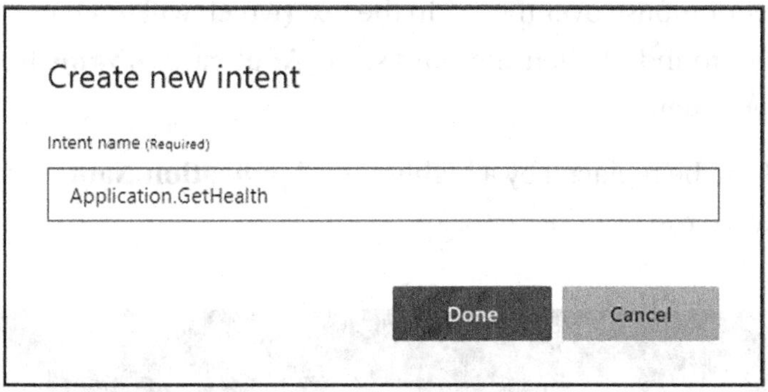

Create new intent

Intent name (Required)

Application.GetHealth

Done   Cancel

Figure 2-57. *The "Create new intent" dialog*

23.   Repeat steps 22 and 23 to create two more intents: **Application. GetComponents** and **Ticket.CreateIncident** (Figure 2-58).

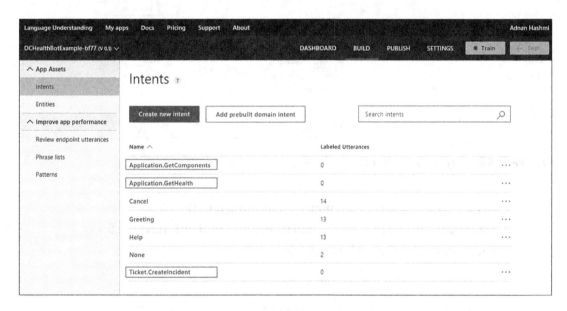

Figure 2-58. *The Intents screen on the LUIS.ai portal*

24.   On the Intents screen, click the **Application.GetHealth** link.

25.   On the Intents screen, type "*What is the status of Application X?*" in the text box and hit Enter on the keyboard.

The entered text will be added to the Utterances list below the text box.

26. Hover your mouse over the "x" in the text (which will put bar brackets around it), then click and select **Application.Name** from the popup menu.

The [x] will be replaced by a highlighted **Application.Name** for the entered text (Figure 2-59).

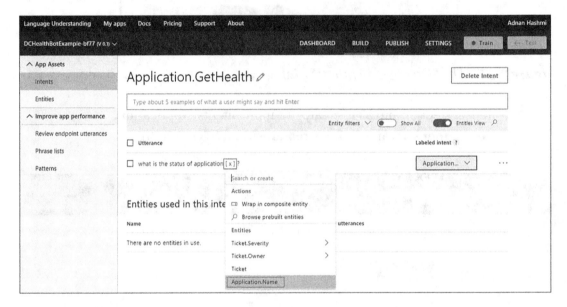

Figure 2-59. *Tag an entity within the utterance text*

27. Repeat Steps 26 and 27 to enter the following additional statements, hovering over "x" and selecting **Application.Name** for each utterance entered (Figure 2-60):

    a. Give me Application X metrics.

    b. How is the health of Application X?

    c. How is Application X performing?

    d. Tell me about the health of the Accounting application.

    e. Show me the status of the Genesis application.

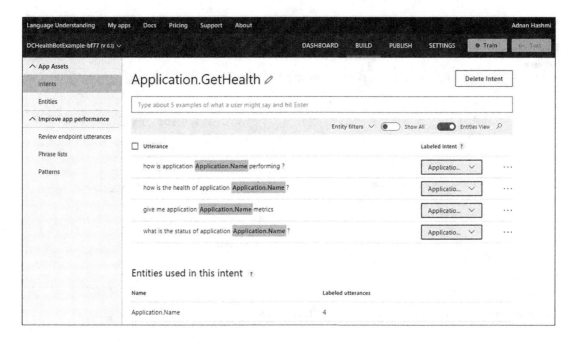

Figure 2-60. *Entities tagged within utterances*

28. Click on the **Intents** link in the left-hand navigation and then click **Application.GetComponents**.

29. Enter the following two example utterances:

    a. List Application X components.

    b. What are the building blocks for Application X?

       You'll notice that this time around, **Application.Name** is automatically selected as the entity for the entered utterances (Figure 2-61).

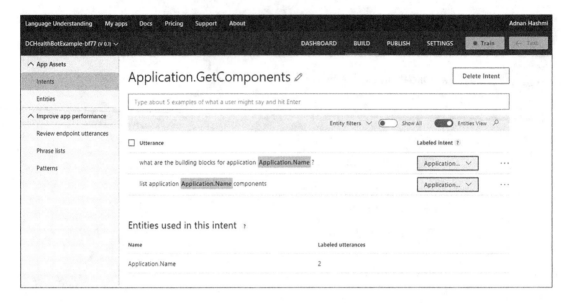

Figure 2-61. *Entities tagged within utterances*

30. Click on the **Intents** link in the left-hand navigation and then click **Ticket.CreateIncident**.

31. Enter utterance "*Create a high-severity service desk ticket for Application X and assign to Y team*" in the text box.

32. Select the appropriate entities created previously for the utterance (Figure 2-62).

Figure 2-62. *Entities tagged within an utterance*

Now that all the entities and intents have been created, the system can be trained to generate a model to be used by the bot application.

33. Click on the **Train** button at the top right-hand corner of the screen.

    Once complete, the red icon on the **Train** button will turn green.

34. Click the **Test** button in the top right-hand corner of the screen to display the **Test** pane.

35. Type *"Show me the health of the Accounting application"* in the test utterance text box and hit Enter.

    Click the **Inspect** link to view the intent confidence (ranges between 0 and 1 and is shown in parentheses) and the extracted entity value (Figure 2-63).

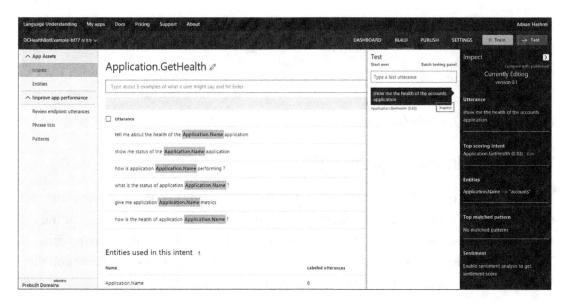

Figure 2-63. *Test the model using a test utterance*

36. As a last step, click on the **Publish** link on the top-right of the screen and then click the **Publish** button (Figure 2-64).

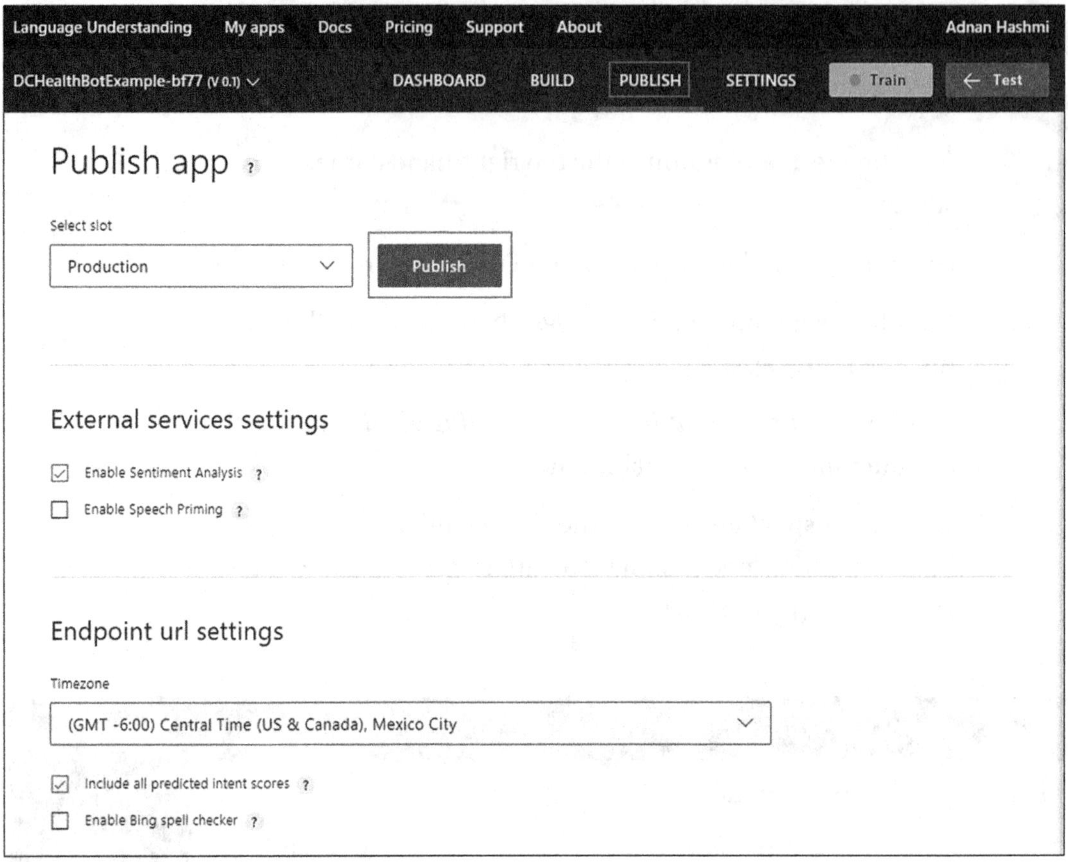

Figure 2-64. *The Publish App screen*

Write Code in Visual Studio 2017

To allow the bot to handle user utterances, the bot code needs to communicate with the LUIS service we created in the previous section. Microsoft takes care of generating a boilerplate Visual Studio solution when you create a Bot Service application in Azure. This section assumes that you have already installed the Microsoft Bot Emulator and the Visual Studio template (see QnA Bot recipe for download links).

1. Navigate to the Bot Service application created earlier using the Azure Portal and click the **Build** link under **Bot Management** in the Navigation blade.

2. Click **Download zip file** to download the Visual Studio solution generated automatically when the Bot Service application was created (Figure 2-65).

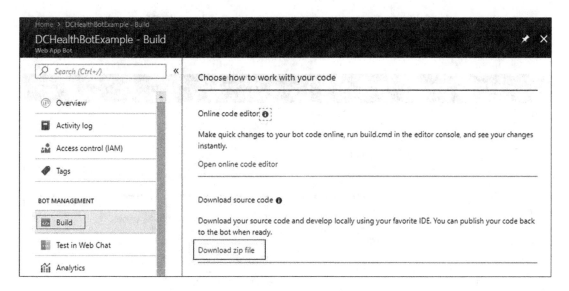

Figure 2-65. *Downloading the bot source code from Azure Portal*

3. Unzip the contents of the downloaded zip file to a folder of your choice.

4. Open the solution file (*.sln) contained in the unzipped contents in Visual Studio 2017.

5. Open the **Web.config** file by double-clicking it in the Solution Explorer and then add the following four configuration settings in the **appSettings** section:

```
<add key="LuisAppId" value="" />
<add key="LuisAPIKey" value="" />
<add key="LuisAPIHostName" value="" />
<add key="AzureWebJobsStorage" value="" />
```

The preceding configuration settings are referenced in the code you just downloaded. You will get a runtime error if you try to run the code without specifying the configuration settings and their values in the **Web.config** file.

6. To get the values for the configuration settings, navigate to the Bot Service application created in Azure Portal and click **Application Settings** under **App Service Settings** on the main blade.

7. Locate the four configuration settings and copy the value for each to the **Web.config** file in Visual Studio 2017 (Figure 2-66).

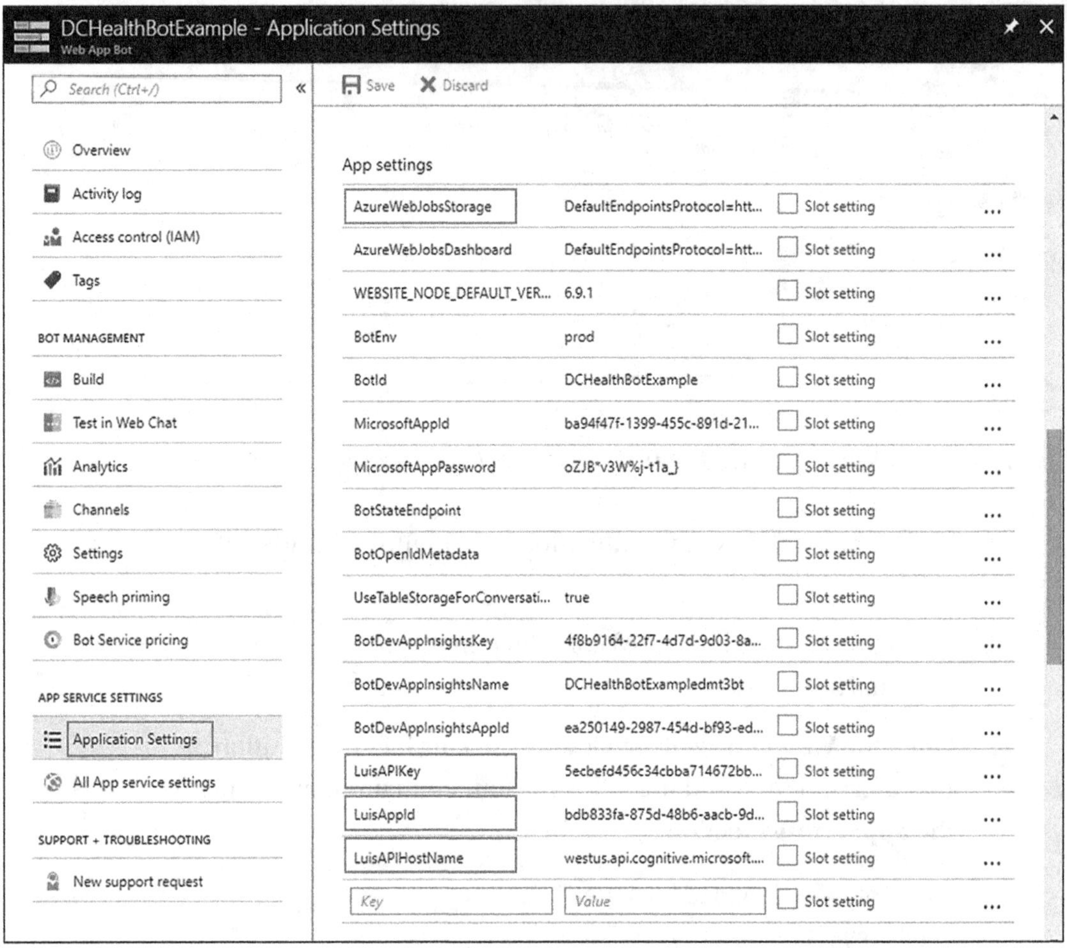

Figure 2-66. *The application settings for the web app bot service*

8. Build the solution by going to Build ➤ Build Solution or by using the **Ctrl+Shift+B** shortcut on your keyboard. (If you get error messages that prevent the solution from compiling, you may need to update the installed NuGet packages to the correct versions).

9. Execute the built solution by clicking the **Run** icon in the top toolbar in Visual Studio 2017.

The application will open in the web browser (Figure 2-67).

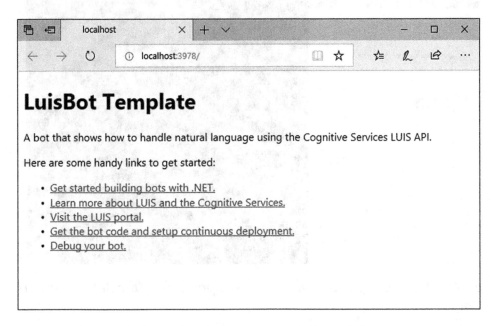

Figure 2-67. *The bot web application running in the web browser*

10. Copy the application's URL (localhost followed by a port number) from the web browser's address bar.

11. With the application running, open the Bot Framework Emulator, paste the copied URL followed by /api/messages in the address bar, and click the **Connect** button (Figure 2-68).

Figure 2-68. *Connecting to the Bot Service endpoint using the Bot Framework Emulator*

12. Once connected, type *"hello"* in the message box and hit Enter on the keyboard (Figure 2-69).

Figure 2-69. *Testing the Bot Service endpoint using the Bot Framework Emulator*

We will now add code to respond to user utterances based on determined intents.

13. Stop the running solution in Visual Studio and open the BasicLuisDialog.cs file by double-clicking it in the Solution Explorer.

    The BasicLuisDialog.cs code file contains the four default intents already added (Figure 2-70).

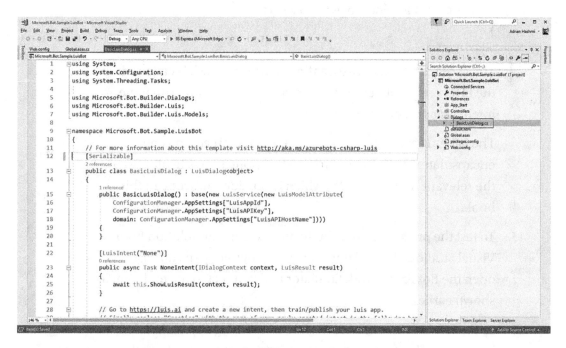

Figure 2-70. *The BasicLuisDialog.cs file in Visual Studio 2017*

14. To handle the Application.GetHealth intent, add the following code to the BasicLuisDialog.cs file:

```
[LuisIntent("Application.GetHealth")]
public async Task ApplicationHealthIntent(IDialogContext
context, LuisResult result)
{
await this.ShowApplicationHealth(context, result);
}
```

```
private async Task ShowApplicationHealth(IDialogContext
context, LuisResult result)
{
    string appName = result.Entities[0].Entity;
    string status = DCHealthBot.Helper.
GetApplicationHealth(appName);

    await context.PostAsync($"The current health of the
    application is {status}.");
    context.Wait(MessageReceived);
}
```

The `ApplicationHealthIntent` asynchronous task is called when the LUIS endpoint determines from the user utterance that the intent is `Application.GetHealth`.

The `DCHealthBot.Helper` class used in the preceding code encapsulates the logic to retrieve the application's health from the relevant APIs or CMDB, which is outside the scope of this book.

15. To test the preceding code, build and execute the solution from Visual Studio 2017, and once the web browser opens up, also open the Bot Framework Emulator and connect to the endpoint as shown earlier.

16. Enter the text *"Give me status of the Accounting application."* The code will determine the intent, retrieve the status from the backend system or API, and return the result (Figure 2-71).

Figure 2-71. *Testing the Bot Service endpoint using the Bot Framework Emulator*

Setting Up Azure Deployment via Resource Manager Template

When automating your machine-learning pipelines, managing your workflows via a web-based user interface is probably the worst possible way to do so. The preferred approach is either using scripting via Azure PowerShell with Resource Manager templates to deploy your resources to Azure (goo.gl/YpK3t1), or via code.

The following code segment shows how you can set up an Azure deployment via a Resource Manager template via a helper class. You can use this to generate your Resource Manager client, create and verify if the resource group exists, and start the deployment.

```
// Requires the following Azure NuGet packages and related dependencies:
// package id="Microsoft.Azure.Management.Authorization" version="2.0.0"
// package id="Microsoft.Azure.Management.ResourceManager" version="1.4.0-
   preview"
// package id="Microsoft.Rest.ClientRuntime.Azure.Authentication"
   version="2.2.8-preview"
```

```csharp
using Microsoft.Azure.Management.ResourceManager;
using Microsoft.Azure.Management.ResourceManager.Models;
using Microsoft.Rest.Azure.Authentication;
using Newtonsoft.Json;
using Newtonsoft.Json.Linq;
using System;
using System.IO;

namespace PortalGenerated
{
    /// <summary>
    /// This is a helper class for deploying an Azure Resource Manager
        template
    /// More info about template deployments can be found here https://
        go.microsoft.com/fwLink/?LinkID=733371
    /// </summary>
    class DeploymentHelper
    {
        string subscriptionId = "your-subscription-id";
        string clientId = "your-service-principal-clientId";
        string clientSecret = "your-service-principal-client-secret";
        string resourceGroupName = "resource-group-name";
        string deploymentName = "deployment-name";
        string resourceGroupLocation = "resource-group-location"; // must
        be specified for creating a new resource group
        string pathToTemplateFile = "path-to-template.json-on-disk";
        string pathToParameterFile = "path-to-parameters.json-on-disk";
        string tenantId = "tenant-id";

        public async void Run()
        {
            // Try to obtain the service credentials
            var serviceCreds = await ApplicationTokenProvider.
            LoginSilentAsync(tenantId, clientId, clientSecret);
```

```
// Read the template and parameter file contents
JObject templateFileContents = GetJsonFileContents(pathToTempla
teFile);
JObject parameterFileContents = GetJsonFileContents(pathToParam
eterFile);

// Create the resource manager client
var resourceManagementClient = new ResourceManagementClient(ser
viceCreds);
resourceManagementClient.SubscriptionId = subscriptionId;

// Create or check that resource group exists
EnsureResourceGroupExists(resourceManagementClient,
resourceGroupName, resourceGroupLocation);

// Start a deployment
DeployTemplate(resourceManagementClient, resourceGroupName,
deploymentName, templateFileContents, parameterFileContents);
}

/// <summary>
/// Reads a JSON file from the specified path
/// </summary>
/// <param name="pathToJson">The full path to the JSON file</param>
/// <returns>The JSON file contents</returns>
private JObject GetJsonFileContents(string pathToJson)
{
    JObject templatefileContent = new JObject();
    using (StreamReader file = File.OpenText(pathToJson))
    {
        using (JsonTextReader reader = new JsonTextReader(file))
        {
            templatefileContent = (JObject)JToken.ReadFrom(reader);
            return templatefileContent;
        }
    }
}
```

```
/// <summary>
/// Ensures that a resource group with the specified name exists.
    If it does not, will attempt to create one.
/// </summary>
/// <param name="resourceManagementClient">The resource manager
    client.</param>
/// <param name="resourceGroupName">The name of the resource
    group.</param>
/// <param name="resourceGroupLocation">The resource group
    location. Required when creating a new resource group.</param>
private static void EnsureResourceGroupExists(ResourceManagement
Client, string resourceGroupName, string resourceGroupLocation)
{
    if (resourceManagementClient.ResourceGroups.CheckExistence(reso
    urceGroupName) != true)
    {
        Console.WriteLine(string.Format("Creating resource
        group '{0}' in location '{1}'", resourceGroupName,
        resourceGroupLocation));
        var resourceGroup = new ResourceGroup();
        resourceGroup.Location = resourceGroupLocation;
        resourceManagementClient.ResourceGroups.CreateOrUpdate(reso
        urceGroupName, resourceGroup);
    }
    else
    {
        Console.WriteLine(string.Format("Using existing resource
        group '{0}'", resourceGroupName));
    }
}
```

```
/// <summary>
/// Starts a template deployment.
/// </summary>
/// <param name="resourceManagementClient">The resource manager
    client.</param>
/// <param name="resourceGroupName">The name of the resource
    group.</param>
/// <param name="deploymentName">The name of the deployment.
    </param>
/// <param name="templateFileContents">The template file
    contents.</param>
/// <param name="parameterFileContents">The parameter file
    contents.</param>
private static void DeployTemplate(ResourceManagementClient,
string resourceGroupName, string deploymentName, JObject
templateFileContents, JObject parameterFileContents)
{
    Console.WriteLine(string.Format("Starting template
    deployment '{0}' in resource group '{1}'", deploymentName,
    resourceGroupName));
    var deployment = new Deployment();

    deployment.Properties = new DeploymentProperties
    {
        Mode = DeploymentMode.Incremental,
        Template = templateFileContents,
        Parameters = parameterFileContents["parameters"].
        ToObject<JObject>()
    };

    var deploymentResult = resourceManagementClient.Deployments.Cre
    ateOrUpdate(resourceGroupName, deploymentName, deployment);
    Console.WriteLine(string.Format("Deployment status: {0}",
    deploymentResult.Properties.ProvisioningState));
    }
  }
}
```

References & Further Reading

Srikanth Machiraju and Ritesh Modi, *Developing Bots with Microsoft Bots Framework: Create Intelligent Bots using MS Bot Framework and Azure Cognitive Services*, Apress. Published 2017.

Joe Mayo, *Programming the Microsoft Bot Framework: A Multiplatform Approach to Building Chatbots*. Published 2017.

CHAPTER 3

Seeing Is Believing: Custom Vision

"If we want machines to think, we need to teach them to see."

—Fei Fei Li, Stanford Professor and chief scientist of
AI/ML of Google Cloud;

"Our mission is to bring AI to every developer and every organization on the planet, and to help businesses augment human ingenuity in unique and differentiated ways. . . . Once you have created and trained your custom vision model through the service, it's a matter of a few clicks to get your model exported from the service. This allows developers a quick way to take their custom model with them to any environment, whether their scenario requires that the model run on-premises, in the cloud, or on mobile and edge devices. This provides the most flexible and easy way for developers to export and embed custom vision models in minutes with 'zero' coding."

—Joseph Sirosh, corporate vice president of artificial
intelligence and research at Microsoft

The integration and use of computer-vision technologies in context with artificial intelligence and machine learning has become a topic of immense interest in both academia and industry. As computation power increases, new algorithms and techniques become available to be used for next generation of computer-vision research and development.

© Adnan Masood, Adnan Hashmi 2019
A. Masood and A. Hashmi, *Cognitive Computing Recipes*, https://doi.org/10.1007/978-1-4842-4106-6_3

All major platforms offer computer vision APIs with which to create AI-based applications, both on-premises and in the cloud. Even though computer vision is typically defined as a machine's ability to "see" an image, similar to how humans see things, the implementations vary from granular tasks like image classification, object detection, image segmentation, similarity analysis, labeling various objects, feature extraction, captioning, dense captioning, to larger and more holistic tasks of figuring out what objects make up a specific image or video frame. Computer vision APIs and services, such as Microsoft Cognitive Services, deal with visual information that is processed in the form of images and videos.

The computer vision APIs helps extract rich context-sensitive information from an image about its contents to help solve real-world problems such as retail-shelf inventory analysis, anomaly detection on pipelines and long-distance wires via drones, welding defects in radiological images, automatic license-plate recognition, real-time human-action recognition, and medical imaging to name a few. The uncanny effectiveness of deep learning led Geoffrey Hinton, the godfather of neural networks, to say that it is "quite obvious that we should stop training radiologists." He further elaborated that as image-perception algorithms get to be evidently better than humans, "I think that if you work as a radiologist you are like Wile E. Coyote in the cartoon, you're already over the edge of the cliff, but you haven't yet looked down. There's no ground underneath."

There is some contention about Hinton's statement in medical circles, but today's specialized approaches for extracting rich information from an image about its contents, getting intelligent captions for textual description of the image, detecting BMI, gender, and age, and racy/adult content detection have real use cases for content moderation to evaluate text, images, and videos for offensive content.

Cognitive Services vision APIs also include the emotion API, which analyzes faces to detect a range of feelings, such as anger, happiness, sadness, fear, and surprise. The face API detects human faces, compares similar ones, and can help organize people into groups according to visual similarity, and also identifies previously tagged people in images—i.e., facial verification. The Cognitive Services video API provides support for intelligent video processing for face detection, motion detection, generating thumbnails, and near real-time video analysis for items like writing captions for each frame.

In this chapter, we will also look at custom vision service use, as well as at using CNTK. This is to help address use cases where you need to perform image recognition on a wider spectrum of objects and scenes. Custom vision allows you to create custom image classifiers, typically focused on a specific domain, such as retail, medical, fintech, etc.. For instance, you can train a custom vision service to identify different types of receipts or forms, and then use the REST API to consume this model using an application, service, cell phone or an edge device. These capabilities also extend to video analysis, where the indexer extracts insights from videos to perform facial recognition, sentiment analysis, and captioning. In retail, these capabilities are highly useful for detecting the shopper's sentiment—i.e., emotion detection—at retail displays to check their level of interest or at smart displays for customized offers; for detection to authorize entry; or to calculate the male/female ratio for demographic targeting and interest. In retail displays and brick and mortar establishments, understanding user behavior for engagement, retention, and up-selling helps deliver a better product experience or a chance to offer upgrades. Real-time A|B multivariate targeting—i.e., experimenting with different images, designs, and user elements, including user-defined uploads and custom images—can be supported with minimal or no human interaction by the capabilities offered by custom vision APIs.

The list of humanitarian-, safety-, and security-related use cases in computer vision is quite long. Workplace safety and alerts, audits, logging and tracing of the capabilities, facial identification to find missing children, search for human trafficking victims, and providing natural language object recognition to enable a blind person to read a menu are just the tip of the iceberg. The use of camera data also includes features like smart doorbells that provide a daily log informing you of deliveries, mailman, family members, a neighbor's dog that strolled by (and you can catch him doing business on your lawn!), and so forth, as well as baby monitors!

Without further ado, let's look into the recipes and how to do these things with code and the Cognitive Services portal.

3-1. Hot Dog, Not Hot Dog

No book on computer vision is complete without the quintessential (albeit cheesy) hotdog/nothot dog example. The MNIST of deep neural networks, hotdog, Not hotdog is the dataset of classifying images. The practical nature of these graphics shall remain obscure so as to protect the sensitivities of readers, from the HBO show *Silicon Valley*.

As noted in *XKCD* 1425 (`https://xkcd.com/1425/`), it is evidently hard in CS to explain the difference between seemingly simple and virtually impossible tasks. The classification of cats versus dogs used to be one such case. In the following example, we will see how to use custom vision to accomplish the image classification task using a small food dataset.

Problem

In most computer vision–related industry cases, we have a set of objects that needs to be categorized, labelled, and classified into different subsets and groups. Humans are very good at these tasks, but machines still struggle. How do we provide a machine a sample of objects and use it to classify items into two categories? It could be husky or corgi, corgi or muffin, hot dog or not hot dog, Bolt A or Bolt B, Ryan Gosling or Ryan Reynolds, Elijah Wood or Daniel Radcliffe, Jessica Chastain or Bryce Dallas Howard, Amy Adams or Isla Fisher—the list goes on.

tldr; let's do object classification by providing training samples

Solution

To demonstrate how easy it is to accomplish this image-classification task using custom vision, we will be using a visual approach, hence the screenshots, so please brace for it. To prepare for this walkthrough, visit `https://github.com/prash29/Hotdog-Not-Hotdog` and download the dataset of images.

Now, to start the visual walkthrough, visit CustomVision.ai and enter your email and password to log in.

Once logged in, click **New Project.**

Figure 3-1. *Create a new project on the CustomVision.ai site*

In the following screen, you would provide the details of your new project, a description, and the category it belongs to. For the purpose of this classifying exercise, select **Classification** as the project type and **Food** as the domain. At the time of this writing, custom vision supports classification, while object detection is still a beta offering.

You can also choose the domain to which your dataset belongs. This helps optimize the search using the pre-trained models already available as part of Cognitive Services.

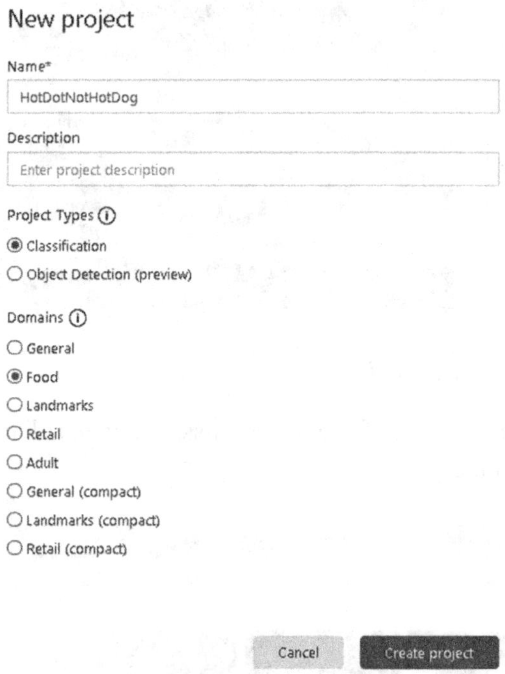

New project

Name*

HotDotNotHotDog

Description

Enter project description

Project Types (i)
- (•) Classification
- ( ) Object Detection (preview)

Domains (i)
- ( ) General
- (•) Food
- ( ) Landmarks
- ( ) Retail
- ( ) Adult
- ( ) General (compact)
- ( ) Landmarks (compact)
- ( ) Retail (compact)

Cancel   Create project

Figure 3-2. *Enter details for the HotDogNotHotDog project*

You'll also see the compact models available for certain domains, which are optimized for the constraints of real-time classification on edge devices such as mobile phones. Classifiers built using compact domains might not be as accurate, but they can be exported and used on edge devices and then trained with more varied images to help improve accuracy.

Now, it's time to tag and upload the training images. Using the dataset extracted earlier, select the training images and tag these with the desired keywords; in this case, *hotdogs* and *hot dogs*.

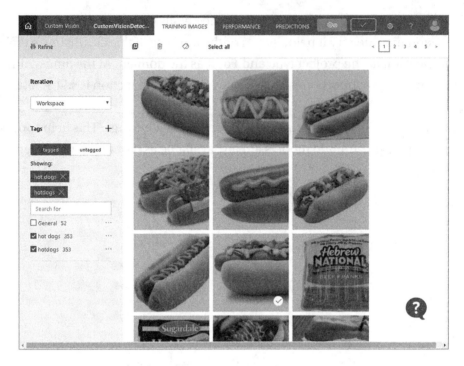

Figure 3-3. *Tag images for training*

You also want to tag members of the other class, i.e., *general*, which are not hot dogs, such as the following images.

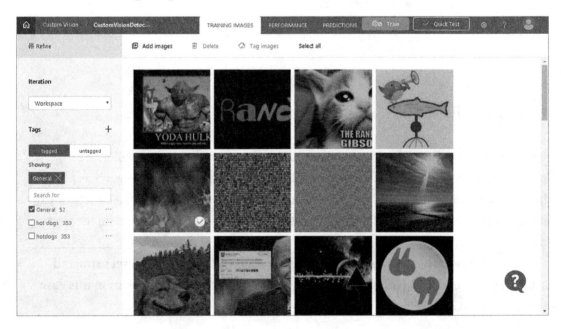

Figure 3-4. *Tag images for other class(es)*

Once uploaded, click on the green **Train** button to train the classifier. You will then see the iterations and corresponding performances.

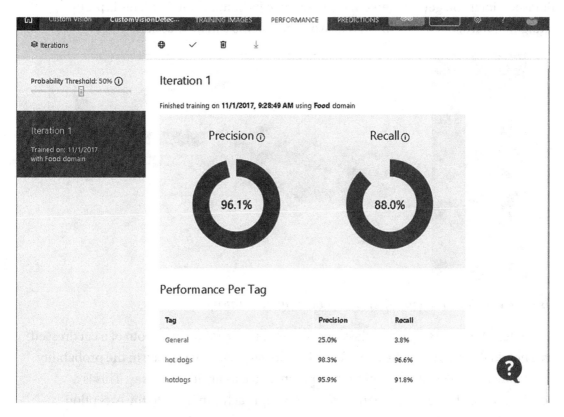

Figure 3-5. *Classifier training performances per tag*

Precision and recall are good together. *Recall* tells you what percentage of images actually have hot dogs that were detected correctly using your classifier, while *precision* talks about the percentage of images that were declared positive using your classifier and were actually hot dogs. Or, alternatively, in mathy terms:

$$Precision = (TruePositives)/(TruePositives + FalsePositives)$$
$$Precision = (TruePositives)/(TruePositives + FalsePositives)$$

and

$$Recall = (TruePositives)/(TruePositives + FalseNegatives)$$
$$Recall = (TruePositives)/(TruePositives + FalseNegatives)$$

Now you can test out your algorithm using different images by clicking on the **Test image** link. Upload and submit a hot dog image that is not part of your training dataset. Viola! You get 100 percent probability of its being a hot dog. This is pretty straightforward, but as we know, real-world problems can be messier.

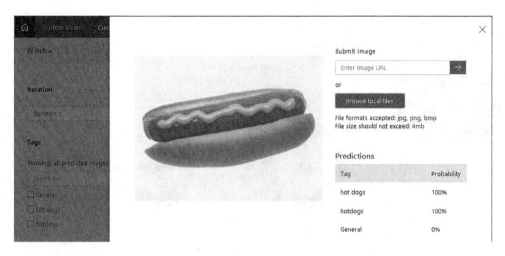

Figure 3-6. *Test the classifier by uploading new images*

To test the accuracy of our classifier, let's try out the following photo of a cat dressed as a hot dog. In this case, the classifier is just not sure. As you can see in the probability breakdown, it does not have enough confidence to classify it either way. This is a good example of where a human-in-the-loop approach can help do the exception classification in real-world business cases.

Figure 3-7. *Test classifier accuracy by uploading a confusing or ambiguous image*

Now, as a final test, let's try out the following photo of a dog dressed as a hot dog. In this case, the classifier misclassifies the image as being of a hot dog, which can have potentially dangerous results.

Figure 3-8. *Test classifier accuracy by uploading a confusing or ambiguous image*

How does one avoid such misclassifications? Having a larger, more diverse dataset would help. Having similar negative samples as part of such a dataset also helps train the classifier and improves overall accuracy.

Having said that, attacking trained models with adversarial examples in order to deliberately deceive them is an active area of research where generative adversarial networks (GAN) are set out to attack state-of-the-art face recognition systems (`https://arxiv.org/pdf/1801.00349.pdf`), and other objects are studied. In their CVR paper "Deep Neural Networks Are Easily Fooled: High Confidence Predictions for Unrecognizable Images" (`http://www.evolvingai.org/fooling`), the Nguyen, Yosinski, and Clune provided examples where neural networks were easily duped into considering unnatural and bizarre images as, well, real objects.

Figure 3-9. *Unrecognizable images*

3-2. Building Custom Vision to Train Your Security System

Now that we have tried binary classification of images, let's get sophisticated. How about training for people—faces, to be exact. In this recipe you will see training images of faces and do classification based on such images.

Problem

How can I train an on-edge device like a cell phone or a smart doorbell to recognize the person visiting using custom vision services?

Solution

Caveat emptor: Don't try this at home.

The following are step-by-step directions for the setup. It is similar to Recipe 3-1; however, the repetitive steps have been removed for clarity and consistency.

Visit the Custom Vision website and click on the **Sign In** button: `https:// customvision.ai/`. Log in using your email.

The app will ask for permission. Click **Yes** to allow the app to access your profile and data.

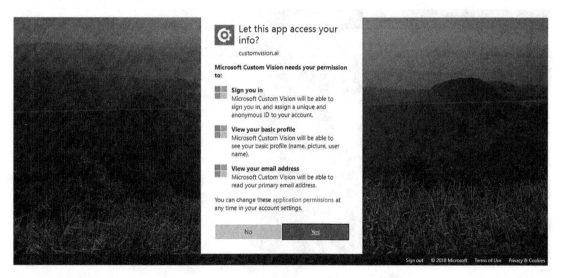

Figure 3-10. *Allow permissions to the CustomVision.ai app*

It will ask you to accept the Terms of Service. Read the agreements carefully. Select the checkbox to accept the terms agreements and click the **I agree** button.

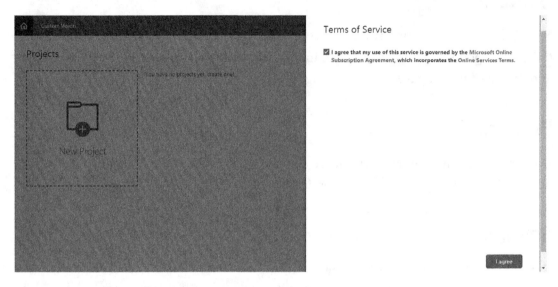

Figure 3-11. *Accepting the Terms for Service for CustomVision.ai*

Next, it will ask for an Azure account. You can sign up for an account, skip it with "I'll do it later," or log in to your Azure account by clicking on the **Switch directories** link if you have one already.

Figure 3-12. *Picking the Azure account to use*

After clicking "Switch directories," the following screen will appear. Click **Ok!** to continue.

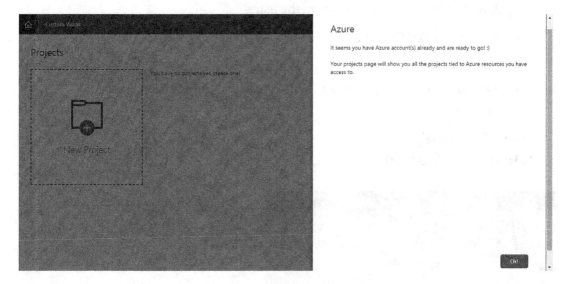

Figure 3-13. *Switch directories to use your Azure account*

Now, click **New Project** to create a new project.

Figure 3-14. *Create a new CustomVision.ai project*

Enter the details of the project:

- Name: [any name]

- Description: [anything that makes sense]

- Resource Group: "Limited Trial" if you have a trial account. If you have a subscription choose from the list.

- Project Types: "Classification" to classify images. This is what we want.

- Domains: "General (compact)." Projects with compact domains can be exported.

Then, click **Create project.**

This is again a classification exercise.

Figure 3-15. *Enter details for the new CustomVision.ai project*

The project will open, and you will see a button to add images. We will add images to train the classifier. Click on **Add images** to add images.

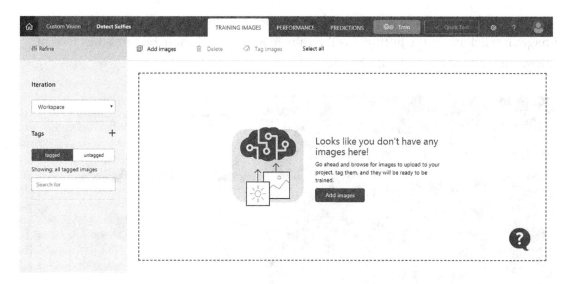

Figure 3-16. *Add images to train the classifier*

Click **Browse local files** to upload images from your machine.

Make sure that the images are taken from different camera angles, lighting, background, types, styles, groups, sizes, and so forth. Use a variety of photo types to ensure that your classifier is not biased and can generalize well. The maximum allowed size is 6 MB per file.

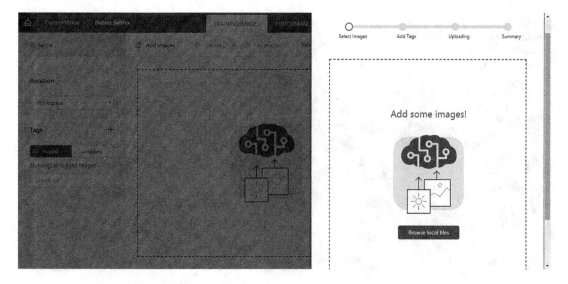

Figure 3-17. *Upload images from your local drive*

Now, add tags to the images by clicking on the "+" sign, and then upload the images by clicking on the button. I will go ahead and upload some pictures they took at Microsoft Ignite at the LinkedIn booth.

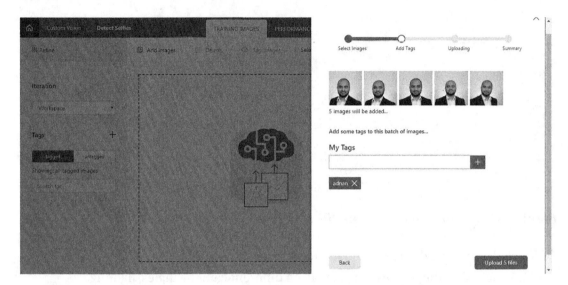

Figure 3-18. *Add tags to the uploaded images*

The upload process will start, and once the images are uploaded click **Done** to continue.

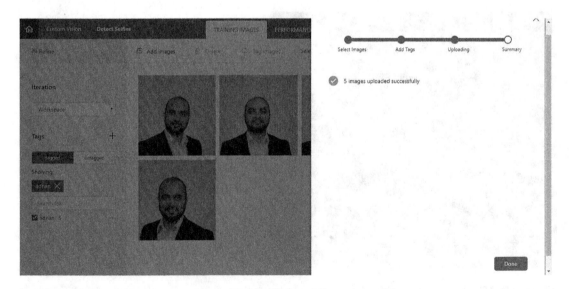

Figure 3-19. *Images uploaded after tagging*

A screen will appear with the uploaded images.

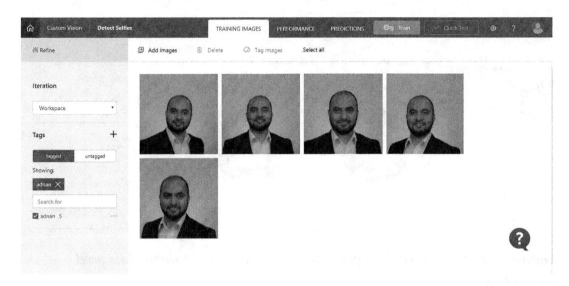

Figure 3-20. *Tagged images uploaded successfully*

Click on the Performance tab and change the probability to 90 percent, then click on the **Train** button to train the classifier. The probability threshold defines what the potential tolerance for accuracy is. In this case we want to be 90 percent sure that the person in the picture is the person at the door.

Figure 3-21. *Set Probability Threshold for image classification*

Once the training is complete the results will be shown for both precision and recall. Since this is just one class, you can see both values are 100 percent.

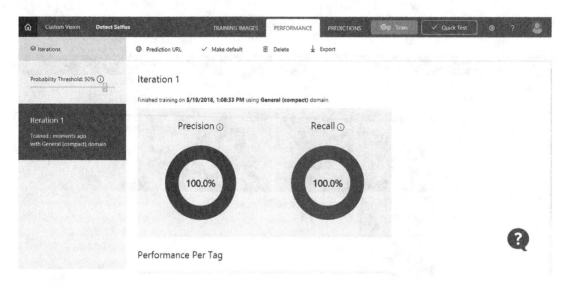

Figure 3-22. *Precision and Recall displayed as 100% for a single class used for training*

You can test the model by clicking on the **Quick Test** button on the top menu bar.

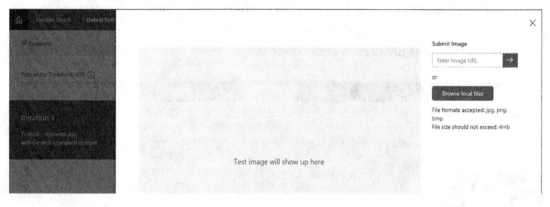

Figure 3-23. *Quick Test of the trained model*

Upload an image that has not been used to train, and it will show a prediction of the picture by tagging.

Figure 3-24. *Upload new image to test classifier*

Great results! Now try another.

Figure 3-25. *Upload another image to test classifier*

Perfect. This means it works. Now, let's test it out with my co-author's picture.

Figure 3-26. *Test classifier with an image from a different class*

Click on the Predictions tab to see the test results; you can see that the probability of this being Adnan (Masood) is 0 percent.

For better results, keep testing images, adding tags, and retraining until you are getting satisfactory results. Once satisfied with the results, click on the Performance tab and then on the **Export** button.

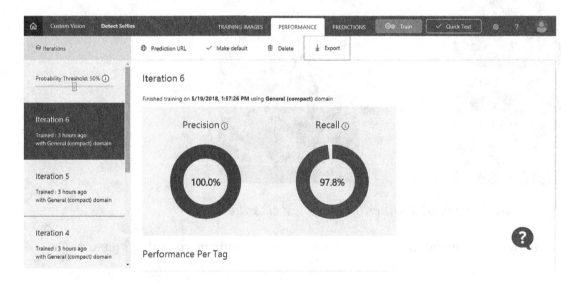

Figure 3-27. *Export the trained classifier model*

Here you can export models in various formats. This includes iOS CoreML for iOS devices, TensorFlow for Android, and ONNX (Open Neural Network Exchange), which is a part of an open ecosystem for interchangeable AI models.

Choose TensorFlow.

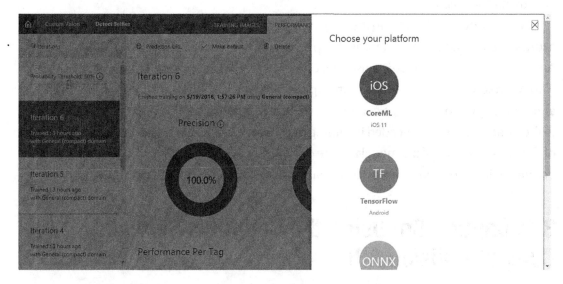

Figure 3-28.   *Export the trained classifier model for used with TensorFlow*

Click on the **Download** button to download the files. The zip file will have two files— one for labels and one for TensorFlow.

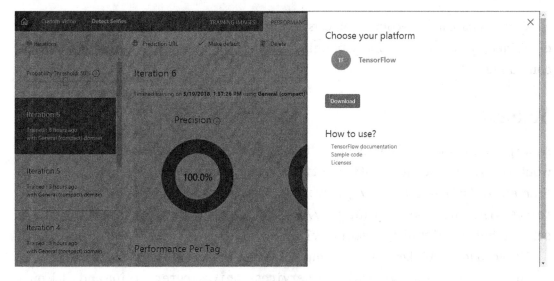

Figure 3-29.   *Download the exported files as a zip archive*

To use this model as part of your mobile app, you can clone this repository and open it in Android Studio. A complete working example of the Android custom vision service can be found here on github:

`https://github.com/Azure-Samples/cognitive-services-android-customvision-sample`

Add the downloaded files to the project assets of the Android app available as part of azure sample listed above. Overwrite the previous files. Create a build and run it on an Android device. The application uses the Camera 2 API, which means it requires devices with Android version > 5. Now you can deploy this model on edge on multiple devices and endpoints. This model of edge computing i.e. bringing memory and computing power closer to the location where it is needed is gaining popularity quickly and being applied in variety of domains. Training of the model is done on computationally powerful servers while the evaluation is performed on the edge i.e. data gets processed as close to the source as possible.

3-3. Caption Bot Using the Cognitive Services Computer Vision API

Going beyond simple face detection and binary classification, we will now look into a more sophisticated use case by generating captions and understanding objects within images.

Problem

How do you have a bot recognize objects within an image and write a textual description of the image—i.e., labelling and captioning—in an automated manner using a cognitive computing API?

Solution

As we proceed to solve this problem with the Computer Vision API, the prerequisite would be to have **Node.js.** Get it from `https://nodejs.org`. You also need **Bot Framework Emulator** (`https://github.com/Microsoft/BotFramework-Emulator/releases`) installed and set up (`https://docs.microsoft.com/en-us/azure/bot-service/bot-service-debug-emulator?view=azure-bot-service-3.0`).

We need to get API keys for the Computer Vision API. Go to `https://azure.microsoft.com/en-in/try/cognitive-services/?api=computer-vision` and click on the **Get API Key** button to get a free API key for seven days.

Now, select your country and accept the Microsoft Cognitive Services Terms to continue.

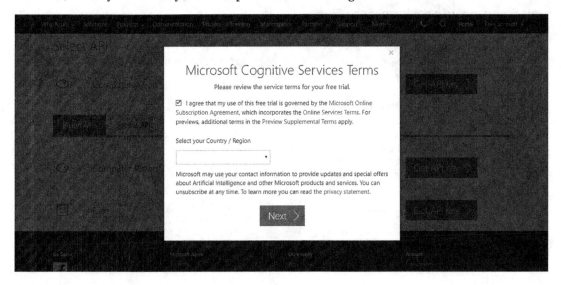

Figure 3-30. *Select country and accept the Microsoft Cognitive Services API Terms of Use*

Sign in using any of the available methods. Once you are logged in, you will get your keys and API endpoints.

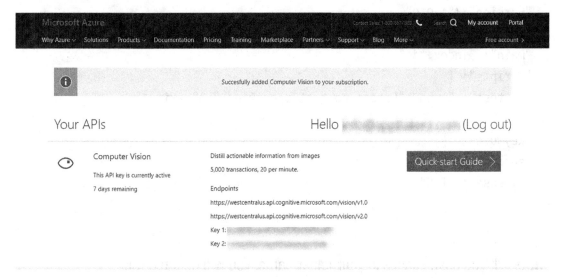

Figure 3-31. *Computer Vision API Keys and Endpoints*

Copy the API keys to a safe place.

Now we will work on creating the Caption Bot. Let's create a new folder with the name CaptionBot or any other name and open the folder in Visual Code or in your favorite IDE.

Open the terminal using "CTRL + ` " and run `npm init -y`. This will initialize the project and create a `package.json` file.

```
$ npm init -y
Wrote to E:_____\CaptionBot\package.json:

{
  "name": "CaptionBot",
  "version": "1.0.0",
  "description": "",
  "main": "index.js",
  "scripts": {
    "test": "echo \"Error: no test specified\" && exit 1"
  },
  "keywords": [],
  "author": "",
  "license": "ISC"
}
```

```
$ npm init -y
Wrote to E: \CaptionBot\package . json:
{
    "name": "CaptionBot",
    "version": "1.0.0",
    "description" : ""
    "main": "index. js"
    "scripts": {
        "test": "echo \"Error: no test specified\" && exit 1"
    },
    "keywords": [],
    "author": "",
    "license": "ISC"
}
```

Note   If you have spaces in your folder name, you will get an error.

Now, install the required packages by running the following:

```
npm install --save botbuilder dotenv restify request-promise
```

- botbuilder is the official module of Microsoft for Node.js to create a bot.

- dotenv allows us to load environment variables easily and safely. We will use this to load our API key.

- restify is used to create a REST endpoint. We need one for our bot.

- request-promise allows us to make HTTP requests easily and efficiently. It is a promise version of the original request module.

```
$ npm install --save botbuilder dotenv restify request-promise
dtrace-provider@0.8.7 install E: * \node_modules \dtrace-provider
node-gyp rebuild | | node suppress-error . js
```

Create a .env file and save the API key in the file.

```
COMPUTER VISION KEY= ************************
```

Create a new file, app.js, and add the modules.

```
// Load environment variables
require( ' dotenv' ) . config( )

const builder = require( 'botbuilder' ) ;
const restify = require( 'restify' ) ;
const request = require( 'request-promise' ) .defaults({ encoding: null } ) ;
```

Store the API endpoint in a constant.

```
Const API_URL = 'https://westcentralus.api.cognitive.microsoft.com/vision/
v2.0/analyze?visualFeatures=Description';
```

Add the code for setting up the restify server. The restify server will listen to the port provided in the environment variable, or to 3978 if not provided.

```
// Setup Restify Server
var server = restify. createServer( ) ;
server . listen(process . env. port | | process. env . PORT | | 3978, ( )
=> {
    console. log( '%s listening to %s', server. name, server. url) ;
});
```

Create the chatbot by adding these lines of code:

```
// Create chat bot
var connector = new builder . ChatConnector( ) ;

// Listen for messages
server.post( '/api/messages', connector. listen( ) );

var inMemoryStorage = new builder. MemoryBotStorage( ) ;

var bot = new builder . UniversalBot(connector, (session) => {

})
    . set( ' storage' , inMemoryStorage) ;
```

On line 26, add these lines of code. This code will check whether the user has sent an attachment/URL. If there is an attachment, the bot will send a message to the user. If there is no attachment or link, the bot will let the user know.

```
var msg = session . message;
var isURL = msg . text . indexof( 'http' ) !== -1 ? msg. text : null;

if (msg.attachments.length || isURL) {
    session. send( "You have sent me an attachment or a URL. ' )
} else {

    // No attachments were sent
    session. send('You did not send me an image or a link of the image to
    caption. ' )
    }

})
    . set( " storage', inMemoryStorage) ;
```

Type node app in the terminal and hit **Enter**.

Open the Bot Framework Emulator and the Caption Bot by clicking on **create a new bot configuration**.

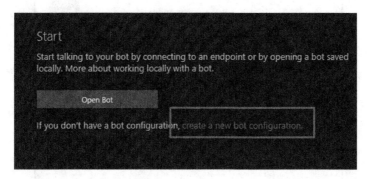

Figure 3-32. *Create a new bot configuration in the Bot Framework Emulator*

Add details and a restify endpoint. Click on **Save and connect** and then save the configuration file.

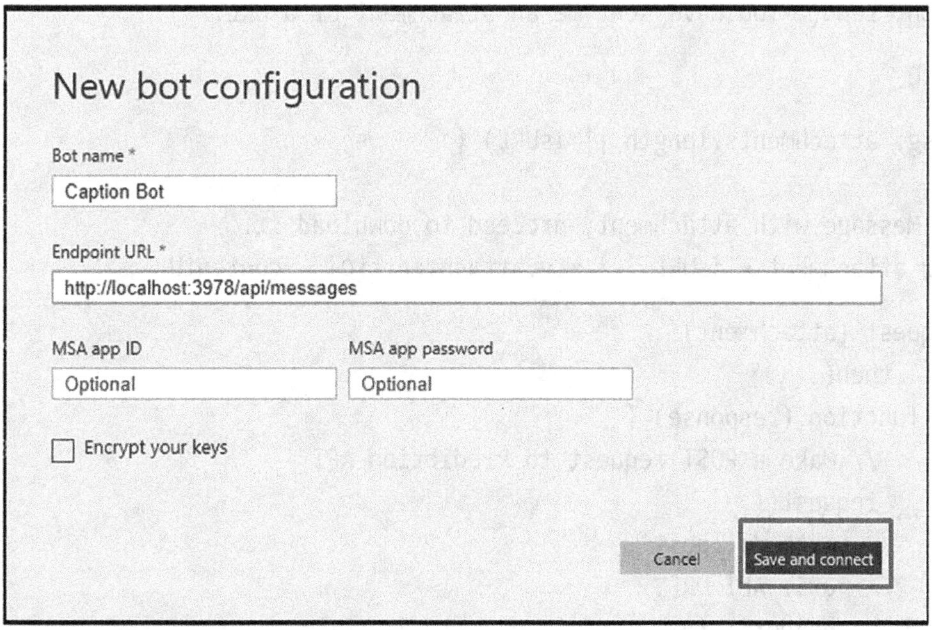

Figure 3-33. *The New Bot Configuration window*

Now you can test the bot.

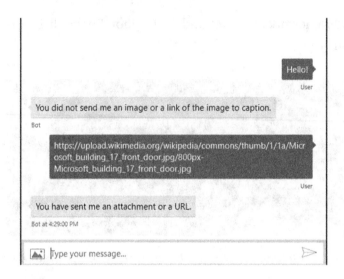

Figure 3-34. *Testing the bot using the Emulator*

On line 30, replace the following

```
session. send( 'You have sent me an attachment or a URL.' )
```

with

```
if (msg. attachments.length || isURL) {

    // Message with attachment, proceed to download it.
    var attachment = isURL | | msg.attachments[0] . contentUrl;

    request (attachment)
      . then(
      function (response) {
        // Make a POST request to Prediction API
        request({
          method: 'post',
          uri: API_URL,
          headers: {
            'Content-Type' : "multipart/form-data",
            'Ocp-Apim-Subscription-Key' : process. env. COMPUTER_VISION_
            KEY
          },
```

```
    formData: { body: response },
    json: true
})
    // If request is successful
    .then((response) => {

    // Check if response has predictions
    if (response && response. description && response. description.
    captions) {

        let caption - response. description. captions;

        // If we have a caption
        if (caption. length) {
            session. send("It is " + caption [0]. text);

            session. send( "It is " + caption[0] . text);
            }

            // If we don't have a caption
            else {
                session. send("Sorry! I can't caption it.");
            }
        }
        // If response does not have data
        else {
            session.send("Sorry! I can't caption it. ");
            }
        })

        // If there is an error in POST request, send this message
        .catch((err) => session. send("I can't process your request
        for some technical reasons. "));
    })
    .catch((err) -> {
        console. log( "Error downloading attachment: ', err);
    }):
} else {
```

On line 34, the bot is downloading the image the user uploads. Once the image is received, the bot makes the request to the Computer Vision API on line 38.

When the response is received, the bot checks if there is any caption. If there is a caption, it sends the caption to the user (line 58). Otherwise, it tells the user that it can't caption the image.

Now stop and run the bot again to test it out. Here is an example.

It is a swan swimming in a body of water

Bot at 5:01:51 PM

Figure 3-35. *Calling the Computer Vision API using the bot*

It takes some time to get a response from API, so add a typing indication by adding this line of code on line 26:

```
var bot = new builder.UniversalBot(connector, (session) => {

    session . sendTyping( ) ;

    var msg = session.message;
```

Add these lines at the end of the file. This code sends a greeting message to the user when the bot connects:

```
. set( storage , inMemoryStorage) ;

bot. on ( ' conversationUpdate', function (activity) {
   if (activity. membersAdded) {
      const hello = new builder . Message( )
      .address(activity. address)
      .text("Hello! I'm a Caption Bot. Send me an image or a URL of an
      image and I'll caption it for you.");
   activity . membersAdded. forEach(function (identity) {
      // Send message when the bot joins the conversation
      if (identity. id === activity.address.bot.id) {
         bot. send(hello);
      }
   });
   }
});
```

Let's test the bot again.

Figure 3-36. *Calling the Computer Vision API using the bot*

Pretty good, eh? Let's try few more.

Figure 3-37. *Calling the Computer Vision API using the bot*

Figure 3-38. *Calling the Computer Vision API using the bot*

It is a piece of chocolate cake on a plate

Bot at 5:08:20 PM

Figure 3-39. *Calling the Computer Vision API using the bot*

It is a white plate topped with a sandwich and fries on a table

Bot at 5:08:42 PM

Figure 3-40. *Calling the Computer Vision API using the bot*

Fairly decent, and all these food pictures are making me hungry!

There is a great paper written about generating human-like image captions, "Speaking the Same Language: Matching Machine to Human Captions by Adversarial Training," available at `https://arxiv.org/abs/1703.10476`. Let's compare our Caption Bot results using Cognitive Services with some of the authors' results.

Figure 3-41. *Comparing results from the Caption Bot with results from the technique used in the research paper*

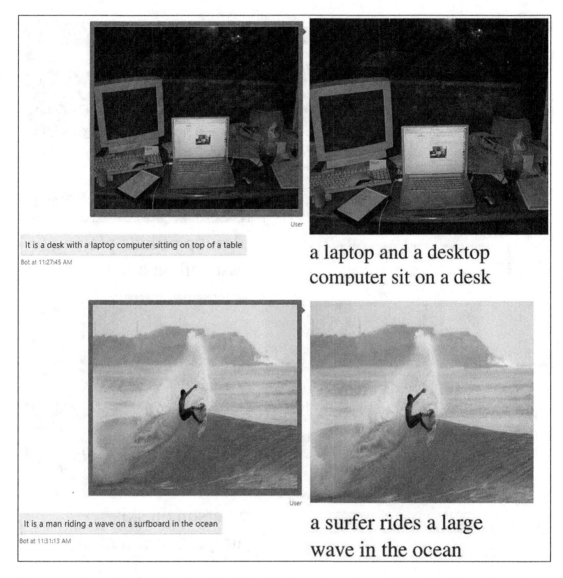

It is a desk with a laptop computer sitting on top of a table
Bot at 11:27:45 AM

a laptop and a desktop computer sit on a desk

It is a man riding a wave on a surfboard in the ocean
Bot at 11:31:13 AM

a surfer rides a large wave in the ocean

Figure 3-42. *Comparing results from the Caption Bot with results from the technique used in the research paper*

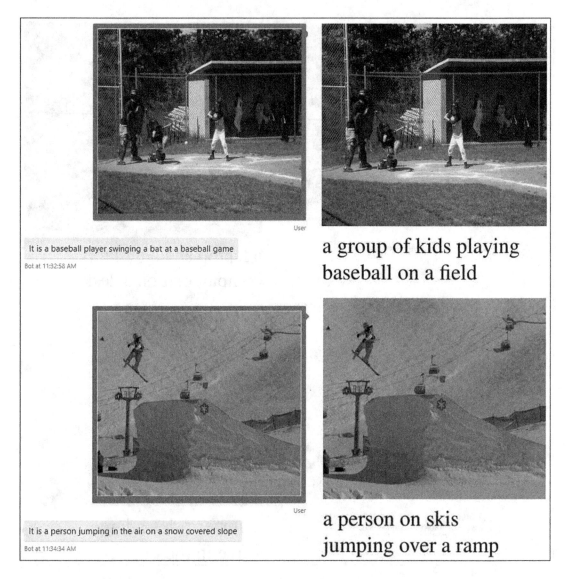

Figure 3-43. *Comparing results from the Caption Bot with results from the technique used in the research paper*

Figure 3-44. *Comparing results from the Caption Bot with results from the technique used in the research paper*

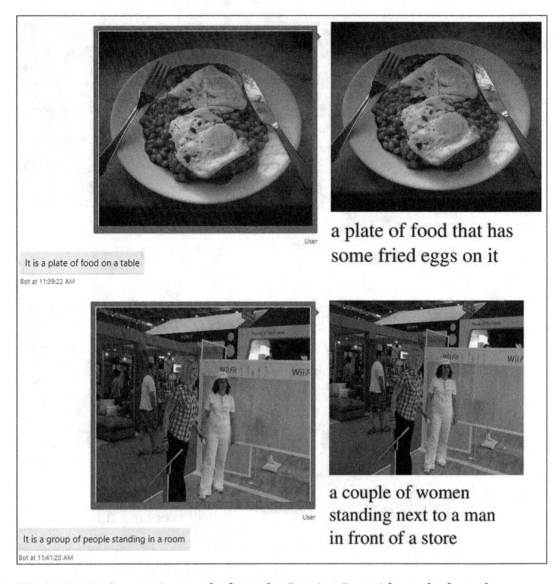

Figure 3-45. *Comparing results from the Caption Bot with results from the technique used in the research paper*

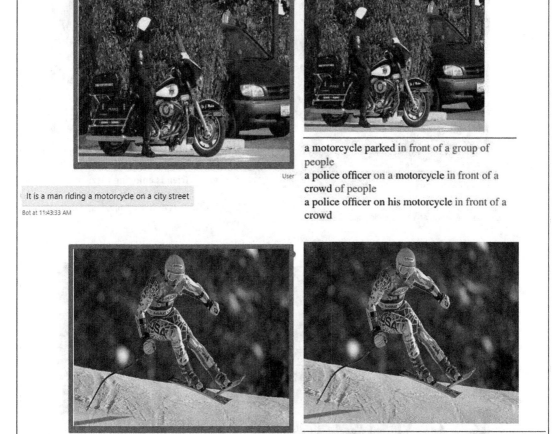

Figure 3-46. *Comparing results from the Caption Bot with results from the technique used in the research paper*

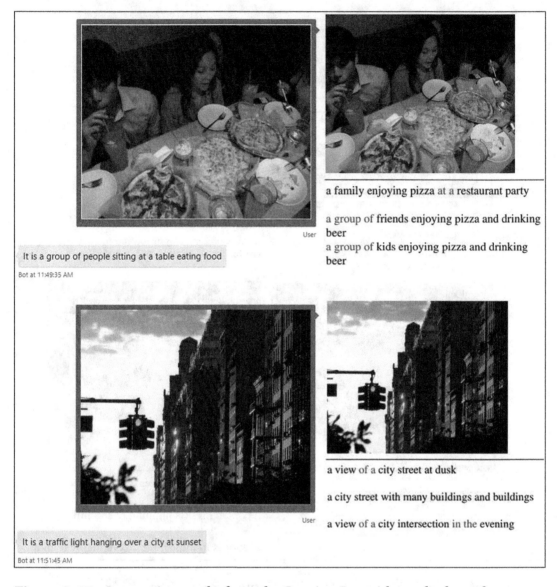

Figure 3-47. *Comparing results from the Caption Bot with results from the technique used in the research paper*

These are fairly decent out-of-the-box results, but it leaves dense captioning and z-indexing with more to be desired. A more sophisticated use case would be testing out the API for the Stanford DAQUAR challenge.

DAQUAR challenge

DAQUAR stands for "DAtaset for QUestion Answering on Real-world images." It is a dataset of images with question–answer pairs for both training and testing. It is not about just recognizing the image using AI. Instead, DAQUAR is about questioning the AI about the images, which is one step further than image recognition. The challenge is to train the AI using the dataset and then test it. More details about the challenge can be found at `https://www.mpi-inf.mpg.de/de/abteilungen/computer-vision-and-multimodal-computing/research/vision-and-language/visual-turing-challenge/`.

3-4. Explore Your Fridge Using CustomVision.AI

Even though we are still waiting for working hoverboards to arrive, we do have smart fridges from a variety of high-tech manufacturers. These fridges create shopping lists, coordinate schedules, play your favorite songs and movies, and double as your therapist. Well, maybe not the last one, but you get the point.

Problem

How can we build a simple grocery detector—i.e., identify the contents of your fridge—using the object-detection capabilities of the custom vision service?

Solution

The usual suspect in our toolbox, custom vision, is used to solve this problem. In this case, we will be bit more sophisticated, as you will see.

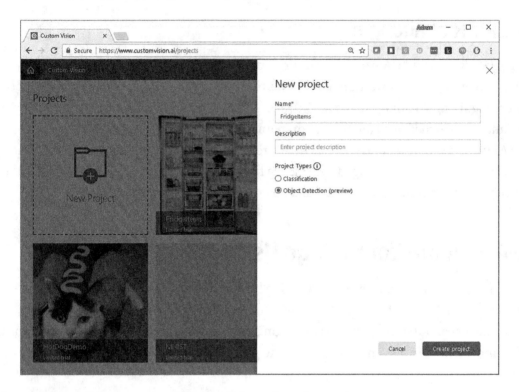

Figure 3-48.   *Create a new CustomVision.ai project*

Since I run out of OJ quickly, let's upload some images of orange juice and see if we can identify the object.

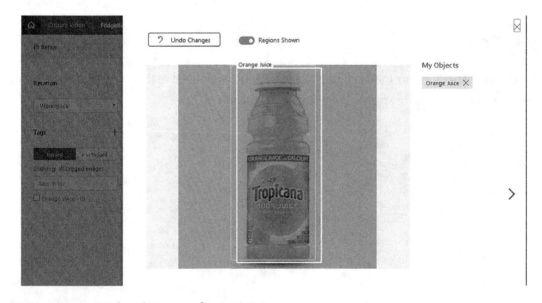

Figure 3-49.   *Upload images for training*

We will start by uploading pictures, tagging them, and identifying the regions.

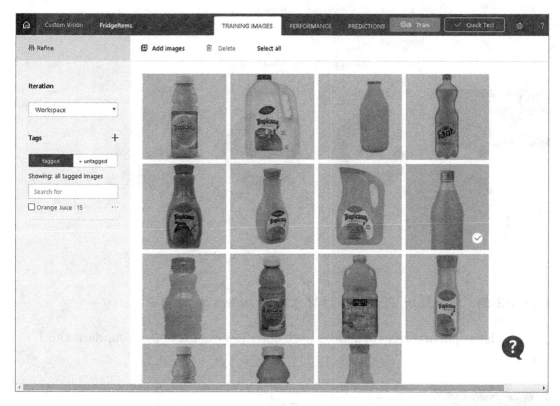

Figure 3-50. *Tag images for training*

You can see the precision and recall next, along with a new measure, MAP, for object detection. Mean Average Precision (MAP) provides a single-figure measure of quality across recall levels and has been shown to have especially good discrimination and stability. MAP is used as the metric by which to measure the accuracy of object detectors, like Faster R-CNN, YOLO, and Single Shot Detector(SSD), and provides the average of the maximum precisions at different recall values.

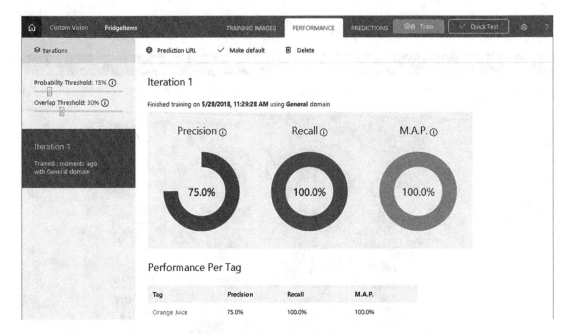

Figure 3-51. *Precision, Recall, and M.A.P. for object detection*

Now, let's upload images of a fridge itself and draw out the object boundaries and tag.

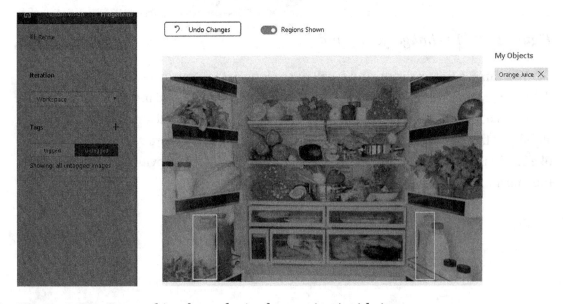

Figure 3-52. *Draw object boundaries for tagging inside image*

Continue tagging with multiple objects and examples to improve model diversity and accuracy.

Figure 3-53. *Draw object boundaries for tagging inside image*

Now, click **Train** to run the iteration.

Figure 3-54. *Train the model*

It's time to put this model to the test by uploading the following image.

Figure 3-55. *Test model using a new image*

You can see that the orange juice bottle is detected with some accuracy. Not stellar, provided our small training set, but still fairly good, especially since you have not had to write a single line of code.

Figure 3-56. *Detect object in new image*

Now, let's see how this works out with the prediction API by using the RESTFul interface. This way you can use it from your application. You can write code to invoke the RESTFul API as well; however, the Postman extension for Google Chrome as a REST client allows you to interact with the RESTFul API much more easily. You can also set up the Postman Interceptor extension so that you can reuse your current Google Chrome session cookies while interacting with the APIs. You can download and install Postman from https://www.getpostman.com.

Click on the gear to get the prediction API endpoint and keys.

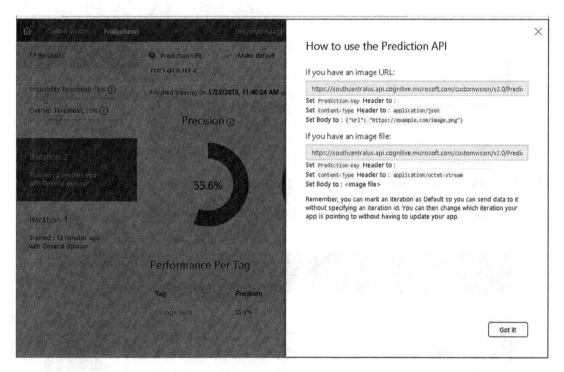

Figure 3-57. *Prediction API endpoint and keys*

You can see the information from the project and account settings.

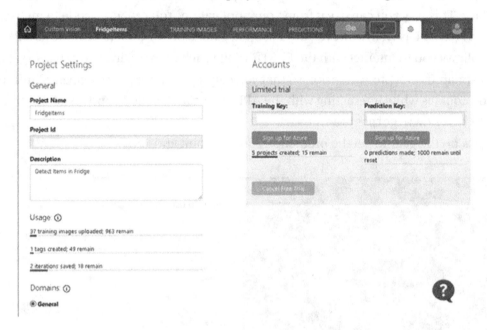

Figure 3-58. *Project and Account settings screen*

Now, create a new request in Postman by clicking on **Request**.

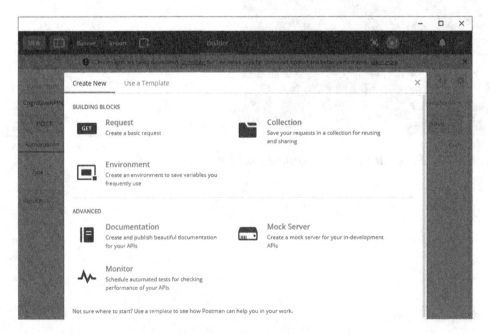

Figure 3-59. *Create new API request using Postman*

Save the request by populating the headers and the body.

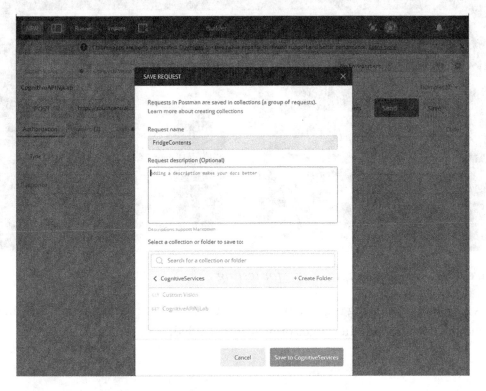

Figure 3-60. *Save Postman Request*

And now provide a link for the image to test out. You can search for any relevant image via Google or Bing image search, similar to the following.

Figure 3-61. *Specify sample image for testing*

As seen in the following request, we have set the body URL parameter with the image link and the headers with the values previously specified.

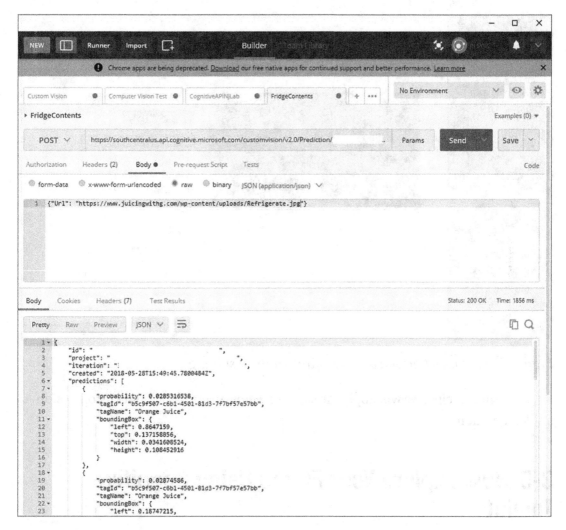

Figure 3-62. *Inspect the request payload in Postman*

When invoked, we get the bounding box information in the image along with the corresponding probability, which can be seen as a JSON response in the preceding figure and as a visual depiction of the same results in the following figure.

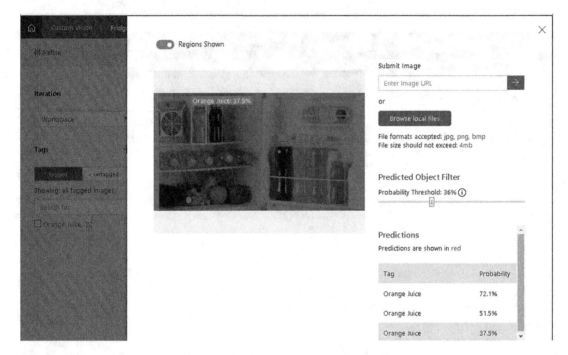

Figure 3-63. *Object detected successfully in the test image*

In the next recipe, we will apply the same principle using CNTK and custom vision implementation.

3-5. Now Explore Your Fridge Using Cognitive Toolkit

Cloud APIs are usually great to get started, and they provide great value so you don't have to reinvent the wheel, do custom training, and spend hours trying to operationalize. However, there are several industry and business use cases, such as an on-premises disconnected implementation, when cloud is not a viable option; in this case, you can do custom on-premises implementations using Microsoft Cognitive Toolkit (CNTK).

Problem

Build a simple grocery detector—i.e., identify the contents of your fridge—using the object-detection capabilities of Cognitive Toolkit.

Solution

In this recipe, we are going to use the Microsoft Cognitive Toolkit (formerly CNTK) fast R-CNN implementation to train an existing neural network, AlexNet, to recognize groceries in a refrigerator by training an external classifier. This approach does not require any expertise and works with a small dataset.

We used a lot of jargon in the previous sentence, so let's break it down.

R-CNN (Girshick et al., 2014) stands for Region-based Convolutional Neural Networks. The algorithm first applies selective search to identify a manageable number of bounding-box object region candidates or regions of interest, which are then used to extract convolutional neural network features from each of those regions. R-CNN, Fast R-CNN, and Faster R-CNN are object-recognition techniques, while Mask R-CNN is used for image segmentation and YOLO (You Only Look Once) for fast object recognition. A region of interest (ROI) is a subset or a part of an image that has been selected for operation and should ideally include the object. The neural network then finds the features from these ROIs for classification. You can find details of R-CNN at Andrej Karpathy (Director AI @ Tesla, Stanford Computer Vision) here: https://cs.stanford.edu/people/karpathy/rcnn/

A detailed overview of these algorithms is beyond the scope of this discussion, but you can find the papers and associated code using the following table.

Table 3-1. *Algorithms and Codes for object recognition*

Model	Goal	Resources
R-CNN	Object recognition	[paper]https://arxiv.org/abs/1311.2524 [code]https://github.com/rbgirshick/rcnn
Fast R-CNN	Object recognition	[paper]https://arxiv.org/abs/1504.08083 [code]https://github.com/rbgirshick/fast-rcnn
Faster R-CNN	Object recognition	[paper]https://arxiv.org/abs/1506.01497 [code]https://github.com/rbgirshick/py-faster-rcnn
Mask R-CNN	Image segmentation	[paper]https://arxiv.org/abs/1703.06870 [code]https://github.com/CharlesShang/FastMaskRCNN
YOLO	Fast object recognition	[paper]https://arxiv.org/abs/1506.02640 [code]https://github.com/pjreddie/darknet/wiki/ YOLO:-Real-Time-Object-Detection

Like LeNet, VGG, GoogLeNet, and ResNet, AlexNet is a convolutional neural network architecture that emerged from a Stanford vision research paper. It uses a deep neural network to automatically find features in an image. AlexNet is a pre-trained neural network, and it can classify images on its own into 1,000 object categories. It has been trained using more than a million images. AlexNet has made great contributions to the computer vision field. The paper can be found at `http://vision.stanford.edu/teaching/cs231b_spring1415/slides/alexnet_tugce_kyunghee.pdf`.

Microsoft Cognitive Toolkit (`https://cntk.ai`), formerly called CNTK, is a unified deep-learning toolkit that describes neural networks as a series of computational steps via a directed graph. The toolkit has been shown to produce great results for Pascal VOC (`http://host.robots.ox.ac.uk/pascal/VOC/`), which is one of the main object-detection challenges in the field. Microsoft defines cognitive toolkit as follows:

> *"It allows users to easily realize and combine popular model types such as feed-forward DNNs, convolutional nets (CNNs), and recurrent networks (RNNs/LSTMs). It implements stochastic gradient descent (SGD, error backpropagation) learning with automatic differentiation and parallelization across multiple GPUs and servers."*

In this implementation, we will be using a small dataset of 25 images of grocery items in refrigerators, of which 20 will be used to train the classifier and 5 will be used to test. Twenty images is indeed a very small number and will not produce highly accurate results, but it is great to get started or for demonstration purposes. There are a total of 180 annotated objects, which include egg box, yogurt, ketchup, mushroom, mustard, orange, squash, and water.

Setting Up the Environment

Let's get started:

1. Download the appropriate package of CNTK 2.0 from the official repository. Only version 2.0 is compatible with this recipe as the latest releases may have some breaking changes:

   `https://github.com/Microsoft/CNTK/releases/tag/v2.0`

   This document uses the GPU package.

2. Click on the **I accept** button to start downloading.

3. Create a folder with the name of `local` or any name in the C: drive or any other drive. Extract the files to that folder. It is a good idea to keep the version number with the CNTK folder so that it does not get mixed with other CNTK versions.

4. CNTK is extracted to `D:\local\CNTK-2-0` in this recipe. Adjust the steps according to your installation directory.

5. Open CMD or PowerShell.

6. Change the directory to the location the installation script is using.

   `"cd D:\local\CNTK-2-0\cntk\Scripts\install\windows"`

7. Run `install.bat` to start installation.

```
Windows PowerShell
Copyright (C) Microsoft Corporation. All rights reserved.

PS C: \Users> cd D:\local\CNTK-2-0\cntk\Scripts\install\windows
PS D: \local\CNTK-2-0\cntk\Scripts\install\windows> ./install.bat

CNTK Binary Install Script

This script will set up CNTK, the CNTK prerequisites, and the CNTK Python
environment onto the system.
More help can be found at:
   https: //github.com/Microsoft/CNTK/wiki/Setup-Windows-Binary-Script

The script will analyze your machine and will determine which components
are required.
The required components will be downloaded in [D:\local\CNTK-2-0\cntk\
Scripts\install\windows \ps \ InstallCache]
Repeated operation of this script will reuse already downloaded components.

  - If required VS2015 Runtime will be installed
  - If required MSMPI will be installed
  - Anaconda3 will be installed into [C: \local \Anaconda3-4.1.1-
    Windows-x86_64]
  - A CNTK-PY35 environment will be created or updated in [C:\local\
    Anaconda3-4.1.1-Windows-x86_64\envs]
  - CNTK will be installed or updated in the CNTK-PY35 environment
```

```
1 - I agree and want to continue
Q - Quit the installation process

1 - I agree and want to continue
Q - Quit the installation process

1
Determining Operations to perform. This will take a moment. . .

The following operations will be performed:
    * Install Anaconda3-4.1.10
    * Set up CNTK PythonEnvironment 35
    * Set up/Update CNTK Wheel 35
    * Create CNTKPY batch file

Do you want to continue? (y/n)

Writing web request
     Writing request stream. . . (Number of bytes written: 8777442)

CNTK Binary Install Script
```

8. Setup may ask you for permission, and dialog box(es) may appear.
   Click **Yes** to continue installation.

```
Using Anaconda Cloud api site https://api .anaconda.org
Using Anaconda Cloud api site https://api.anaconda.org
Fetching package metadata .........
Solving package specifications: ..........
Fetching packages ...
ca-certificate 100% |############################| Time: 0:00:02 76.10 KB/s
vs2015_runtime 100% |############################| Time: 0:00:02 727.49 kB/s
bzip2-1.0.6-vc 100% |############################| Time: 0:00:02 71.71 kB/s
openss1-1.0.20 100% |############################| Time: 0:00:11 488.74 kB/s
vc-14-0.tar.bz 100% |############################| Time: 0:00:00 78.57 kB/s
zlib-1.2.11-vc 100% |############################| Time: 0:00:02 58.73 kB/s
icu-57.1-vc14_ 100% |############################| Time: 0:00:14 2.42 MB/5
jpeg-8d-vc14_2 100% |############################| Time: 0:00:00 315.72 kB/s
libpng-1.6.34- 100% |############################| Time: 0:00:03 181.01 kB/s
tk-8.5.19-vc14 100% |############################| Time: 0:00:06 379.64 kB/s
```

```
colorama-0.3.9 100% |##############################| Time: 0:00:00 195.84 kB/s
decorator-4.1. 100% |##############################| Time: 0:00:00 157.76 kB/s
entrypoints-0. 100% |##############################| Time: 0:00:00 622.98 kB/s
freetype-2.5.5 100% |##############################| Time: 0:00:01 399.95 kB/s
ipython_genuti 100% |##############################| Time: 0:00:00 297.80 kB/s
jedi-0.10.2-py 100 |##############################| Time: 0:00:00 453.49 kB/s
jsonschema-2.6 100% |##############################| Time: 0:00:00 349.53 kB/s
markupsafe-1.0 0% |
    | ETA: --:--:--   0.00 B/S
```

9. Once the installation is complete, you will get a success message.

```
CNTK v2 Python install complete.

To activate the CNTK Python environment and set the PATH to include CNTK,
start a command shell and run
    D:\local\CNTK-2-0\cntk\scripts\cntkpy35.bat

Please check out tutorials and examples here:
    D:\local\CNTK-2-0\cntk\Tutorials
    D: \local\CNTK-2-0\cntk\Examples

PS D:\local\CNTK-2-0\entk\Scripts\install\windows>
```

We will verify the installation using CNTK Python. But to use this, we will have to activate the environment by running the cntkpy35.bat script.

This will add the CNTK Python environment variables to the current command prompt.

1. Open a command prompt and enter D:, then cd D:\local\CNTK-2-0\cntk\scripts, and, at last, cntkpy35.bat.
    This will activate the CNTK Python environment for the current command prompt.

    ```
    D: \local\CNTK-2-0\cntk\Scripts>cntkpy35.bat
    ```

    ```
    (C: \local\Anaconda3-4.1.1-Windows-x86_64\envs\cntk-py35) D: \
    local\CNTK-2-0\cntk\Scripts>
    ```

    Clone this repository in the local folder: https://github.com/Azure/ObjectDetectionUsingCntk

2. Now, in the CMD, enter

    ```
    cd D:\local\ObjectDetectionUsingCntk\resources\python35_64bit_
    requirements
    ```

3. Then run

    ```
    pip.exe install -r requirements.txt
    ```

    If you get an error that CMake must be installed, then install it using

    ```
    pip install cMake
    ```

    Then, run the `pip` command again to start installation:

    ```
    pip.exe install -r requirements.txt
    ```

4. Download the `AlexNet.model` file from the following link and copy it to the `ObjectDetectionUsingCntk\resources\cntk` folder:

    ```
    https://www.cntk.ai/Models/AlexNet/AlexNet.model
    ```

    Now that we are done with the setup, let's start training.

Training the Model

From the command prompt, browse to the cloned directory and run `python 1_computeRois.py`. This script will calculate ROIs (regions of interest) for each image in the dataset using the following three steps:

1. Selective search is used to generate hundreds of ROIs per image. These ROIs could be smaller or larger than the actual object.

2. ROIs that are too similar or smaller are discarded.

3. Finally, ROIs that uniformly cover the image are added at different scales and aspect ratios.

The following script will pass each of the computed ROIs in the previous step through the CNTK model to generate its 4,096-float deep neural network representation:

```
Run python 2_cntkGenerateInputs.py
```

This requires three CNTK-specific input files to be generated for the training and the test set as shown here:

- `{train,test}.txt`: Each row contains the path to an image.

- `{train,test}.rois.txt`: Each row contains all ROIs for an image in relative (x,y,w,h) coordinates.

- `{train,test}.roilabels.txt`: Each row contains the labels for the ROIs in one-hot encoding.

```
(C:\local\Anaconda3-4.1.1-Windows-x86_64\envs\cntk-py35) D:\local\ObjectDet
ectionUsingCnitk>python 2_cnitkGenerateInput
2018-06-05 16:20:06
PARAMETERS: datasetName = grocery
Number of images in set 'train' = 25
Processing image set 'train', image 0 of 25
wrote gt roidb to D:\local\ObjectDetectionUsingCntk/proc/grocery/cntkFiles/
train.cache_gt_roidb.pkl
Only keeping the first 200 ROIs. .
wrote ss roidb to D:\local\ObjectDetectionUsingCntk/proc/grocery/cntkFiles/
train.cache_selective_search_roidb.pkl
    0: Found 4820 objects of class _background_
    1: Found 20 objects of class orange.
    2: Found 20 objects of class eggBox.
    3: Found 20 objects of class joghurt.
    4: Found 20 objects of class ketchup.
    5: Found 40 objects of class squash.
    6: Found 20 objects of class mushroom.
    7: Found 20 objects of class water.
    8: Found 20 objects of class mustard.

Number of images in set 'test' = 5
Processing image set 'test', image 0 of 5
wrote gt roidb to D:\local\ObjectDetectionUsingCntk/proc/grocery/cntkFiles/
test.cache_gt_roidb.pkl
Only keeping the first 200 ROIs. .
```

wrote ss roidb to D:\local\ObjectDetectionUsingCntk/proc/grocery/cntkFiles/
test.cache_selective_search_roidb.pkl
DONE

(C:\local\Anaconda3-4.1.1-Windows-x86_64\envs\entk-py35) D:\local\
ObjectDetectionUsingCnitk>

You can run python B2_cntkVisualizeInputs.py to visualize an input. This script will visualize the inputs generated by mapping them on the image.

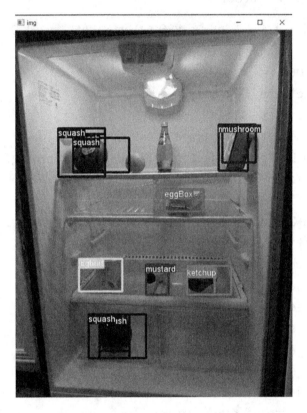

Figure 3-64. *Visualizing inputs on the image*

Now run python 3_runCntk.py.

This script will now run the CNTK training, which will take the inputs generated in the previous step and write the 4,096-float embedding for each ROI and for each image.

This may take some time because it requires heavy computation. The script will automatically run on GPU if a GPU is detected. If the GPU package is used you will see the message "Using GPU for training."

One suggestion, if you are serious about deep learning, is to invest in a GPU. This is what my machine looks like. You are welcome.

Figure 3-65. *My GPU*

If you don't have a GPU or if you are using CPU-only package, it will take more time:

```
(C:\local\Anaconda3-4.1.1-Windows-x86_64\envs\entk-py35) D:\local\
ObjectDetectionUsingCntk>python 3_runCntk.py
2018-06-05 16:24:34
PARAMETERS: datasetName = grocery
classifier = svm
cntk_lr_per_image = [0.01, 0.01, 0.01, 0.01, 0.01, 0.01, 0.01, 0.01, 0.01,
0.01, 0.001, 0.001, 0.001, 0.001, 0.001, 0.0001]
Selected GPU[0] Geforce GTX 1060 as the process wide default device.
Using GPU for training.
Loading pre-trained model. .
Loading pre-trained model. . . DONE.
Using pre-trained DNN without refinement
Writing model to D:\local\ObjectDetectionUsingCntk/proc/grocery/models/
fren_svm.model
Evaluating images 1 of 5
Writing DNN output of dimension (200, 4096) to disk
```

```
Evaluating images 1 of 25
Writing DNN output of dimension (200, 4096) to disk
DONE.
```

Run python 4_trainSvm.py.

This script will train a classifier using the ROIs for each image as input and will output N+1 linear classifiers, one for each class (grocery item), plus one for the background.

This script uses a slightly modified version of the published R-CNN code to train a linear SVM classifier. The main change is to load the 4,096-float ROI embedding from disk rather than to run the network on the fly.

```
optimization finished, #iter = 141
Objective value = -0.058624
nSV - 204
[LibLinear ]      0: meanAcc=1.000 .. pos wrong:      0/      39; neg
wrong:      0/ 2171;      obj val: 0.378 = 0.000 (posUnscaled) + 0.013
(neg) + 0.365 (reg)
      1: meanAcc=0, 999 -- pos wrong:      0/ 39; neg
wrong:      2/   901;      obj val: 0.484 = 0.000 (posUnscaled) + 0.022
(neg) + 0.462 (reg)
    Pruning easy negatives
        before pruning: aneg . 901
        after pruning: Ineg . 381
    Cache holds 39 pos examples and 381 neg examples
    0 pos support vectors
    190 neg support vectors
DONE.
```

Run python 5_evaluateResults.py. Now the model is ready, and it can be used to classify the objects it has been trained for. This script will measure the accuracy of the classifier. The output will be the mean Average Precision (mAP) for the test data set (five images).

The number of test images is just five and may not produce highly accurate outputs.

```
(C:\local\Anaconda3-4.1.1-Windows-x86_64\envs\entk-py35) D:\local\ObjectDet
ectionUsingCnitk>python 5_evaluateResults.py
2018-06-05 16:29:06
PARAMETERS: datasetName = grocery
```

```
classifier = Svm
image_set = test
test. cache ss roidb loaded from D:\local\ObjectDetectionUsingCntk/proc/
grocery/cntkFiles/test.cache_selective_search_roidb.pkl
      Processing image 0 of 5. .
Number of rois before non-maxima surpression: 1592
Number of rois after non-maxima surpression: 595
Evaluating detections
AP for orange = 0.2727
AP for eggBox = 0.7455
AP for joghurt = 0.3273
AP for ketchup = 0.7636
AP for squash = 0.4935
AP for mushroom . 0.7013
AP for water = 0.5455
AP for mustard = 0.4485
Mean AP = 0.5372
DONE .
```

Run python 5_visualizeResults.py. This script will visualize the result calculated in the previous step.

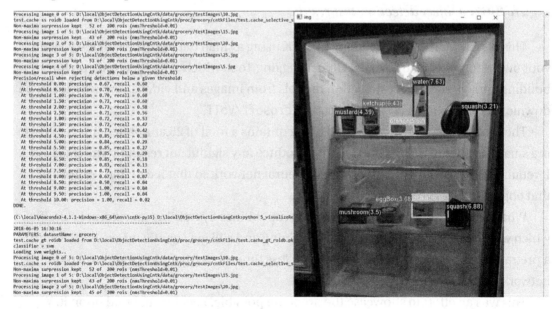

Figure 3-66. *Visualizing calculated results*

Here is a test result.

Figure 3-67. *Object detection test results*

This was a small demonstration of CNTK using a small dataset. You can also create your own dataset using the Visual Object Tagging Tool, which is an Electron app for building end-to-end object-detection models from images and videos, and which can be downloaded from `https://github.com/Microsoft/VoTT`.

The grocery dataset we have used here contains a total of 25 annotated images. This is a small number of images and will not produce any significant result for practical uses. It requires thousands of images to train a neural network so that it can find features of that object and classify it.

What we have done here is extended its capabilities by training an external classifier, which was able to use just 20 images for training and still get significant results. Using a pretrained network requires less data and less time as compared to training a neural network from scratch.

This was an effort to showcase the art of the possible. Feel free to build upon it. We will see another CNTK-based recipe later in this chapter.

3-6. Product and Part Identification Using Custom Vision

Have you heard of Birdsnap? The birdwatching app uses computer vision and learning to identify birds. Or how about Birder in the Hand, a Merlin Bird ID mobile app that can identify hundreds of North American species and was developed by Caltech and Cornell Tech computer-vision researchers in partnership with the Cornell Lab of Ornithology. A commercial application of this technology is in retail, where people can find matching parts, accessories, or articles of clothing. Let's see how can we recognize parts.

Problem

In retail, there are variety of use cases where you need to detect products, and identify parts of products using images. For example, if you would like to know from pictures of shelves, which items are in stock or the sku of a product from its photo to search the inventory. How do we do it?

Solution

First things first, there are a few things you need to get started. Some of these you may already have from recipes you did earlier:

- Custom Vision account: Unless you already have one, get a free trial from `https://www.customvision.ai`.

- Node.js: Get it from `https://nodejs.org`.

- Git: Get it from `https://git-scm.com/downloads`.

- Bot Framework Emulator

1. Let's train Custom Vision. Visit `customvision.ai` and create a new project by clicking **New Project**. Enter your project details and then click on the **Create project** button.

Figure 3-68. *Create a new CustomVision.ai project*

- Project type: Classification—We want to classify images.

- Domains: Retail—Retail is for products we find on shopping websites.

2. Now click on **Add images** to add your product and parts images.

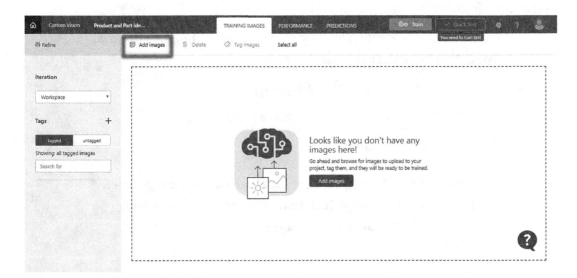

Figure 3-69. *Add images for model training*

3. Click the **Browse local files** button to select images from your
    computer. Add tag(s) and upload images.

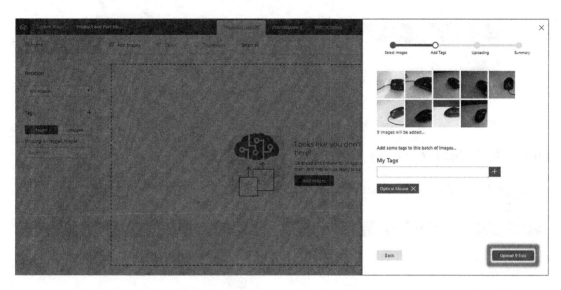

Figure 3-70. *Specify tags for images*

4. Once the images are uploaded, click **Done** to continue. Repeat
    Steps 4–7 for your other products.

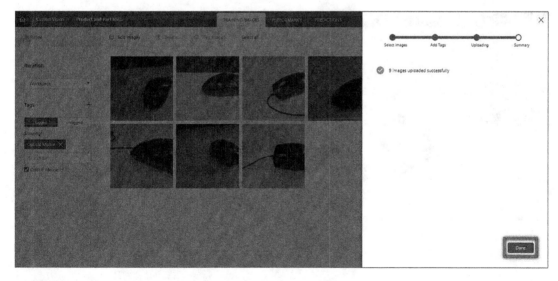

Figure 3-71. *Finalize uploading*

Once you have added images of your all products, click on the Performance tab and set **Probability Threshold** to 90%. The higher the threshold the better the results.

Figure 3-72. *Set Probability Threshold*

Click the **Train** button to start training.

Figure 3-73. *Train the model*

Once training is complete, click the **Quick Test** button to test the performance.

Figure 3-74. *Perform a Quick Test of the trained model*

Click the **Browse local files** button to upload an image for testing. Do a few tests to ensure the training is satisfactory.

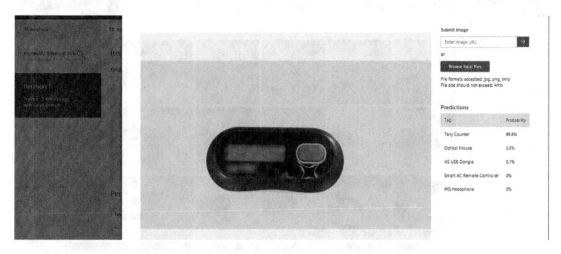

Figure 3-75. *Upload image for testing*

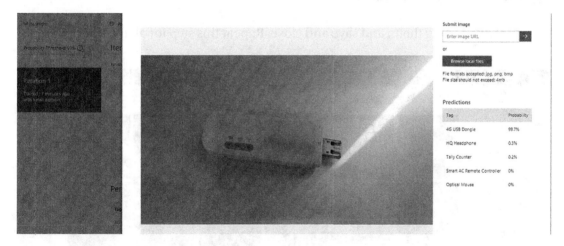

Figure 3-76. *Test using different images*

Once you are finished testing, click on the Predictions tab.

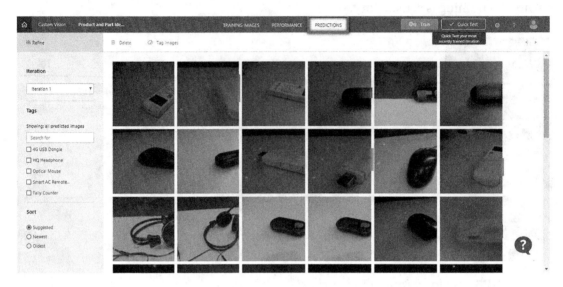

Figure 3-77.   *Click Predictions tab*

Select images, tag them, and save and close. Repeat this step for all the images.

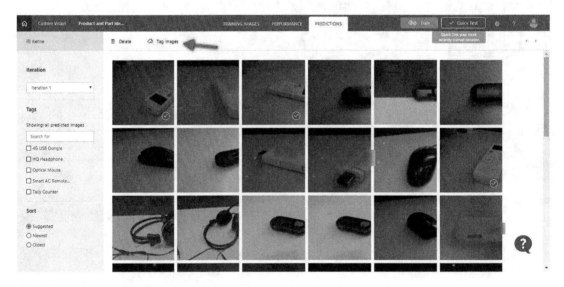

Figure 3-78.   *Tag images in the Predictions tab*

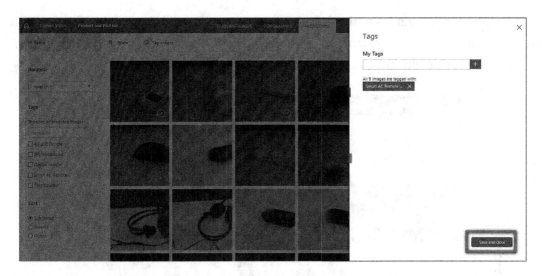

Figure 3-79. *Tag images in the Predictions tab*

Once you have added tags to all the images, go to the Performance tab to train again. Keep testing and training until you are satisfied with the results.

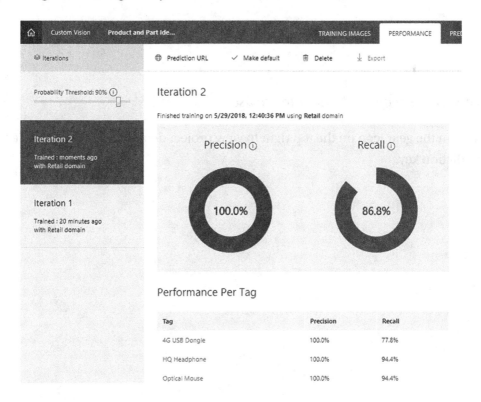

Figure 3-80. *Re-train model*

Mark the latest iteration as the default so that it can be used via the API. The iteration is the last trained model. You can also use other iterations with the API as well; however, if you don't provide any iteration ID then the default will be used.

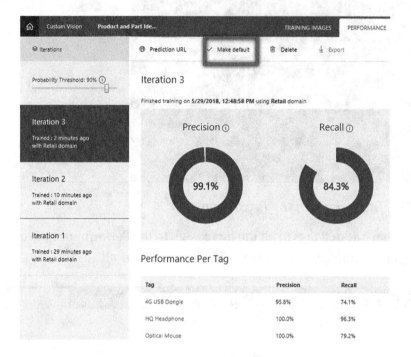

Figure 3-81. *Specify model iteration to use*

Click on the gear icon on the top right to view project details and copy the project ID and prediction key.

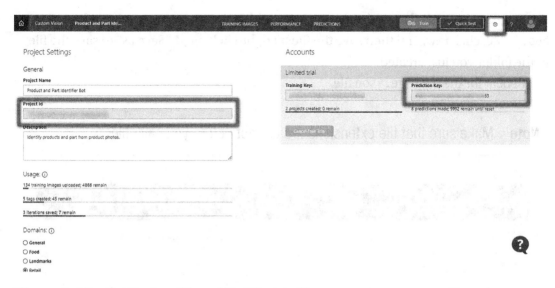

Figure 3-82. *Get Project ID and Prediction Key*

Now we will be using a sample bot from the Microsoft GitHub repository to test the predictions. Here is the link to the bot: `https://github.com/Microsoft/BotBuilder-Samples/tree/master/Node/core-ReceiveAttachment`.

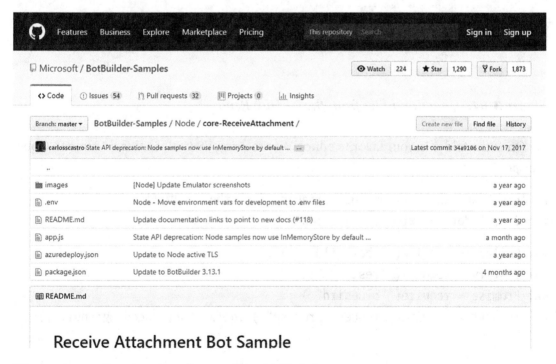

Figure 3-83. *Receive Attachment Bot GitHub Repo*

You can either git clone the repo or create a folder on your computer. Click on the app.js file, click **raw**, and then save the file by right-clicking ↗ "Save as" to save the file in the folder you just created.

Repeat for the package.json file.

Note   Make sure that file extensions are correct before you save files.

Figure 3-84. *Download files from the GitHub Repo*

Open the folder in your favorite editor. We are using VS Code in this document. Open the app.js file.

```
// This Loads the environment variables from the . env file
require( " dotenv-extended' ) . load( ) ;

var builder = require( ' botbuilder" ) ;
var restify - require( 'restify' );
var Promise = require( "bluebird" ) ;
var request - require( 'request-promise" ) .defaults({ encoding: null });
```

```
// Set up Restify Server
var server - restify.createServer( );
server . listen(process . env. port | | process. env. PORT | | 3978,
function () {
    console. log('Xs listening to %s', server. name, server. url);

// Create chat bot
var connector = new builder . ChatConnector({
    appId: process.env.MICROSOFT_APP_ID,
    appPassword: process. env. MICROSOFT_APP_PASSWORD
});

// Listen for messages
server.post('/api/messages' , connector. listen( ));

// Bot Storage: Here we register the state storage for your bot.
// Default store: volatile in-memory store - Only for prototyping!
// We provide adapters for Azure Table, CosmosDb, SQL Azure, or you can
impl
// For samples and documentation, see: https://github. com/Microsoft/
BotBuild
var inMemoryStorage = new builder.MemoryBotStorage( );
```

Remove the key/value pairs from lines 17 and 18 because we don't need the app ID and password for Emulator.

```
// Create chat bot
var connector = new builder . ChatConnector({
    appId: process . env. MICROSOFT APP ID,
    appPassword: process . env . MICROSOFT APP PASSWORD
});

// Create chat bot
var connector = new builder . ChatConnector( ) ;
```

Open the terminal using the "CTRL + `" key combination and run npm install to install dependencies.

```
$ npm install

> dtrace-provider@0.8.6 install E: \Products and Parts Identifier Bot\node_
modules\dtrace-provider
> node-gyp rebuild || node suppress-error. js
```

Run npm start to run the bot.

```
$ npm install

> botbuilder-sample-receiveattachment@1.0.0 start E: \Products and Parts
Identifier Bot
> node app. js
```

Run Bot Emulator and create a new bot configuration.

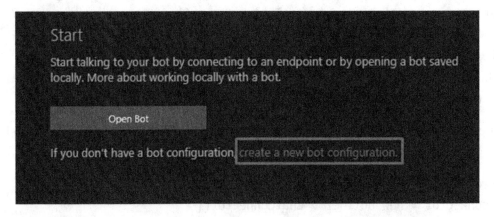

Figure 3-85. *Create a new bot configuration using the Bot Emulator*

Enter the bot details and save. The default endpoint URL for us would be http://localhost:3978/api/messages.

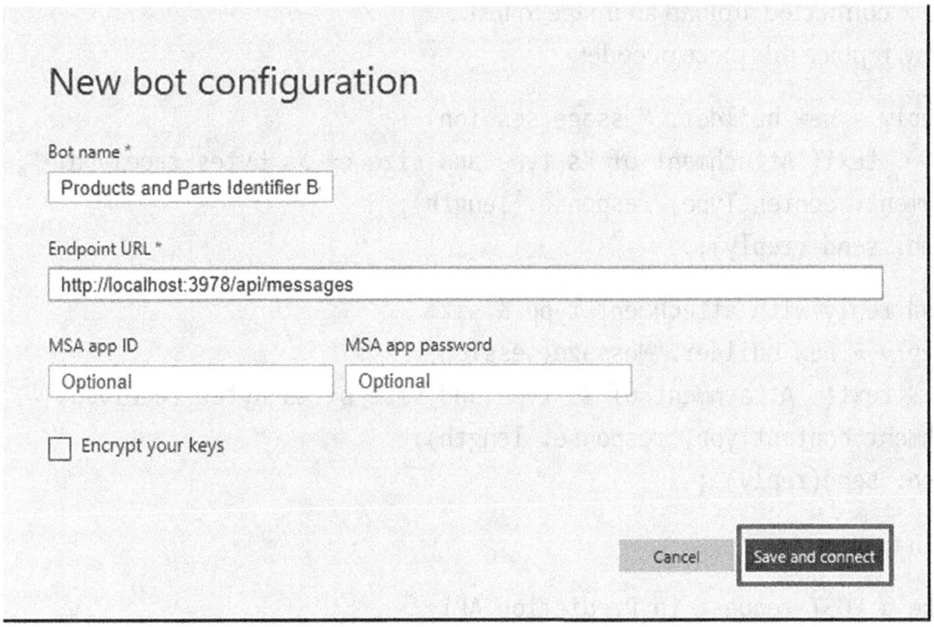

New bot configuration

Bot name *

Products and Parts Identifier B

Endpoint URL *

http://localhost:3978/api/messages

MSA app ID

Optional

MSA app password

Optional

☐ Encrypt your keys

Cancel   Save and connect

Figure 3-86. *The New Bot Configuration window*

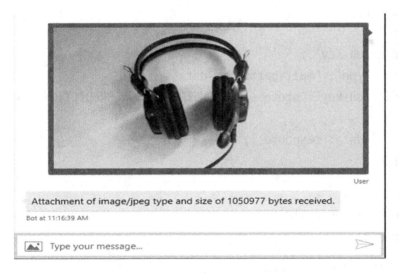

User

Attachment of image/jpeg type and size of 1050977 bytes received.

Bot at 11:16:39 AM

🖾 Type your message...   ▷

Figure 3-87. *Upload image to bot*

Once connected, upload an image to test.

Now, replace this piece of code:

```
var reply - new builder. Message(session)
       . text("Attachment of Xs type and size of Xs bytes received. ",
attachment. contentType, response. length);
Session. send (reply);

// Send reply with attachment type & size
var reply = new builder. Message(session)
       . text( 'Attachment of %s type and size of %s bytes received. ',
attachment.contentType, response. length);
session. send(reply) ;
```

with this

```
// Make a POST request to Prediction API
request({
    method: 'post',
    uri: API_URL,
    headers: {
       'Prediction-Key' : ' '
       Content-Type': "multipart/form-data"
       'Prediction-key': process.env.CUSTOM_VISION_PREDICTION_KEY
    };
    formData: { data: response },
    json: true
})

// If request is successful
.then((response)

// Check if response has predictions
if (response && response.predictions && response.predictions.length) {
       let predictions = response. predictions;
       let best = predictions[0];

       // Find best prediction - with the highest probability
       for (let i - 1; i < predictions.length; i++) {
```

```
        if (predictions[i] . probability > best. probability) {
            best = predictions[i];
        }
    }

    // If the probability is higher than the threshold, send message
    if (best. probability > parseFloat(process. env. CONFIDENCE_THRESHOLD) )
{
        session. send"This is a " + best. tagName);
    }
    // If the probability is lower than the threshold
    else {
        session. send("Sorry! I don't know what it is.");
    }

    // If response does not have predictions
    else {
        session. send("Sorry! I don't know what it is." );
    }
})

    // If there is an error in POST request, send this message
    .catch((err) => session. send("I can't process your request for some
technical reasons.") ) ;

}).catch(function (err) {
```

Create a ".env" file and add keys.

```
#Custom Vision Keys
CUSTOM_VISION_PROJECT_ID= ***************
CUSTOM_VISION_PREDICTION = **************

#Confidence or Probability Threshold
CONFIDENCE_THRESHOLD= . 9
```

On line 9, add this code.

```
const API_URL = 'https://southcentralus.api.cognitive.microsoft.com/
customvision/v2. 0/Prediction/' +
    process. env. CUSTOM_VISION_PROJECT_ID + '/image';
```

Run the bot again (using npm start) and send the image of the product again to the bot.

Figure 3-88. *Re-upload image to bot*

It takes some time to get a response from the API, so let's send a typing indicator to the user so he knows that the bot is doing something.

Add the following code on line 33, run the bot again, and send the product image. (use "CTRL + C" to stop):

```
Session.sendTyping();
Var msg = session.message;
```

Figure 3-89. *Display the Typing image while the bot waits for a response from the API*

Replace the code on line 102

```
} else {

    // No attachments were sent
    var reply = new builder.Message(session)
        .text("Hi there! This sample is intented to show how can I receive
        attachments")
    session. send (reply) ;
}
```

with

```
} else {

    // No attachments were sent
    session. send( 'You did not send me a product image to recognize. ' )
}
```

Add the following code at the end of the file. This is for sending a message to the user when the bot connects:

```
bot.on ( "conversationUpdate', function (activity) {
   if (activity. membersAdded) {
      const hello = new builder.Message( )
         .address (activity.address)
         .text("Hello! Send me an image of the product and I'll send you
         the actual image of the product.");
      activity.membersAdded.forEach(function (identity) {
         // Send message when the bot joins the conversation
         if (identity.id === activity.address.bot.id) {
            bot . send (hello) ;
         }
      });
   }
});
```

Figure 3-90. *Send response if an image is not uploaded*

Add S3 Bucket URL in the .env file.

```
#S3 BUCKET PRODUCT IMAGE URL
S3 BUCKET URL=https://s3 . amazonaws.com/<bucketname>/
```

On line 78, replace

```
session.send("This is a " + best.tagName);
```

with

```
if (best . probability > parseFloat(process. env. CONFIDENCE_THRESHOLD) )
    let fileName = best.tagName.replace(' ', + '+') + '.jpg' ;
    session. send({
        text: 'You have sent me an image of ' + best.tagName + '. This is the
image of the product. ",
        attachments: [
            {
                contentType: ' image/jpeg' ,
                contentUrl: process.env.S3_BUCKET_URL + fileName,
                name: best.tagName
            }
        ]
    });
}
```

Product images on S3 have the same filenames as the tags on Custom Vision. That's why we can easily get the images by building the concatenated URL.

Let's try our bot now by running npm start.

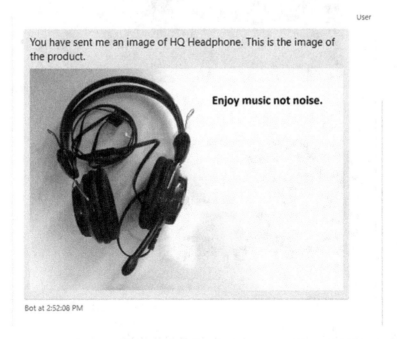

Figure 3-91. *Send bot response after an image is uploaded*

Now, try another one.

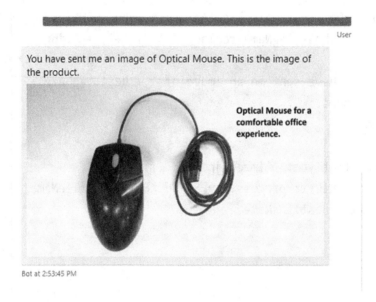

Figure 3-92. *Send bot response after an image is uploaded*

Now, a dongle:

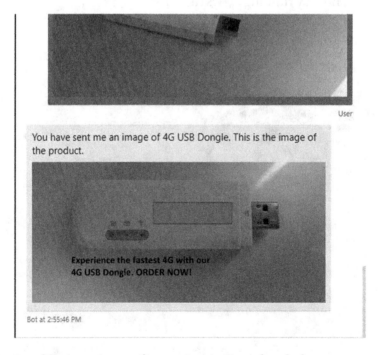

Figure 3-93. *Send bot response after an image is uploaded*

And a remote control:

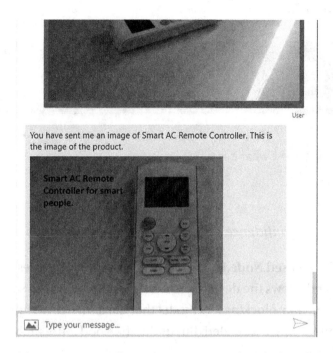

Figure 3-94. *Send bot response after an image is uploaded*

And a tally counter:

Figure 3-95. *Send bot response after an image is uploaded*

If you get the following message for any trained products, change the CONFIDENCE_
THRESHOLD in the .env file.

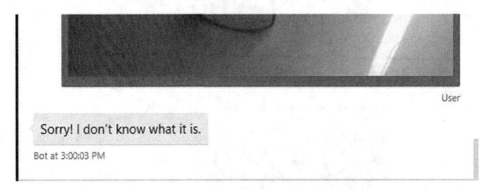

Figure 3-96. *Change confidence threshold if uploaded image is not recognized*

In this example, we used **Node.js**, the JavaScript runtime that uses Chrome's V8
JavaScript engine and allows the developers to run JavaScript on the server side. It
uses an event-driven, non-blocking I/O model that makes it lightweight and efficient.
The main event loop is single threaded, but under the hood it uses libuv to provide
asynchronous behavior.

Microsoft Bot Framework allows developers to easily create efficient, intelligent,
and scalable bots in no time. These bots can be connected with Microsoft Cognitive
Services, making them more natural. The NPM modules used in this example include
the following:

- dotenv-extended allows us to load environment variables from a
  .env file. It makes it easy and safe to handle environment variables.

- botbuilder is the official Node.js module for Microsoft Bot Builder
  Framework.

- restify creates REST endpoints so that we can connect with the bot
  in an easy way.

- bluebird module lets us use Promises in Node.js. (Bluebird is a full
  featured promise library however JavaScript now supports Promise
  without any module.)

- request-promise is the Promise version of the request module; it
  allows us to easily and efficiently make HTTP requests.

3-7. Apparel Search with Custom Vision Models in CNTK

Problem

Build a clothes search engine using a Custom Vision model.

Solution

As seen in the earlier recipes, image recognition and classification can be used to solve very common business problems nowadays and are being used in a lot of fields and industries, from captioning to lung cancer diagnostics, and from inventory detection to finding you the best fit of clothes for the day. Most people who have worked with deep learning have come across the MNIST dataset. It contains 28 x 28 grayscale images of handwritten digits from 0 to 9. The creator of Keras and author of an amazing book on deep learning "Deep Learning with Python" by O'Reilly Media, Francois Chollet had this to say about MNIST:

Figure 3-97. *Francis Chollet's tweet about MNIST*

Zalando, an eCommerce company, came up with a new dataset called Fashion-MNIST. It contains a training set of 60,000 examples and a test set of 10,000 examples. Each example is a 28 x 28 grayscale image of a fashion product associated with a label from ten classes. The official repository for the dataset is found here: `https://github.com/zalandoresearch/fashion-mnist`.

We will solve this challenge as part of Azure Notebook. If you did not set up Azure Notebook as part of Chapter 2, the following are the steps for setting up the Microsoft Azure Notebook.

Open `https://notebooks.azure.com` and log in to your account. If you are using your corporate account, you may need special permissions. It might be faster, provided it's compliant with your corporate policies, that you start with a personal account.

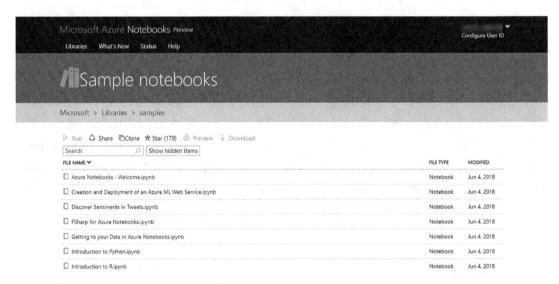

Figure 3-98. *Microsoft Azure Notebooks*

Click on the Libraries to go to your library. It would be empty.

Figure 3-99. *User Libraries on Azure Notebooks*

Click on **New Library** to create a new one.

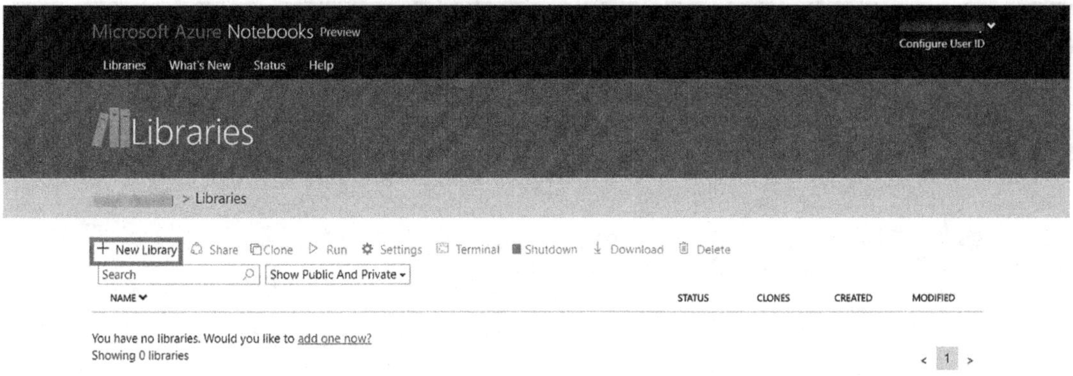

Figure 3-100. *Create a new Library*

Enter the name of your new library and a unique URL for your library, then click on the **Create** button.

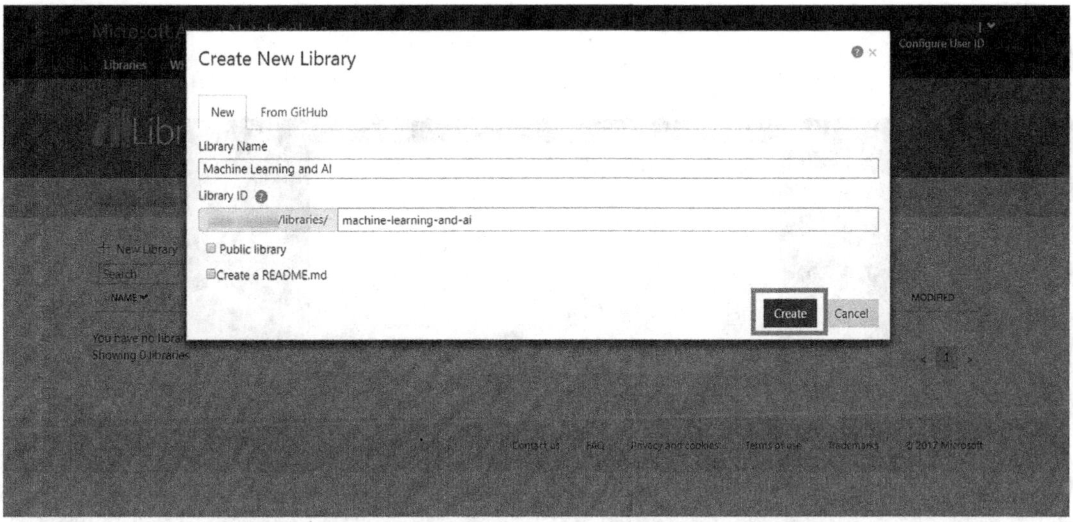

Figure 3-101. *Create a new Library*

Click the **New** button to create a new file.

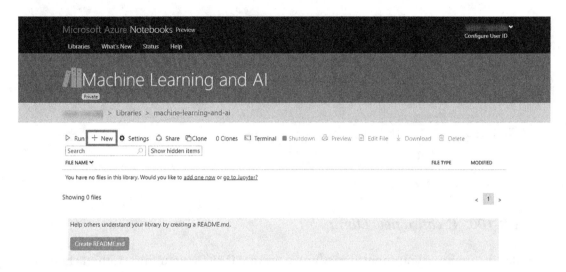

Figure 3-102. *Create a new file in the Library*

Fill in the required details to continue. Don't forget to select Python 3.6 from the drop-down list.

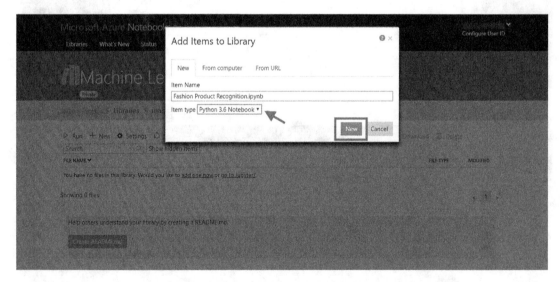

Figure 3-103. *Specify notebook file name and Python version to use*

Before we start, let's download the Fashion-MNIST dataset from https://github.com/zalandoresearch/fashion-mnist#get-the-data.

These `.gz` files contain both training and test datasets, including images and labels. More information can be found in the following image. Download all four files shown.

Many ML libraries already include Fashion-MNIST data/API, give it a try!

You can use direct links to download the dataset. The data is stored in the **same** format as the original MNIST data.

Name	Content	Examples	Size	Link	MD5 Checksum
train-images-idx3-ubyte.gz	training set images	60,000	26 MBytes	Download	8d4fb7e6c68d591d4c3dfef9ec88bf0d
train-labels-idx1-ubyte.gz	training set labels	60,000	29 KBytes	Download	25c81989df183df01b3e8a0aad5dffbe
t10k-images-idx3-ubyte.gz	test set images	10,000	4.3 MBytes	Download	bef4ecab320f06d8554ea6380940ec79
t10k-labels-idx1-ubyte.gz	test set labels	10,000	5.1 KBytes	Download	bb300cfdad3c16e7a12a480ee83cd310

Alternatively, you can clone this GitHub repository; the dataset appears under `data/fashion`. This repo also contains some scripts for benchmark and visualization.

    git clone git@github.com:zalandoresearch/fashion-mnist.git

Labels

Each training and test example is assigned to one of the following labels:

Figure 3-104. *Download files for GitHub Repo*

Once downloaded, create a new directory with the name `input` in the notebook.

Figure 3-105. *Create new folder*

Click on the input directory to open it and then create another directory with the name fashion.

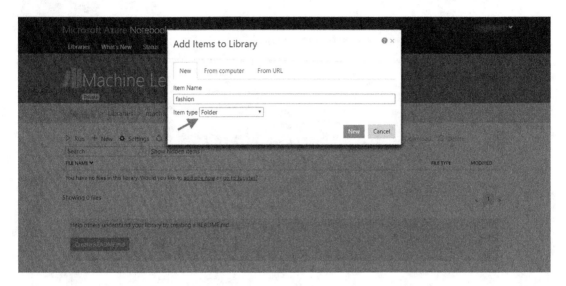

Figure 3-106. *Create sub folder named 'fashion'*

Open the fashion directory by clicking on it and then upload the dataset you have downloaded in the step above. Upload all the files to your notebook.

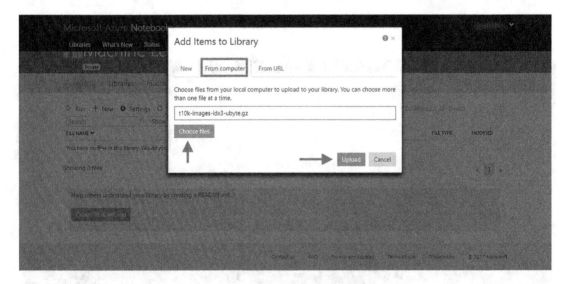

Figure 3-107. *Upload dataset to the 'fashion' sub-folder*

Now, go back to the directory and click on the notebook file to open it.

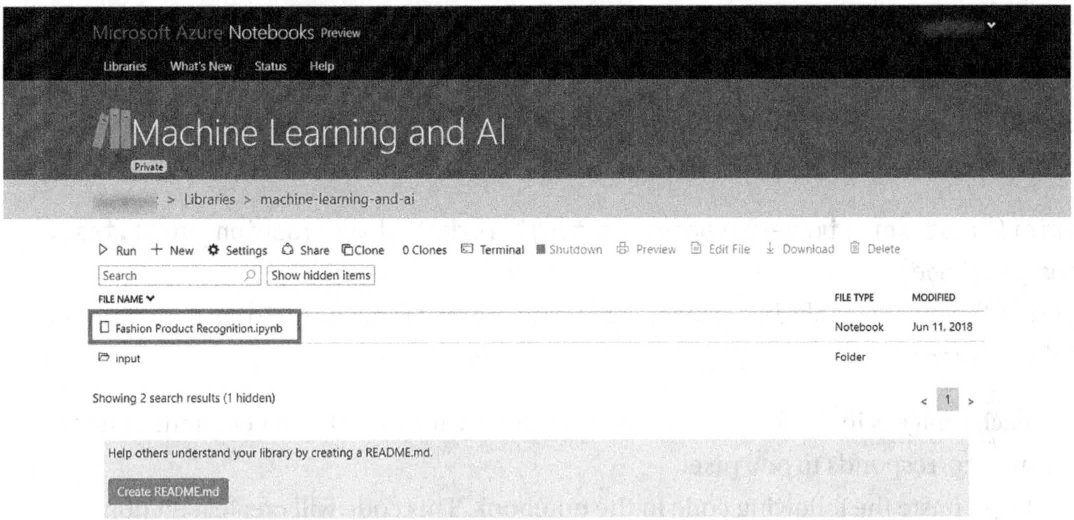

Figure 3-108. *Open Python Notebook*

Now copy-paste the following code into the notebook. This code will import the required Python libraries, including TensorFlow.

```
import numpy as np
import matplotlib.pyplot as plt
import seaborn as sns
import tensorflow as tf
from tensorflow.python.framework import ops
from tensorflow.examples.tutorials.mnist import input_data
```

Copy-paste the following code into the notebook. This code will import the required dataset from the directory we have created.

```
fashion_mnist = input_data.read_data_sets('input/fashion', one_hot=True)
```

Here, one_hot = True means that we want to use one-hot encoding. It is a method to represent the variables in the form of binary vectors. The value is first mapped to an integer, and then the integer is converted to a binary vector.

Copy-paste the following code in the notebook. This code will show the shapes of both the training and the test datasets. It is important to know the shapes before you create a neural network.

Here, *shape* means the structure and dimension of the data we have in terms of rows and columns.

```
print("Training set (images) shape: {shape}".format(shape=fashion_mnist.
train.images.shape))
print("Training set (labels) shape: {shape}".format(shape=fashion_mnist.
train.labels.shape))

print("Test set (images) shape: {shape}".format(shape=fashion_mnist.test.
images.shape))
print("Test set (labels) shape: {shape}".format(shape=fashion_mnist.test.
labels.shape))
```

Each image is in the form of a 1D NumPy array with 28 * 28 = 784 elements. Each element corresponds to one pixel.

Copy-paste the following code in the notebook. This code will create a dictionary of integers and labels so that we can easily identify labels.

```
label_dict = {
0: 'T-shirt/top',
1: 'Trouser',
2: 'Pullover',
3: 'Dress',
4: 'Coat',
5: 'Sandal',
6: 'Shirt',
7: 'Sneaker',
8: 'Bag',
9: 'Ankle boot'
}
```

Now, let's check one of the sample images so that we know that we have the correct dataset. Copy-paste the following code in the notebook. This code will load a sample image, get its label, and plot it on the screen.

```
sample_1 = fashion_mnist.train.images[47].reshape(28,28)
sample_label_1 = np.where(fashion_mnist.train.labels[47] == 1)[0][0]
print("y = {label_index} ({label})".format(label_index=sample_label_1,
label=label_dict[sample_label_1]))
plt.imshow(sample_1, cmap='Greys')
```

For detection, we will create a three-layer feedforward neural network with 128 units in each hidden layer. Then, we will use a Softmax function on the output from our network to get outputs for our target classes, which number ten in this case. A Softmax function is a generalization of the logistic function that "squashes" a K-dimensional vector of arbitrary real values to a K-dimensional vector of real values. Each entry is in the range of 0 to 1, and the sum of all entries will be 1.

Copy-paste the following code in the notebook. This code will help declare the parameters to describe our network. This will simplify hyperparameter-tuning during later phases.

Here, *hyperparameter* simply means a parameter that is set by the developer or trainer for the algorithm. Hyperparameters are used to adjust the algorithm and outputs.

```
n_hidden_1 = 128
n_hidden_2 = 128

n_input = 784
n_classes = 10
n_samples = fashion_mnist.train.num_examples
```

Next, copy-paste the following code in the notebook. This code will create a function that will take in some data about input-vector dimension and return TensorFlow placeholders.

TensorFlow placeholders will allow us to feed the data later easily to TensorFlow.

```
def create_placeholders(n_x, n_y):
 X = tf.placeholder(tf.float32, [n_x, None], name="X")
 Y = tf.placeholder(tf.float32, [n_y, None], name="Y")
 return X, Y
```

Now, it's time to initialize parameters. Copy-paste the following code in the notebook.

```
def initialize_parameters():

 tf.set_random_seed(42)

 W1 = tf.get_variable("W1", [n_hidden_1, n_input], initializer=tf.contrib.
layers.xavier_initializer(seed=42))
 b1 = tf.get_variable("b1", [n_hidden_1, 1], initializer=tf.zeros_
initializer())

 W2 = tf.get_variable("W2", [n_hidden_2, n_hidden_1], initializer=tf.
contrib.layers.xavier_initializer(seed=42))
 b2 = tf.get_variable("b2", [n_hidden_2, 1], initializer=tf.zeros_
initializer())

 W3 = tf.get_variable("W3", [n_classes, n_hidden_2], initializer=tf.
contrib.layers.xavier_initializer(seed=42))
 b3 = tf.get_variable("b3", [n_classes, 1], initializer=tf.zeros_
initializer())

 parameters = {
 "W1": W1,
 "b1": b1,
 "W2": W2,
 "b2": b2,
 "W3": W3,
 "b3": b3
 }

 return parameters
```

This code will initialize the weights and biases for each layer of our three-layer neural network. We will update them later in training. It uses Xavier initialization for our weights and Zero initialization for our biases. Xavier initialization makes sure that the weights are neither too small nor too large, which keeps the signal in a reasonable range of values through many layers.

Our neural network will make predictions using forward propagation. In forward propagation data flows from the previous layer to the next layer in a forward direction, and only selective values are transferred.

To accomplish this, copy-paste the following code in the notebook. This code will create a function that will take the input image and our dictionary of parameters and return the output from the last linear unit. ReLU is the max function(x, 0), which takes a matrix from a convolved image. It then sets all negative values to 0, and the rest of the values are kept constant. This simplifies and speeds up the learning process.

```
def forward_propagation(X, parameters):

    # Get parameters from dictionary
    W1 = parameters['W1']
    b1 = parameters['b1']
    W2 = parameters['W2']
    b2 = parameters['b2']
    W3 = parameters['W3']
    b3 = parameters['b3']

    # Carry out forward propagation
    Z1 = tf.add(tf.matmul(W1,X), b1)
    A1 = tf.nn.relu(Z1)
    Z2 = tf.add(tf.matmul(W2,A1), b2)
    A2 = tf.nn.relu(Z2)
    Z3 = tf.add(tf.matmul(W3,A2), b3)

    return Z3
```

The next step is to compute the cost function. The following code segment will help create a function to calculate cost using the data received from the second hidden layer and the actual class we are trying to predict.

The cost is simply a measure of the difference between the target class predicted by our neural network and the actual target class in Y. In other words, it is a measure of the difference between the predicted value of the class by our neural network and the actual class. This cost will be used during backpropagation to update the weights. The greater the cost, the greater the need for each parameter update. Cost is inversely proportional to accuracy i.e. the higher the cost would be, the least accurate the results hence the bigger adjustment we would need to make.

To give a very simple example, if the actual price of a smartphone is $500 and the predicted price is $425, the cost will be $75. Now, it needs to improve the algorithm to make a prediction with lower cost. Then, a prediction will be made again, and it may be $440. Now the cost is $60. This needs to be repeated until we get the desired results.

Copy-paste the following code in the notebook.

```
def compute_cost(Z3, Y):
 # Get logits (predictions) and labels
 logits = tf.transpose(Z3)
 labels = tf.transpose(Y)

 # Compute cost
 cost = tf.reduce_mean(tf.nn.softmax_cross_entropy_with_
logits(logits=logits, labels=labels))

 return cost
```

Backprop (back propagation) is an essential step in order for our neural network to work because it decides how much to update our parameters (weights and biases) based on the cost from the previous computation.

To put this all together, let's create a function called model() that will do everything for us from initializing parameters to calculating cost. It will take in the training and the test datasets, and, after building the network and training it, the function will compute the model's accuracies and return the final updated parameters dictionary.

Copy-paste the following code to create the model.

```
def model(train, test, learning_rate=0.0001, num_epochs=16, minibatch_
size=32, print_cost=True, graph_filename='costs'):

 # Ensure that model can be rerun without overwriting tf variables
 ops.reset_default_graph()

 # For reproducibility
 tf.set_random_seed(42)
 seed = 42
```

```python
# Get input and output shapes
(n_x, m) = train.images.T.shape
n_y = train.labels.T.shape[0]

costs = []

# Create placeholders of shape (n_x, n_y)
X, Y = create_placeholders(n_x, n_y)

# Initialize parameters
parameters = initialize_parameters()

# Forward propagation
Z3 = forward_propagation(X, parameters)

# Cost function
cost = compute_cost(Z3, Y)

# Backpropagation (using Adam optimizer)
optimizer = tf.train.AdamOptimizer(learning_rate).minimize(cost)

# Initialize variables
init = tf.global_variables_initializer()

# Start session to compute TensorFlow graph
with tf.Session() as sess:

# Run initialization
sess.run(init)

# Training loop
for epoch in range(num_epochs):

epoch_cost = 0.
num_minibatches = int(m / minibatch_size)
seed = seed + 1

for i in range(num_minibatches):

# Get next batch of training data and labels
minibatch_X, minibatch_Y = train.next_batch(minibatch_size)
```

```python
# Execute optimizer and cost function
_, minibatch_cost = sess.run([optimizer, cost], feed_dict={X:
minibatch_X.T, Y: minibatch_Y.T})

# Update epoch cost
epoch_cost += minibatch_cost / num_minibatches

# Print the cost every epoch
if print_cost == True:
print("Cost after epoch {epoch_num}: {cost}".format(epoch_num=epoch,
cost=epoch_cost))
costs.append(epoch_cost)

# Plot costs
plt.figure(figsize=(16,5))
plt.plot(np.squeeze(costs), color='#2A688B')
plt.xlim(0, num_epochs-1)
plt.ylabel("cost")
plt.xlabel("iterations")
plt.title("learning rate = {rate}".format(rate=learning_rate))
plt.savefig(graph_filename, dpi=300)
plt.show()

# Save parameters
parameters = sess.run(parameters)
print("Parameters have been trained!")

# Calculate correct predictions
correct_prediction = tf.equal(tf.argmax(Z3), tf.argmax(Y))

# Calculate accuracy on test set
accuracy = tf.reduce_mean(tf.cast(correct_prediction, "float"))

print ("Train Accuracy:", accuracy.eval({X: train.images.T, Y: train.
labels.T}))
print ("Test Accuracy:", accuracy.eval({X: test.images.T, Y: test.
labels.T}))

return parameters
```

Now copy and paste the following code to run the model.

```
train = fashion_mnist.train
test = fashion_mnist.test
parameters = model(train, test, learning_rate=0.0005)
```

Learning rate means how quickly the model should change its belief about something. *High learning rate* means that it will quickly ignore the previous knowledge and learn from new knowledge, which will give low accuracy. On the other hand, a very low learning rate will make the process extremely slow, as the model will remember features of everything.

The optimal learning rate must be neither low nor high. *Epoch* means one forward and one backward pass of all training images. So, the number of epochs will represent the number of times the model has learned from the training dataset.

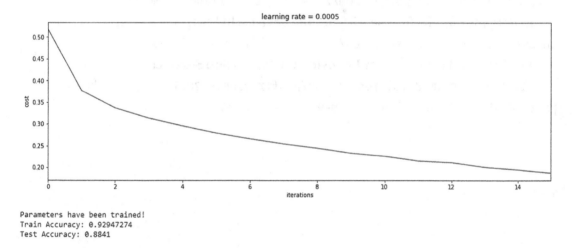

```
Parameters have been trained!
Train Accuracy: 0.92947274
Test Accuracy: 0.8841
```

Figure 3-109. *Learning rate for the model*

The model works decent enough as the accuracy is more than 88 percent.

References & Further Reading

Intelligent Kiosk—Face and Emotion APIs: https://github.com/Microsoft/Cognitive-Samples-IntelligentKiosk

    Deal With It Bot—Face API: http://aifunclub.azurewebsites.net

    Caption Bot—Computer Vision API: http://captionbot.ai

Computer Vision Description—tags, clip art, line drawing, black & white, IsAdultContent/Score, IsRacy/Score, categories, faces, dominant colors, accent color etc.: https://www.microsoft.com/cognitive-services/en-us/computer-vision-api

Emotions—Anger, contempt, disgust, fear, happiness, sadness, surprise, and neutral: https://www.microsoft.com/cognitive-services/en-us/emotion-api

Face Bounding box, 27 facial landmarks, age, gender, head pose, smile, facial hair, glasses: https://www.microsoft.com/cognitive-services/en-us/face-api

Samples and SDKs for ObjectiveC/Swift/iOS, Java/Android, C#/Windows, and Python (Jupyter notebook): https://www.microsoft.com/cognitive-services/en-us/SDK-Sample?api=computer%20vision

Classifying Fashion Articles—Code and dataset samples: https://medium.com/tensorist/classifying-fashion-articles-using-tensorflow-fashion-mnist-f22e8a04728a; https://github.com/zalandoresearch/fashion-mnist

Export your model for use with mobile devices: https://docs.microsoft.com/en-us/azure/cognitive-services/custom-vision-service/export-your-model

Product and Part Identifier Bot using Custom Vision Service: https://blogs.msdn.microsoft.com/geoffreyinnis/2017/06/13/product-and-part-identifier-bot-using-custom-vision-service/

CHAPTER 4

Text Analytics: The Dark Data Frontier

Human: What do we want?
Computer: Natural-language processing!
Human: When do we want it?
Computer: When do we want what?

—Reddit

Text is everywhere. Analysts at Gartner estimate that upward of 80 percent of enterprise data today is unstructured. Our everyday interactions generate torrents of such data, including tweets, blog posts, advertisements, news, articles, research papers, descriptions, emails, YouTube comments, Yelp reviews, surveys from your insurance company, and call transcripts; there is a tremendous amount of unstructured data, and the majority of it is text. Another general way to describe this large amount of mostly monetizable data (except YouTube comments—those are toxic!) is by classifying it as *dark data*. The origin of this term is not well known, but it was popularized by Stanford's Dr. Chris Re, who founded the DeepDive program for extracting valuable information from dark data. The term pertains to the mountains of raw information collected in various ways, and such data remains difficult to analyze.

Text analysis is a multi-step process that includes building a pipeline to process large unstructured datasets. The process starts with data wrangling; i.e., capturing, sorting, sifting, stemming, and matching the text contents. This data can then be visualized into word clouds, giving meaning to concepts clustered together. Clustering and the classification of documents have lots of uses, from triage to similarity analysis and finding relevant details in a haystack. Document classification, clustering, and summarization have a real business impact.

© Adnan Masood, Adnan Hashmi 2019
A. Masood and A. Hashmi, *Cognitive Computing Recipes*, https://doi.org/10.1007/978-1-4842-4106-6_4

Understanding the customer sentiment reflected on social media is very important for businesses, especially in the era of today's Twitter-style information firehose. Reputations can be ruined, and a company's credibility can be put at stake if an enterprise does not come in front of a negative sentiment with its own narrative, especially if the sentiment comes from a not-so-reliable source. Today's machine-learning algorithms provide excellent capabilities to perform topic modeling to understand sentiments, including anger, happiness, disgust, fear, and sadness, with social and language tones and degree of confidence.

Understanding unstructured data is so important that you will see its implementation in a variety of places. Apple recently acquired Lattice.IO, a dark data mining company that built a platform on top of Stanford's open source DeepDive technology. DeepDive is an open source tool aimed at extracting value from a variety of dark data sources, including text documents, PDFs, and so on. DeepDive is officially a "programming and execution framework for statistical inference, which allows us to solve data cleaning, extraction, and integration problems jointly." DeepDive and its associated projects, including Snorkel and Fonduer, are some of the efforts ongoing in academia to understand unstructured text processing. It is used for understanding and processing journal articles as well as for MEMEX (human trafficking) research. Dr. Regina Barzilay, one of my professors at MIT and a professor of electrical engineering and computer science, has recently won a MacArthur genius grant for her work in unstructured text analytics and natural-language processing. Dr. Barzilay's research covers multiple areas of NLP, from syntactic parsing and the deciphering of dead languages, to developing new ways to train neural networks that can provide rationales for their decisions.

Let's explore some of these applications using Cognitive Services.

Overview of the Text Analytics Ecosystem

The analysis of textual information in mining unstructured data is one of the original implementations of machine learning and has been called a variety of names, including dark data mining, unstructured data analysis, and text mining. Even though unstructured data is not limited to raw text, most of the time text is what is being referred to in terms of application logs, telemetry information, standard operating procedures, wikis, corporate document repositories, PDF files, emails, and so on.

As one can imagine, to process, analyze, visualize, and eventually monetize this wealth of information, a variety of solutions have been produced. These solutions range from on-premises software solutions to cloud toolkits and hybrid SDKs that bring the best of both worlds. In this chapter, we will briefly review the current landscape of text analytics libraries with some short examples and then jump into Cognitive Services APIs for text analytics.

CoreNLP

https://stanfordnlp.github.io/CoreNLP/simple.html

Stanford's CoreNLP is an integrated natural language–processing toolkit with a wide variety of natural language–processing tools, including part-of-speech (POS) tagging, grammatical analysis tools, entity recognition, pattern learning, and parsing that is fast, accurate, and able to support several major languages. Entity detection is the ability to detect the names of companies, people, objects, and concepts and then to correlate it and make a context-sensitive search.

CoreNLP also supports the featurization and normalization of data, such as normalizing dates, times, and numeric quantities. It supports a variety of languages as well as the annotation of arbitrary text at scale. CoreNLP, as the product page states, "provide[s] marking up the structure of sentences in terms of phrases and syntactic dependencies, indicate[s] which noun phrases refer to the same entities, indicate[s] sentiment, [and] extract[s] particular or open-class relations between entity mentions."

The library has APIs available for most major modern programming languages and provides simple yet highly useful features such as the ability to run as a simple web service.

The licensing, however, has associated costs for commercial projects and can be expensive for larger enterprises.

NLTK—Python Natural Language Toolkit

https://www.nltk.org

Arguably the most popular Python library, NLTK solves significant natural language-processing challenges and is widely used in education and research. The library supports applications in text processing, information extraction, document classification and sentiment analysis, document similarity, automatic summarizing, and discourse analysis.

NLTK has built-in support for over 50 corpora and trained models including Open Multilingual Wordnet, NPS Chat, and SentiWordNet.

You can get started with NLTK in its simplest form as follows:

```
monty = "Monty Python's "\
... "Flying Circus."
monty*2 + "plus just last word:" + monty[-7:]
"Monty Python's Flying Circus.Monty Python's Flying Circus.plus
just last word:Circus."
monty.find('Python') #finds position of substring within string
6
monty.upper() +' and ' = monty.lower()
"MONTY PYTHON'S FLYING CIRCUS. and monty python's flying circus."
monty.replace('y', 'x')
"Montx Pxthon's Flxing Circus
```

NLKT's advanced implementations may have a steeper learning curve, but it is a production-ready solution for a variety of business use cases.

SpaCY

```
https://spacy.io/
```

Subtitled as an "industrial-strength" Python library, SpaCY is built using Cython. It is a free open source software for natural-language processing. SpaCY features NER (named entity recognition), POS (part of speech) tagging, dependency parsing, word vectors, and more.

Unlike NLTK, which brings everything and the kitchen sink, SpaCY is minimal and opinionated. SpaCY's philosophy is to only present one algorithm (the best one) for each purpose. Even though it currently only supports English, its main limitation, the library is very fast.

However, there is debate about benchmarks, as Dr. Manning had this to say recently:

Christopher Manning
@chrmanning

Following

Hey @spacy_io people (@honnibal, @_inesmontani), those speed comparisons on spacy.io/usage/facts-fi ... are not only outdated—as you note—but the speed for the Stanford Tokenizer is just way wrong. Time to take them down? Here are our measurements:
nlp.stanford.edu/software/token ... #NLProc

Here is a link for CoreNLP for comparison: `https://nlp.stanford.edu/software/tokenizer.html#Speed`

Gensim

`https://radimrehurek.com/gensim/tutorial.html`

Gensim, dubbed topic modeling for humans, is a well-optimized library for topic modeling and document-similarity analysis. Gensim started off as a collection of various Python scripts for the Czech Digital Mathematics Library.

Topic models provide a straightforward way to analyze large volumes of unlabeled text. A "topic" consists of a cluster of words that frequently occur together. Using contextual clues, topic models can connect words with similar meanings and distinguish between uses of words with multiple meanings. Gensim can be used for specific challenges around topic modeling, and it does it quite well. Its topic-modeling algorithms, such as its Latent Dirichlet Allocation (LDA) implementation, are best-in-class. In addition, it's robust, efficient, and scalable.

Word2Vec

`https://www.tensorflow.org/tutorials/word2vec`

Even though it is not a library, we thought it important to talk about vector representation of words. Word2Vec is a two-layer neural net that processes text. The model used for learning-vector representations of words is called "word embeddings."

The input to Word2Vec is a text corpus, which is turned into a set of vectors—to be more precise, feature vectors—for words in that corpus. Technically speaking, Word2Vec is not a deep neural network, and its utility stems from grouping the vectors of similar words together in a vectorspace. However, it helps convert text into a numerical form that deep neural nets can process. The text corpus can be virtually anything encodable, such as genetic coding, graphs, music playlists, or any other verbal or symbolic series, which results in Word2Vec variants like Gene2Vec, Doc2Vec, Like2Vec, and Follower2Vec.

GloVe—Global Vectors for Word Representation

https://nlp.stanford.edu/projects/glove/

Like Word2Vec, GloVe is an unsupervised learning algorithm that converts words into a geometrical encoding of vectors; however, Word2Vec can be classified as predictive, while GloVe is a count-based model. In GloVe the training data is based on aggregated global word–word co-occurrence statistics from a text corpus, resulting in useful co-occurrence information; i.e., frequency of co-occurrence in large text corpora.

There are pre-trained word vectors that can be downloaded from the Stanford GloVe website and the associated GitHub repository.

DeepDive—Features, not Algorithms

http://deepdive.stanford.edu

As discussed earlier, DeepDive is a machine learning–based system used to extract value from unstructured dark data. It has been the foundation of several important projects including the following:

- MEMEX – Human trafficking detection from large internet corpora
- PaleoDeepDive – knowledge base for paleobiologists
- GeoDeepDive – geology journal articles information extraction
- Wisci – adding structured data to Wikipedia

Snorkel—A System for Fast Training-Data Creation

`https://hazyresearch.github.io/snorkel/`

Built by the DeepDive team, Snorkel (pun intended) provides a system for creating training datasets when large, trained, labeled datasets are not available. This is done via weak supervision functions as part of the data-programming paradigm.

Fonduer—Knowledge-Base Construction from Richly Formatted Data

`https://github.com/HazyResearch/fonduer`

Similar to Snorkel, Fonduer provides the capability of doing knowledge-base construction (KBC) from richly formatted data such as tables, PDF files, and so forth. You can define weak supervision functions in multi-modal sources, as shown in Figure 4-1, to identify patterns across different types of documents (table shown later) that can be extracted out. In the following example, you can see how cell entries are being extracted from PDF documents based on their structure, location, and data type and value.

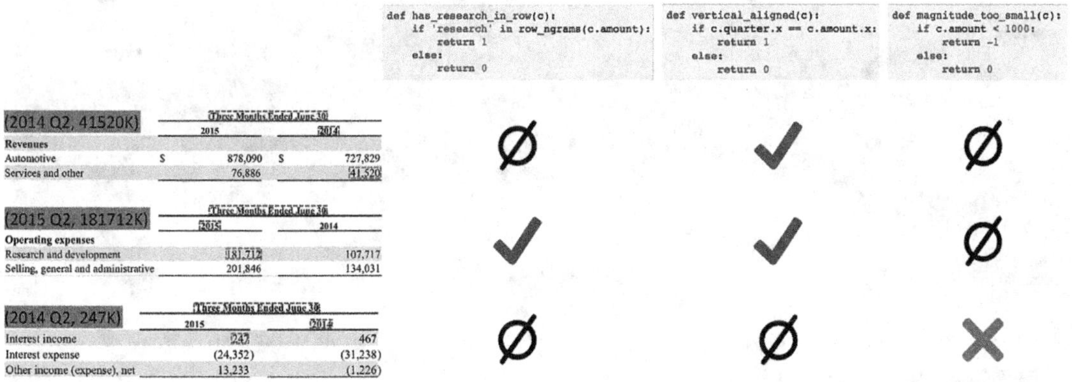

Figure 4-1. *Fonduer functions to extract richly formatted data out of the tables*

TextBlob—Simplified Text Processing

`https://textblob.readthedocs.io/en/dev/`

TextBlob is a Python library that provides an intuitive interface to NLTK for processing text data. Like its predecessors, TextBlob has features including noun-phrase extraction, part-of-speech tagging, sentiment analysis, classification (naive Bayes, decision tree), tokenization, frequency detection, n-grams, word inflection (pluralization and singularization) and lemmatization, spell check, and wordNet integration, to name a few.

Most of the libraries just mentioned can be used with Python and R. There is a cran.R project (`cran.r-project.org/web/views/NaturalLanguageProcessing.html`) that provides many packages with features set for NLTK. For Java and R, we also have OpenNLP and LingPipe. There are a variety of commercial applications, such as SAS Text Analytics and SPSS tools, which provide industry-specific solutions and implementations.

Cloud-based Text Analytics and the APIs

Apart from the libraries mentioned, there are a variety of APIs available, including Watson Natural Language Understanding, Amazon Comprehend, Google Cloud Natural Language, Microsoft LUIS (Language Understanding Intelligent Service), and so forth. In this book we will mainly focus on Microsoft LUIS; the following is a comparative analysis of the feature sets.

Features	Amazon Comprehend	Google Cloud Natural Language	Microsoft Azure Text Analytics	IBM Watson Natural Language Processing
Entity Extraction	✔	✔	✔	✔
Sentiment Analysis	✔	✔	✔	✔
Syntax Analysis (Spell check etc.)	✘	✔	✔	✘
Topic Modeling	✔	✔	✘	✘
POS Tagging	✔	✔	✔	✔

4-1. Claim Classification

Problem

Perform text classification for auto versus home insurance claims. Labeled training data for previous claims provides classification examples. Using this data, build a model to classify the future claims into the right categories.

Solution

The dataset provided has classification for auto versus home. For instance, the auto claims look like the following:

> Coming home, I drove into the wrong house and collided with a tree I don't have.

> The other car collided with mine without giving warning of its intentions.

> I thought my window was down, but I found out it was up when I put my head through it.

While the home claims have textual description similar to this:

> There was a strong rumble from the earthquake and then we heard a crack as the patio collapsed into the ocean.

> The burglars broke into the house through our living room window.

> We left a candle on in the bathroom. A towel hanging nearby caught fire and then burned the whole bathroom.

How It Works

Install TensorFlow using the following:

```
pip install tensorflow
```

This will install TensorFlow and its dependencies.

Install TFLearn using the following:

```
pip install tflearn
```

This is a high-level deep-learning API for TensorFlow.

Start the Python interpreter using python and enter the following commands:

```
import nltk
nltk.download("all")
This will take some time as it will download all data packages. Once the
download is completed, you will get a success message.[nltk_data]
[nltk_data]   Done downloading collection all
True
```

If you get an error:

```
ModuleNotFoundError: No module named 'nltk'
```

you will have to install nltk using the following:

```
pip install nltk
```

Import Modules

We will be using the TFLearn library to build and train the classifier. In addition, it relies on a supplied helper library that performs common text-analytic functions, called *textanalytics*. You can view the contents of this file by opening textanalytics.py in your favorite editor. Ours happens to be Visual Studio code.

Run the following commands in the Python interpreter:

```
import numpy as np
import re
import tflearn
from tflearn.data_utils import to_categorical
import textanalytics as ta
```

You can safely ignore any warnings about "hdf5 is not supported on this machine" or "curses is not supported in this machine" in the output.

If you get an error that sklearn or scipy is not installed, use pip install sklearn and pip install scipy to install.

Prepare the Training Data

In this example, you are provided with a small document containing examples of the text received as claim text, courtesy of Solliance, Inc. They have provided this in a text file with one line per sample claim.

Enter the following commands to read the contents of claims_label.txt:

```
claims_corpus = [claim for claim in open("claims_text.txt")]
claims_corpus
["coming home, I drove into the wrong house and collided with a tree I
don't have. \n",
 through my window was down, but I found out it was up when I put my head
through it. \n
through my windshield into my wife's face.\n", 'A pedestrian hit me and
went under my \n
telephone pole.\n", "I had been driving for forty year when I fell asleep
at the whee
red where no stop sign had ever appeared before.\n, 'My car was legally
parked as it
r and vanished.\n, 'I told the police that I was not injured but on
removing my hat,
on to run, so I ran over him.\n', ' I saw a slow moving, sad old faced
gentleman as he
I was later found in a ditch by some stray cows. \n ' , 'I was driving down
El camino a
dan pulled up behind me. When the left turn light changed green, the black
sedan hit me
it was still red. After hitting my car, the black sedan backed up and then
sped past me
```

In addition to the claims sample, Contoso, Ltd. has provided a document that labels each of the sample claims provided as either 0 ("home insurance claim") or 1 ("auto insurance claim"). This too is presented as a text file with one row per sample, in the same order as the claim text.

Enter the following commands to read the contents of claims_labels.txt:

```
labels = [int(re.sub("\n", "", label)) for label in open("claims_labels.txt")]
labels
[1, 1, 1, 1, 1, 1, 1, 1, 1, 1, 1, 1, 1,1, 1, 1, 1, 1, 1, 1, 0, 0, 0, 0, 0,
0, 0, 0, 0, 0, 0, 0, 0, 0, 0, 0, 0, 0, 0, 0]
```

We can't use integer values. We can use the to_categorical method from TFlearn to convert these values into binary categorical values.

Run the following commands to convert the values from integer to binary categorical values:

```
labels = to_categorical(labels, 2)
labels

array([[0. , 1.],
       [0. , 1.],
       [0. , 1.],
       [0. , 1.],
       [0. , 1.],
       [0. , 1.],
       [0. , 1.],
       [0. , 1.],
       [0. , 1.],
       [0. , 1.],
       [0. , 1.],
       [0. , 1.],
       [0. , 1.],
       [0. , 1.],
       [0. , 1.],
       [0. , 1.],
       ....,
       [0. , 1.],
       [0. , 1.],
       [0. , 1.]])
```

Normalize the Claims Corpus

The `textanalytics` module supplied takes care of implementing our desired normalization logic. In summary, what it does is as follows:

- Expand contractions (for example "can't" becomes "cannot")

- Lowercase all text

- Remove special characters (like punctuation)

- Remove stop words (these are words like *a*, *an*, and *the* that add no value)

Run the following commands and observe how the claim text is modified:

```
norm_corpus = ta.normalize_corpus(claims_corpus)
norm_corpus
[' coming home drove wrong house collided tree', 'car colloid'
 way', 'truck backed windshield wifes face', 'pedesttrian
', 'attempt kill fly drove telephone pole' , 'driving forty
'car legally parked backed car', 'invisible car came nowh
run ran, 'saw slow moving sad old faced gentleman bounce
rnoon sun bright shining behind stoplight made hard see l
 black sedan hit thinking light changed us moved light st
'caught end yellow light car moved intersection light turn
ing tore roof house wind took hour precious paintings', '
emolished one wall', 'snow began pile high tree front yar
ollect second story patio collapsed weight', 'strong winds
uake heard crack patio collapsed ocean', 'earthquake crea
```

Feature Extraction: Vectorize the Claims Corpus

Feature extraction in text analytics has the goal of creating a numeric representation of the textual documents. During feature extraction, a "vocabulary" of unique words is identified, and each word becomes a column in the output. In other words, the table is as wide as the vocabulary.

Each row represents a document. The value in each cell is typically a measure of the relative importance of that word in the document, where if a word from the vocabulary does not appear that cell has a zero value in that column. In other words, the table is as tall as all of the documents in the corpus.

This approach enables machine-learning algorithms, which operate against arrays of numbers, to also operate against text, because each text document is now represented as an array of numbers.

Deep-learning algorithms operate on tensors, which are also vectors (or arrays of numbers), and so this approach is also valid for preparing text for use with a deep-learning algorithm.

Run the following commands to see what the vectorized version of the claims in norm_corpus looks like:

```
vectorizer, tfidf_matrix = ta.build_feature_matrix(norm_corpus)
data = tfidf_matrix.toarray()
print(data.shape)
(40, 258)

data

array ([[0., 0., ..., 0., 0., 0.,],
        [0., 0., ..., 0., 0., 0.,],
        [0., 0., ..., 0., 0., 0.,],

              ....,

        [0., 0., ..., 0., 0., 0.,],
        [0., 0., ..., 0., 0., 0.,],
        [0., 0., ..., 0., 0., 0.,]])
```

Build the Neural Network

Now that you have normalized and extracted the features from the training text data, you are ready to build the classifier. In this case, we will build a simple neural network. The network will be three layers deep, and each node in one layer will be connected to every other node in a subsequent layer. This is what is meant by *fully connected*. We will train the model by applying a regression.

Run the following commands to build the structure for your neural network:

```
net = tflearn.input_data(shape=[None, 258])
net = tflearn.fully_connected(net, 32)
net = tflearn.fully_connected(net, 32)
net = tflearn.fully_connected(net, 2, activation="softmax")
net = tflearn.regression(net)
```

Observe that we declared in the first line that the input data will be 258 columns wide (lining up to our "vocabulary") and an unspecified number of documents tall. This is what is defined by shape=[None,258].

Also, take a look at the second-to-last line, which defines the outputs. This is a fully connected layer as well, but it only has two nodes. This is because the output of our neural network has only two possible values.

The layers in between the input data and the final fully connected layer represent our hidden layers. How many layers and how many nodes for each layer you should have is typically something you arrive at empirically and through iteration, measuring the model's performance. As a rule of thumb, most neural networks have the same dimensions for all of their hidden layers.

Train the Neural Network

Now that we have the structure of our neural network, we will create an instance of the DNN class and provide it our network. This will become our model.

Run the following command:

```
model = tflearn.DNN(net)
```

Now we are ready to let the DNN learn by fitting it against our training data and labels.

Run the following command to fit your model against the data:

```
model.fit(data, labels, n_epoch=10, batch_size=16, show_metric=True)
```

Test Classifying Claims

Now that you have constructed a model, try it out against a set of claims. Recall that we need to normalize and featurize the text using the exact same pipeline we used during training.

Run the following command to prepare the test data:

```
test_claim = ['I crashed my car into a pole.', 'The flood ruined my
house.', 'I lost control of my car and fell in the river.']
test_claim = ta.normalize_corpus(test_claim)
test_claim = vectorizer.transform(test_claim)
test_claim = test_claim.toarray()
print(test_claim.shape)
```

Now, use the model to predict the classification by running the following commands:

```
pred = model.predict(test_claim)
pred
array([[0.48525476, 0.5147453 ],
       [0.5027783 , 0.4972217 ],
       [0.49397638, 0.50602365]], dtype=float32)
```

The way to read the preceding output is that there is one array per document. The first element in an array corresponds to the confidence it has in a label of 0, and the second corresponds to the confidence it has in a label of 1. Another way to examine this output is as labels.

Run the following commands to show the prediction in this way:

```
pred_label = model.predict_label(test_claim)
pred_label

array([[0. , 1.],
       [0. , 1.],
       [0. , 1.]],  dtype=int64)
```

Note that for each array representing a document, the labels are presented in sorted order according to their confidence level. So the first element in the array represents the label the model is predicting.

Model Exporting and Importing

Now that we have a working model, we need to export the trained model to a file so that it can be used downstream by the deployed web service. To export the model, run the save command and provide a filename.

```
model.save('claim_classifier.tfl')
```

To test reloading the model into the same session, you first need to reset the default TensorFlow graph. Run the following commands to reset the graph:

```
import tensorflow as tf
tf.reset_default_graph()
```

Before you can load the saved model, you need to recreate the structure of the neural network. Then you can use the load method to read the file from disk. Run the following commands to load the model:

```
net2 = tflearn.input_data(shape=[None, 258])
net2 = tflearn.fully_connected(net2, 32)
net2 = tflearn.fully_connected(net2, 32)
net2 = tflearn.fully_connected(net2, 2, activation="softmax")
net2 = tflearn.regression(net2)
model2 = tflearn.DNN(net2)
model2.load('claim_classifier.tfl', weights_only=True)
```

As before, you can use the model to run predictions. Run the following commands to try the prediction with the reloaded model:

```
pred_label = model2.predict_label(test_claim)
pred_label
pred_label[0][0]
```

The reloaded prediction model provides the results of the prediction claim, with the resulting value of 1 being a valid claim based on the dataset.

4-2. Know Your Company's Health Problem

Publicly traded companies and some foreign entities are required by law to disclose the state and health of their business to the U.S. Securities and Exchange Commission (SEC). The SEC uses their EDGAR (Electronic Data Gathering, Analysis, and Retrieval) system to collect, validate, index, accept, and forward the submitted disclosures, and it makes the data publicly available for analysis of time-sensitive corporate information.

See a complete description here: https://www.sec.gov/edgar/aboutedgar.htm.

The disclosures or filings comprise mainly unstructured data in the form of text contained within HTML files and contain a wealth of information that can subsequently be extracted and mined for use by financial analysts to gauge the health of a company or entity before any investment in stocks can be made. However, the process of extracting the files from the SEC HTTP site, parsing the retrieved files for the relevant sections, and finally obtaining insights and meaning from the information is fairly cumbersome and requires knowledge about how the SEC structures and publishes the information, something that investors are not fully aware of. In addition, the task of sifting through vast amounts of text manually requires significant time and energy.

Solution

The SEC already provides a web-based UI to search the disclosures data store on their site. While this provides a way to access and view the disclosures in the web browser, a complete solution to retrieve and mine the information would entail setting up an ETL pipeline that continually retrieves data from the SEC site as and when information is published. This can be implemented in a number of ways; a possible high-level solution would look like Figure 4-2.

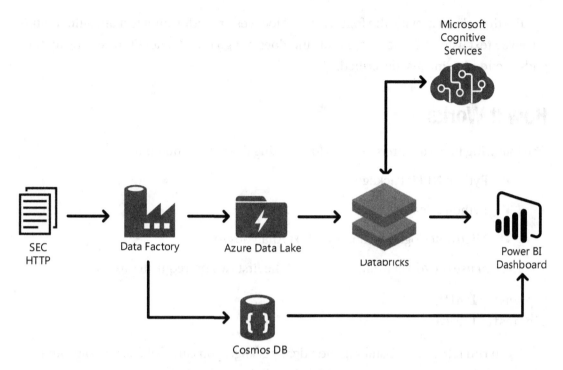

Figure 4-2. *An architectural schematic for the solution.*[1]

The diagram can be summarized as follows:

1. Data is retrieved from the SEC HTTP using an ETL tool or service such as Azure Data Factory.

2. The retrieved files are loaded into an unstructured storage medium such as Azure Storage or Azure Data Lake Store; additional metadata is stored in a NoSQL data store; e.g., Cosmos DB.

3. Python notebooks running inside a cluster on Databricks make calls to the Azure Text Analytics API, which allows for the analysis of the text contained within the retrieved files.

4. The results of the analyzed text along with the metadata is surfaced to end users using a dashboard tool or service such as Microsoft Power BI.

---

[1]A comprehensive list of Azure solution architectures to help you design and implement secure, highly available, performant, and resilient solutions on Azure can be found here: https://azure.microsoft.com/en-us/solutions/architecture/.

For the sake of brevity, the following text focuses on performing text analytics on the retrieved text using a Python notebook and does not go into the details of setting up the end-to-end pipeline just described.

How It Works

The following items are prerequisites for creating the Python notebook:

- Python NLTK Package

- Python Edgar Package

- Microsoft Cognitive Services Text Analytics API

You can use the `pip` command to install the first two prerequisites as follows:

```
pip install nltk
pip install edgar
```

If you run into issues installing the Edgar package, you can also use the following commands in your notebook to explicitly install the package:

```
import sys
!{sys.executable} -m pip install edgar
```

Use the following steps to provision a Microsoft Cognitive Services Text Analytics API:

1. Log in to Azure Portal and click on the **Create a resource** link on the top-left corner of the page.

2. Select the **AI + Machine Learning** category under **Azure Marketplace** and then click the **Text Analytics** link (Figure 4-3).

Figure 4-3. *Selection of AI + Machine Learning and Text Analytics quickstart from the Azure Marketplace*

3. Fill out the information for the service and click the **Create** button
    to provision the Text Analytics API endpoint (Figure 4-4).

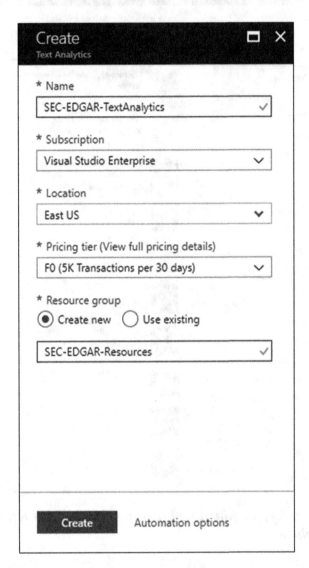

Figure 4-4. *Select the name, location, pricing tier, and resource group for the application*

Now we are ready to create the Python notebook:

1. Start by importing the 10-K filings for an organization using the Edgar package we installed earlier. The listed name and CIK, or Central Index Key (which serves as a unique identifier for each company), can be retrieved from the SEC site at https://www. sec.gov/edgar/searchedgar/cik.htm.

```
import edgar
company = edgar.Company("Microsoft Corp", "0000789019")
tree = company.getAllFilings(filingType = "10-K")
docs = edgar.getDocuments(tree, noOfDocuments=5)
```

2. For this example, we will analyze one filing and strip the text of any unwanted characters or symbols using the following statement (code formatted for readability only):

```
filingText = docs[0].replace('\n'  , ' ')
                     .replace('\r'  , ' ')
                     .replace('/s/' , ' ')
                     .replace('\xa0', ' ')
```

3. It is always a good idea to further trim the text being analyzed by removing punctuation marks and stop words before any actual analysis. Use the NLTK package to achieve this through the following statements:

```
from nltk.corpus import stopwords
from nltk.tokenize import word_tokenize
import string

stopWords = set(stopwords.words('english'))
wordTokens = word_tokenize(filingText)
filingTextArray = [w for w in wordTokens if not w in stopWords]
filingTextFiltered = ' '.join(filingTextArray)
filingTextFiltered = filingTextFiltered.translate(string.
punctuation)
```

4. To call the Microsoft Cognitive Service Text Analytics API we provisioned earlier, store the subscription key and the endpoint URLs to be called using the statements here:

```
subscriptionKey = "[TODO: Paste Subscription Key here]"
baseUrl = "[TODO: Paste URL here]"
sentimentApiUrl = baseUrl + "/sentiment"
```

Navigate to the Text Analytics API instance and click the **Overview** link on the main blade to copy the subscription key and endpoint URL. Once copied, paste the two values into the preceding code (Figure 4-5).

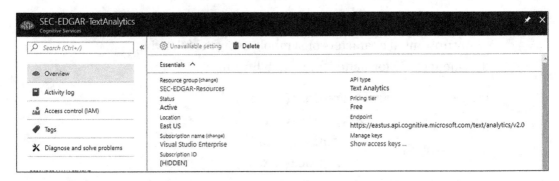

Figure 4-5. *The Text Analytics dashboard shows the key configuration values*

You'll need to click the **Show access keys...** link to get to the subscription key for the API (Figure 4-6).

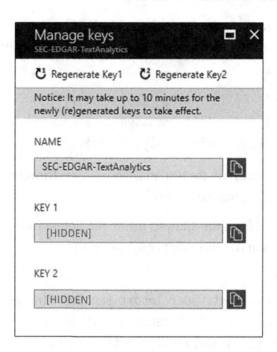

Figure 4-6. *The Key Management console for generating and using the subscription keys*

5. To call the Text Analytics API, construct the JSON to pass to the endpoint as follows:

```
documents = {'documents' : [
  { 'id': '1', 'text': filingTextFiltered[:5000] }
]}
```

The value passed as the Id in the preceding code can be any arbitrary numeric value. Also, since each disclosure from the SEC site comprises a large body of text, we had to truncate the text down to the first 5,000 characters in the constructed JSON.

6. Use the following code to make the call to the Text Analytics API, passing in the filtered filing text retrieved using the Edgar package:

```
headers = {"Ocp-Apim-Subscription-Key": subscriptionKey}
response = requests.post(sentimentApiUrl, headers=headers,
json=documents)
sentiments = response.json()
print(sentiments)
```

213

The last statement in the preceding code displays the returned sentiment score in JSON format, which might look something similar to this:

```
{'documents': [{'id': '1', 'score': 0.7}],
 'errors': [{'id': '1', 'message': 'Truncated input to
first 100 tokens during analysis.'}]}
```

Calling an external API for text analysis requires trimming the payload for performance reasons.

7. We can also perform the analysis inside the notebook using the Vader Sentiment Analyzer that comes with NLTK:

```
import nltk
from nltk.sentiment.vader import SentimentIntensityAnalyzer
sentimentAnalyzer = SentimentIntensityAnalyzer()
scores = sentimentAnalyzer.polarity_scores(filingTextFiltered)
for score in scores:
    print('{0}: {1}\n'.format(score, scores[score]), end=")
```

You should see a more granular view of the sentiment contained within the text with an output similar to the following:

```
neg: 0.048
neu: 0.796
pos: 0.156
compound: 1.0
```

4-3. Text Summarization

Problem

Text summarization is a subfield in natural-language processing that deals with summaries from text corpora. A summary provides important information from an original text source but is shorter, preferably no longer than half of the original text's size, and preserves important information.

In the ever-growing world of information, summaries are highly useful in financial advisory, legal, and news-media domains, where capturing the gist of message in a concise and concrete manner is quite important.

So, let's try to find out how to summarize text documents to get meaningful summaries.

Solution

In this recipe we will summarize the documents using a data science virtual machine and pointer generator networks. The steps are as follows:

1. Visit the following link to visit the DSVM page and select "Data Science Virtual Machine—Windows 2016." You can choose other editions if you prefer:

   `https://azure.microsoft.com/en-us/services/virtual-machines/data-science-virtual-machines/`

2. Click on **GET IT NOW** to choose the DSVM (Figure 4-7).

Data Science Virtual Macl

Microsoft

Overview   Plans + Pricing

Virtual machine with deep learning framewor
machine learning and data science

The Data Science Virtual Machine for Linux is an Ubuntu-basec makes it easy to get started with deep learning on Azure. The I TensorFlow, MXNet, Caffe, Caffe2, Chainer, NVIDIA DIGITS, Dee and PyTorch are built, installed, and configured so they are rea NVIDIA driver, CUDA 9, and cuDNN 7 are also included. All frar but work on the CPU as well. Many sample Jupyter notebooks Serving, MXNet Model Server, and TensorRT are included to te

GET IT NOW

TEST DRIVE

What's Test Drive?

Test Drive duration
8 hours

Pricing information

Figure 4-7. *Click on "Get It Now" to set up the data science virtual machine*

3. Confirm the software plan and click **Continue** (Figure 4-8).

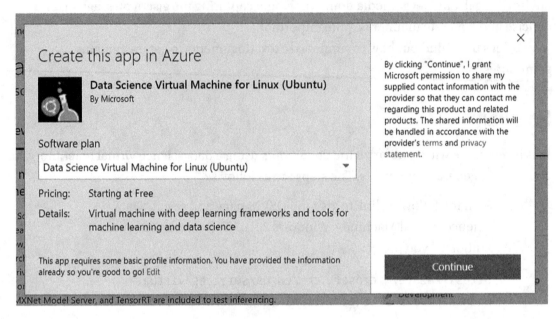

Figure 4-8. *"Create the application in Azure" screen to select the plan and then continue*

4. Click on the **Create** button to start creating the VM (Figure 4-9).

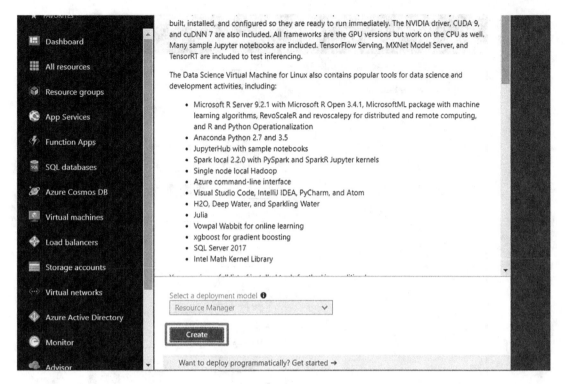

The following text is visible within the figure:

built, installed, and configured so they are ready to run immediately. The NVIDIA driver, CUDA 9, and cuDNN 7 are also included. All frameworks are the GPU versions but work on the CPU as well. Many sample Jupyter notebooks are included. TensorFlow Serving, MXNet Model Server, and TensorRT are included to test inferencing.

The Data Science Virtual Machine for Linux also contains popular tools for data science and development activities, including:

- Microsoft R Server 9.2.1 with Microsoft R Open 3.4.1, MicrosoftML package with machine learning algorithms, RevoScaleR and revoscalepy for distributed and remote computing, and R and Python Operationalization
- Anaconda Python 2.7 and 3.5
- JupyterHub with sample notebooks
- Spark local 2.2.0 with PySpark and SparkR Jupyter kernels
- Single node local Hadoop
- Azure command-line interface
- Visual Studio Code, IntelliJ IDEA, PyCharm, and Atom
- H2O, Deep Water, and Sparkling Water
- Julia
- Vowpal Wabbit for online learning
- xgboost for gradient boosting
- SQL Server 2017
- Intel Math Kernel Library

Select a deployment model ❶

Resource Manager

Create

Want to deploy programmatically? Get started →

Navigation sidebar items: Dashboard, All resources, Resource groups, App Services, Function Apps, SQL databases, Azure Cosmos DB, Virtual machines, Load balancers, Storage accounts, Virtual networks, Azure Active Directory, Monitor, Advisor

Figure 4-9. *The Create button will start creating the VM. It can take some time*

5.   Enter details for the VM and click **OK** (Figure 4-10).

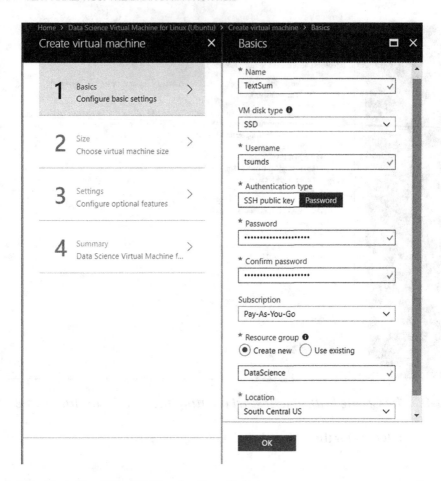

Figure 4-10. *Details of the VM including disk type, username, password, subscription, and location*

6. Choose a VM with a decent amount of RAM, preferably 16 GB (Figure 4-11).

Available

F2s_v2	Standard	Compute optim	2	4	4	4000	16 GB	SSD	$75.89
F4s_v2	Standard	Compute optim	4	8	8	8000	32 GB	SSD	$151.78
F8s_v2	Standard	Compute optim	8	16	16	16000	64 GB	SSD	$303.55
F16s_v2	Standard	Compute optim	16	32	32	32000	128 GB	SSD	$607.10
F32s_v2	Standard	Compute optim	32	64	32	64000	256 GB	SSD	$1,214.21
F64s_v2	Standard	Compute optim	64	128	32	128000	512 GB	SSD	$2,428.42
F72s_v2	Standard	Compute optim	72	144	32	144000	576 GB	SSD	$2,731.97

Prices presented are estimates in your local currency that include Azure infrastructure applicable software costs, as well as any discounts for the subscription and location.

Select

Figure 4-11. *Shows a variety of different virtual machines available for different configurations and budgets*

7. Nothing needs to change here. Click **OK** to continue (Figure 4-12).

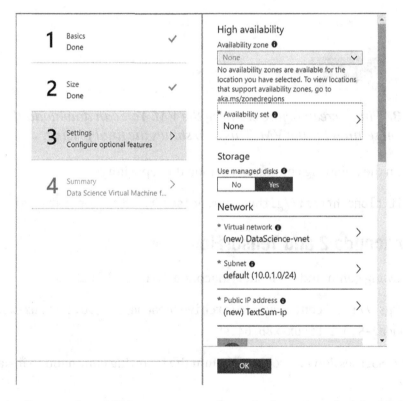

Figure 4-12. *Screen shows HA, storage, and network settings for the VM*

8. Click on the **Create** button to start the deployment (Figure 4-13).

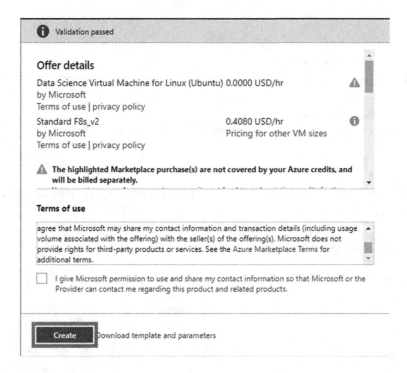

Figure 4-13. *Final screen before creating the VM. You can download the configuration settings for the VM. This also shows the final pricing.*

9. Run the following command to clone the repository:

```
git clone https://github.com/abisee/pointer-generator.git
```

Install Anaconda 2 and TensorFlow

Run the following commands to install Anaconda 2 with Python 2:

```
curl -O https://repo.continuum.io/archive/Anaconda2-5.0.1-Linux-x86_64.sh
bash Anaconda2-5.0.1-Linux-x86_64.sh
```

Close this SSH session and reconnect. Run the following command to install TensorFlow:

```
pip install tensorflow
```

Get the Dataset

You can use the CNN data for this task. Someone has processed the data and uploaded to Google Drive. You can download the data by following these steps or process the data yourself.

```
https://github.com/abisee/cnn-dailymail
```

Install gdown to download data from Google Drive:

```
pip install gdown
```

Visit this link and get the link of the Google Drive file (Figure 4-14):

```
https://github.com/JafferWilson/Process-Data-of-CNN-DailyMail
```

Figure 4-14.   *Copy link from the GitHub repo page*

Copy the download URL from the address bar and remove &export=download:

```
gdown https://drive.google.com/uc?id=0BzQ6rtO2VN95a0c3TlZCWkl3aU0
```

Unzip the downloaded file and rename the folder to data (optional):

```
unzip finished_files.zip
mv finished_files data
cd pointer_generator
```

Install dependencies. This code only works with the old version of TensorFlow.

```
pip install pyrouge
pip install tensorflow==1.3
```

Start the training by using run_summarization.py. This is the top-level file to train, evaluate, or test your summarization model.

```
python run_summarization.py—mode=train—data_path=/home/tsumds/data/
train.bin—vocab_path=/home/tsumds/data/vocab—log_root=/home/tsumds/log/
--exp_name=textsum
```

Note   tsumds is the username.

Press CTRL + C to interrupt the training, and then run the following code to start testing the model:

```
python run_summarization.py—mode=decode—data_path=/home/tsumds/data/
test.bin—vocab_path=/home/tsumds/data/vocab—log_root=/home/tsumds/log/
--exp_name=textsum
```

Leave the following settings as default:

```
er('batch_size', 16, 'minibatch size
er('max_enc_steps', 300 'max timest
er('max_dec_steps', 75, 'max timestep
er('beam_size', 4 'beam size for bea
```

Now run the summarization:

```
python run_summarization.py—mode=eval—data_path=/home/tsumds/data/
val.bin—vocab_path=/home/tsumds/data/vocab—log_root=/home/tsumds/log/
--exp_name=textsum
```

You can see the results of summarized output below with initial results, and how it improves over multiple iterations.

How It Works

The initial results from the summarized output follows. You can see how the number of epochs and training over time improves the summary.

```
INFO:tensorflow:REFERENCE SUMMARY: marseille prosecutor says " so far no
videos were used in the crash investigation " despite media reports .
```

journalists at bild and paris match are " very confident " the video clip is
real , an editor says . andreas !!__lubitz__!! had informed his lufthansa
training school of an episode of severe depression , airline says .

The summary improves as the training cycles iterates through. An improved (we
know, it is still subjective) summary after 28 hours looks like the following:

INFO:tensorflow:GENERATED SUMMARY:
investigation into the crash of germanwings flight 9525 he not aware of
crash . robin 9525 as it not aware of any video footage . paris match
flight 9525 as it crashed into crash investigation.

This improves as training cycles pass by, and after 47 hours it is readable:

INFO:tensorflow:GENERATED SUMMARY: french prosecutor says he added no
videos were were not aware of any video footage . crash of prosecutor says
he was not aware of video footage . crash of french alps as it crashed into
the french alps .

The same approach when tried on a different news story provides the following
summary:

INFO:tensorflow:REFERENCE SUMMARY: membership gives the icc jurisdiction
over alleged crimes committed in palestinian territories since last june .
israel and the united states opposed the move , which could open the door
to war crimes investigations against israelis .

And the following improvement after some time:

INFO:tensorflow:GENERATED SUMMARY: palestinian authority officially became
the 123rd member of the international criminal court on alleged crimes .
the formal accession was marked with a ceremony at palestinian territories
. as members of the palestinians signed the icc 's founding rome statute in
january.

How does your news story unfold when you apply summarization on it?

References & Further Reading

- A curated list of resources dedicated to Natural Language Processing (NLP): https://github.com/keon/awesome-nlp

- Oxford Deep NLP 2017 course with videos and Practical Examples: https://github.com/oxford-cs-deepnlp-2017/lectures

- Christopher Manning, "Building Neural Network Models That Can Reason": https://www.youtube.com/watch?v=5qf_MZXOYCw

- NLTK Book—Complete course on Natural Language Processing in Python with NLTK: https://www.nltk.org/book/

- Dive into NLTK—Detailed eight-part tutorial on using NLTK for text processing: https://textminingonline.com/dive-into-nltk-part-i-getting-started-with-nltk

- Gensim documentation—Official documentation and tutorials. The Tutorials page is very helpful: https://radimrehurek.com/gensim/tutorial.html

- spaCy documentation—Official documentation and quickstart guide: https://spacy.io/

- Intro to NLP with SpaCy—Short tutorial showcasing spaCy's functionality: https://nicschrading.com/project/Intro-to-NLP-with-spaCy/

- CoreNLP documentation—Official documentation and resource compilation: https://stanfordnlp.github.io/CoreNLP/

- List of Python wrappers for CoreNLP—Kept up-to-date by Stanford NLP: https://stanfordnlp.github.io/CoreNLP/other-languages.html

- TextBlob documentation—Official documentation and quickstart guide: https://textblob.readthedocs.io/en/dev/quickstart.html

- Natural Language Processing Basics with TextBlob—Excellent, short NLP crash course using TextBlob: http://rwet.decontextualize.com/book/textblob/

CHAPTER 5

Cognitive Robotics Process Automation: Automate This!

"If you're trying to understand AI's near-term impact, don't think 'sentience.' Instead think 'automation on steroids.'"

—Andrew Ng, Stanford CS adjunct faculty;
Former head of Baidu AI Group/Google Brain

"AI systems can help develop more powerful ways of thinking, but there's at most an indirect sense in which those ways of thinking are being used in turn to develop new AI systems."

— Research Paper by Shan Carter, Google Mind, and
Michael Nielsen, YC Research

As automation becomes a norm in digital businesses, technology professionals are fast embracing it as a tool for creating operational efficiencies. In more recent years, robotics process automation (RPA), or IPA (intelligent process automation), has been helping out businesses by providing much-needed relief from doing mundane and repetitive tasks.

It has been repeatedly said that artificial intelligence is not here to take people's jobs but rather to help them escape the mundane. Human beings can focus on a higher cognitive plane and leave the tedious and repeated tasks to the machines. The goal is to augment the human expertise; enable and accelerate. AI is changing the future of work as we know it; the future of jobs is turning purpose into performance through automation and intelligence.

225

© Adnan Masood, Adnan Hashmi 2019
A. Masood and A. Hashmi, *Cognitive Computing Recipes*, https://doi.org/10.1007/978-1-4842-4106-6_5

Today we see automation in action in a variety of forms in a multitude of industries. From automating the processing of forms and invoices to purchase-order and mortgage-application processing, machine-learning techniques have been helping to improve data quality, reduce processing time, and increase efficiency. This helps reduce turnaround time while keeping humans in the loop on tasks that require human judgment within complex scenarios. These tasks include processes like radiology reports, where an algorithm provides a basic overview and final judgment comes from a human expert. Similarly complex is claims processing, for which robotics process automation is insufficient; it requires cognitive capabilities along with human perception, subject-matter expertise, and judgment.

Recognizing this need for intelligent processing, RPA companies are shifting to adapt the cognitive RPA or IPA approaches. UI Path, the current market leader in the RPA space, supports cognitive automation, as it reports:

> *"Automated bot managers reduce automation costs & meet service levels by synchronizing queued work and robot deployments with scheduled work-flows and events; monitoring & triggering failover procedures, as needed."*

Blue Prism, which has a significant marketshare in the RPA space, also equips its bots with "intelligent automation skills," while Automation Anywhere markets IQ Bot as a cognitive RPA solution that has AI capabilities. Another well-known RPA capabilities provider, WorkFusion, cites their bot's cognitive capabilities under Smart Process Automation.

The use cases for intelligent process automation vary between industries, but as a general rule any repeatable process that can easily be understood and replicated without a higher degree of cognition is typically a good RPA candidate. For instance, in financial technology and banking, doing KYC (know your customer) requirements, such as background checks using public records, SDN (Specially Designated Nationals and Blocked Persons List), OFAC matches, risk assessment, internal records, and also OCR on handwritten customer input and scanned documents makes a great candidate for automation. For investment banking, these use cases include financial advisory rule reviews and reviewing and processing finance and trade transactions against rules and regulatory checks, such as special designated national and personal lists, sanctions evaluation, local regulatory analysis, and buyer and seller apportioning, to name a few.

In the insurance industry, RPA can help deal with servicing policies, as natural-language processing and entity detection can help extract policy data and potential downstream impacts of policy changes. RPA can also validate if any of these changes impact or violate clients' rights or conflict with federal or state regulations so as to avoid potential fines. Insurance claim processing is a long and tedious process that, with help from automation, can be expedited.

In retail, inventory management via computer vision is an excellent use case for cognitive RPA. Automation via robots on the warehouse floor and auto-scaling of servers by analyzing trends and anomalies help businesses meet the demands of customers as they arrive.

In this chapter, we will take a look at what goes on beyond typical RPA jobs by working on some recipes that provide building blocks for intelligent or cognitive robotics process automation.

5-1. Extract Intent from Audio
Problem

The main objective behind introducing automation in the enterprise is to drastically cut down the time used for repetitive tasks that otherwise take time away from productive, mission-critical work. Robotics process automation (RPA) comprises automated processes triggered by an external event, such as the uploading of a file, arrival of an email with a certain subject line, and so forth. However, in some instances, a trigger event might entail a manual intervention by a human operator to initiate the automation workflow.

Interaction points with these otherwise automated processes may be spread across multiple systems with varying user interfaces, requiring continuous user training and a time-consuming manual maintenance of bookmarks for all the disparate systems by each individual user.

Solution

We covered chatbots earlier in Chapter 3, where intents were extracted from user utterances using Microsoft's Language Understanding Intelligent Service (LUIS) API. The solution for the problem in this recipe is similar, with the exception that the user now provides spoken input as opposed to typing some text. Figure 5-1 illustrates how speech is processed to extract user input.

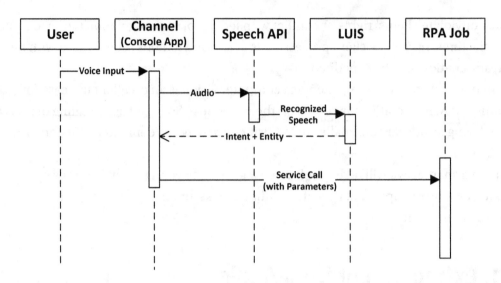

Figure 5-1. *Speech-processing pipeline*

1. The user communicates with a channel such as Skype by using their voice to provide input.

2. The channel takes the received audio input and makes a call to the Microsoft Cognitive Services Speech API to convert the speech to text.

3. The Speech API converts the speech to text and passes it on to the trained LUIS model.

4. LUIS extracts the intents and entities from those utterances and returns them to the calling application, which then makes a service call to an automation job.

How It Works

The scenario this recipe is modeled after allows a user to interact with a speech-enabled scheduling application.

To demonstrate how intent is extracted from speech, we will be looking at a console application that simulates the first four lifelines (swim lanes) from the preceding sequence diagram: User, Channel (Console Application), Speech API, and LUIS.

At a high level, the steps for creating the solution are as follows:

1. Create a LUIS endpoint using Azure Portal (`https://portal.azure.com`).

2. On the LUIS site (`https://www.luis.ai`), create a LUIS application and train the application to extract intents from user utterances.

3. Write console application code in Visual Studio 2017 to convert a speech input from the user into text using the Microsoft Cognitive Services Speech API and to then pass the extracted intents and entities to an automation job to execute a particular task.

The preceding steps are explained in detail in the next section.

Create a LUIS Endpoint

Let's get started:

1. Navigate to Azure Portal (`https://portal.azure.com`) using your web browser and log in using your credentials.

2. Click **Create a resource** in the top-left corner of the menu blade and then click **See all**.

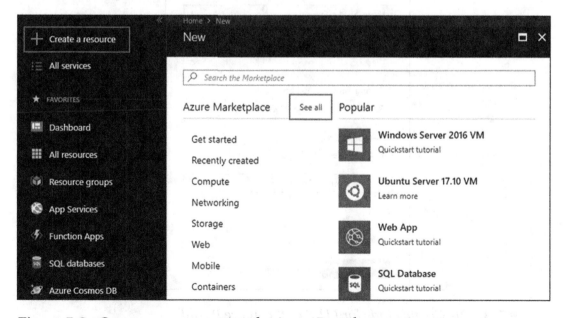

Figure 5-2. *Create a resource using the Azure Portal*

3. In the search box, type *LUIS* and hit **Enter** on your keyboard.

4. Click the **Language Understanding** template in the search results.

5. Click the **Create** button on the Welcome blade.

6. Fill out the details in the Create blade as follows and click the **Create** button when done.

Property	Value
Name	MyScheduler
Subscription	[Select your subscription name]
Location	West US [or select the Azure region closest to you]
Pricing Tier	[Select an appropriate pricing tier]
Resource Group	MyScheduler-LUIS-Resources

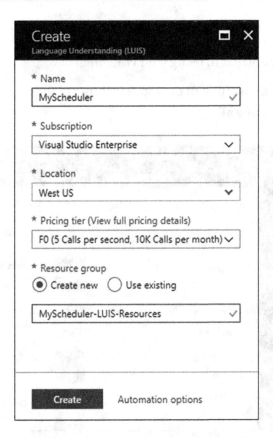

Figure 5-3. *The Create blade for LUIS in the Azure Portal*

7. Navigate to the created LUIS endpoint instance in Azure Portal by clicking **Keys** in the main blade to view the keys that will be used later.

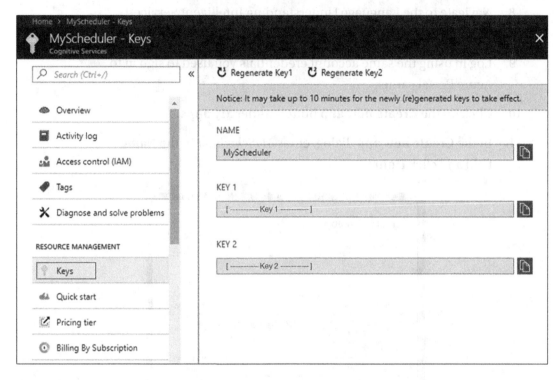

Figure 5-4. *The Keys blade for the LUIS endpoint in the Azure Portal*

Create a LUIS Application and Train for User Utterances

Just as we did in Chapter 2 for the Data Health Monitor Bot, we will create entities and intents in this section. The LUIS application will be trained for the utterances shown in the following table.

Example Utterance(s)	Intent	Entities
"Set my out of office from [X] to [Y]."	Schedule.	Calendar.StartDate
"I will be on vacation starting [X] and will be back on [Y]."	SetOutOfOffice	Calendar.EndDate
"My vacation starts on [X] and ends on [Y]."		
"I am taking PTO from [X] to [Y]."		
"Please set my calendar to out of office from [X] to [Y]."		

The steps to train the model to process the preceding listed intents and entities are shown here:

8. Navigate to the Language Understanding Intelligent Service (LUIS) site at `https://www.luis.ai`.

9. Log in using the same account credentials you used to sign in to Azure Portal earlier.

10. Click on the **Create new app** button under **My apps**.

11. In the **Create new app** dialog, enter *MyScheduler* in the **Name** field and click **Done**.

Figure 5-5. *The Create new app dialog for LUIS.ai*

Once the app is created, the browser will automatically navigate to the **Intents** screen.

12. Click the **Create new intent** button, enter *Schedule.SetOutOfOffice* in the **Intent name** text box, and click **Done**.

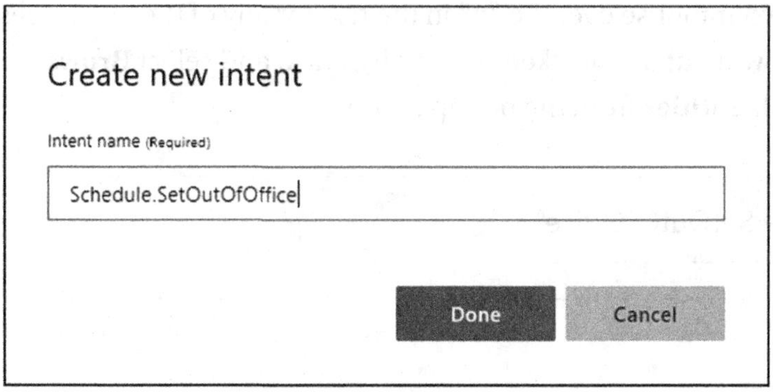

Create new intent

Intent name (Required)

Schedule.SetOutOfOffice|

Done   Cancel

Figure 5-6. *The Create new intent dialog for the LUIS.ai application*

13. On the Intent screen, type *Set my out of office from X to Y* in the text box and hit Enter on the keyboard.

    The entered text will be added to the Utterances list below the text box.

14. Repeat Step 6 and add the following utterances:

    - I will be on vacation starting X and will be back on Y.

    - My vacation starts on X and ends on Y.

    - I am taking PTO from X to Y.

    - Please set my calendar to out of office from X to Y.

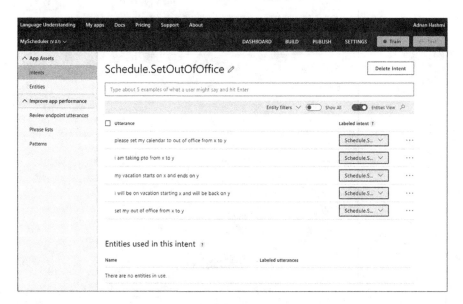

Figure 5-7. *List of utterances for the created intent*

15. Hover your mouse over the **"x"** in the text for any of the utterances (which will put bar brackets around it), click, and select **Browse prebuilt entities** from the popup menu.

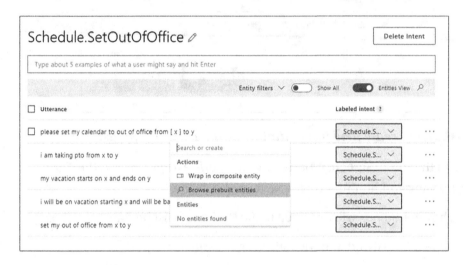

Figure 5-8. *Tag entities in each utterance*

16. In the **Add or remove prebuilt entities** dialog, scroll down, check the **datetimeV2** box, and click the **Done** button.

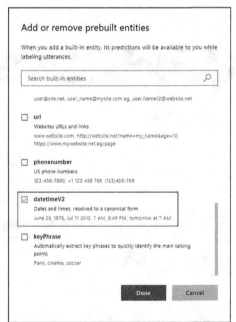

Figure 5-9. *The Add or remove prebuilt entities dialog*

17. Click the **Train** button at the top right-hand corner of the screen. Once complete, the red icon on the **Train** button will turn green.

18. Click the **Test** button in the top right-hand corner of the screen to display the **Test** pane.

19. Type *set my out of office from 08/10/2018 to 08/14/2018* in the test utterance text box and hit Enter.

    You might notice that LUIS incorrectly identified **None** as the recognized intent.

    Click the **Inspect** link to view the intent confidence (ranges between 0 to 1 and is shown in parenthesis) and the extracted entity value.

20. Click the **Edit** link under **Top scoring intent**.

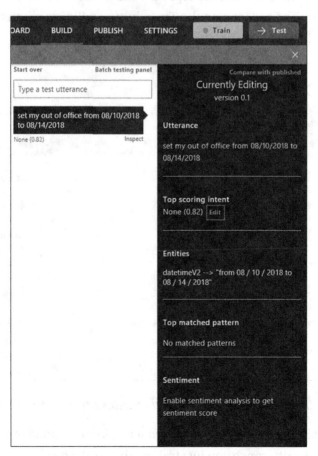

Figure 5-10. *Inspect recognized intent*

21. When the Intents drop-down appears, select **Schedule. SetOutOfOffice**.

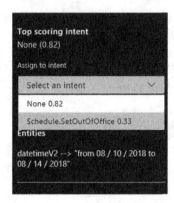

Figure 5-11. *Select intent for recognized utterance*

22. Click the **Train** button at the top right-hand corner of the screen once more. The red icon on the **Train** button will turn green after the model training completes.

Figure 5-12. *List of utterances with tagged entities on the intent screen*

You will also notice that a new utterance has been added to the list to reflect the utterance you just trained the model on.

23.   Click the **Test** button in the top right-hand corner of the screen to display the **Test** pane.

24.   Type *I will be on vacation from 09/27/2018 to 10/3/2018* in the test utterance text box and hit Enter.

This time, the model will correctly identify the intent based on the utterance.

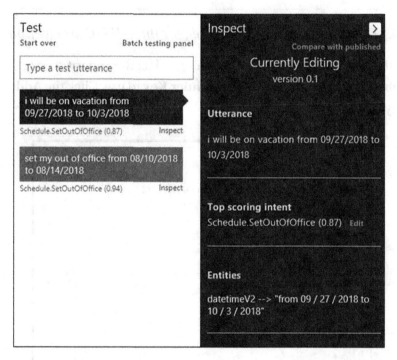

Figure 5-13. *The Inspect panel for the recognized utterance and intent*

25.   Click the **Publish** link on the top-right of the screen to navigate to the **Publish app** page.

26.   Under **Endpoint url settings**, select **Pacific Time** (or the time zone that applies to your application location) as the time zone.

27.   Scroll down to the bottom of the screen and click the **Add Key** button under **Resources and Keys**.

Resources and Keys

Add Key

⦿ North America Regions   ◯ South America Regions   ◯ Europe Regions   ◯ Asia Regions   ◯ Australia Regions

Resource Name	Region	Key String	Endpoint
Starter_Key	westus	Secbef ...	https://westus.api.cognitive.microsoft.com/luis/v2.0/apps/(APP ID)?subscription-key=(SUBSCRIPTION KEY)&spellCheck=true&bing-spell-check-subscription-key= (YOUR_BING_KEY_HERE)&verbose=true&timezoneOffset=-480&q=

Figure 5-14. *The Resources and Keys screen for the LUIS.ai application*

28. In the **Assign a key to your app** dialog, select the **Tenant Name**, **Subscription Name**, and **MyScheduler Key** to use. Click the **Add Key** button to finish.

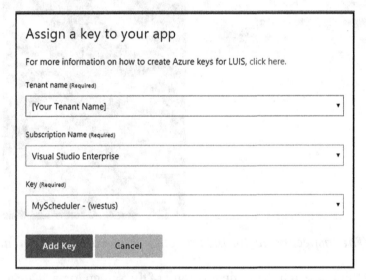

Figure 5-15. *The Assign a key to your app dialog*

A new resource endpoint will be added to the list.

You will also notice the keys you saw in Step 7 in the "Create a LUIS Endpoint" section listed in the Key String column.

Figure 5-16. *The Resources and Keys screen for the LUIS.ai application*

29. Copy the endpoint URL listed in the **Endpoint** column for the
    MyScheduler resource for use later.

30. Scroll back to the top of the page and click the **Publish** button.

Write Code for a Console Application in Visual Studio 2017

Follow these steps:

31. Open Visual Studio 2017 and go to File ➤ New ➤ Project.

32. In the **New Project** window, select **Console App (.NET
    Framework)** for **Visual C#** as the project template to use.

33. Enter *MySchedulerConsoleApp* as the application name and click
    the **OK** button.

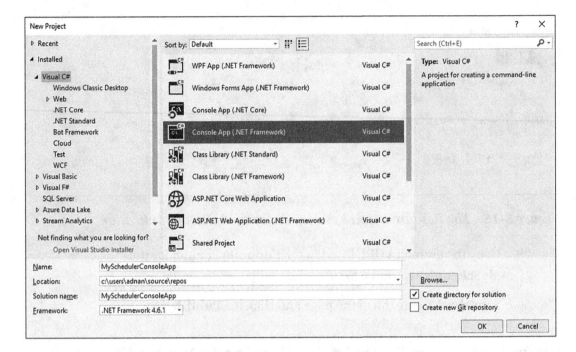

Figure 5-17. *The New Project window in Visual Studio 2017*

34. After the project gets generated, right-click **References** in the
     Visual Studio **Solution Explorer** and select **Manage NuGet
     Packages…** from the menu.

35. Click **Browse** in the NuGet tab and enter *Microsoft.
     CognitiveServices.Speech* in the textbox.

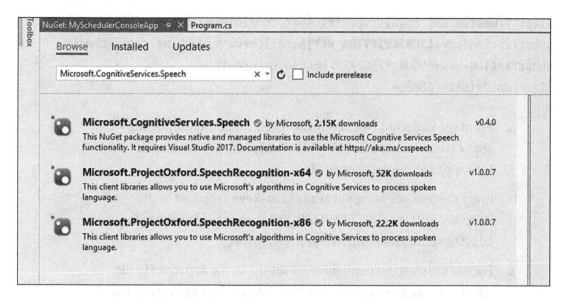

Figure 5-18. *The NuGet packages tab in Visual Studio 2017*

36. Select **Microsoft.CognitiveServices.Speech** from the list and then click the **Install** button on the right.

37. Click the **OK** button on the **Preview Changes** window.

You'll see a new reference to **Microsoft.CognitiveServices. Speech.csharp** has been added to the project.

38. Open the **App.config** file by double-clicking it in the Solution Explorer and add the following four configuration settings in the **appSettings** section:

```
<appSettings>
    <add key="LuisAppId" value="" />
    <add key="LuisSubscriptionKey" value="" />
    <add key="LuisRegion" value="" />
    <add key="speechAPIRegion" value="" />
</appSettings>
```

39. Specify the values for the application settings added in the previous step by copying segments of text from the resource endpoint URL copied in Step 1.

```
https://westus.api.cognitive.microsoft.com/luis/v2.0/apps/{APP_ID}?
subscription-key={SUBSCRIPTION_KEY}&spellCheck=true&bing-spell-check-
subscription-key={YOUR_BING_KEY_HERE}&verbose=true
&timezoneOffset=-480&q=
```

    a. From the endpoint URL, copy the text immediately following /
apps/ (shown above as {APP_ID}) and paste as the value of
LuisAppId in the App.config file.

    b. Copy the text following subscription-key= (appears in the
endpoint URL as {SUBSCRIPTION_KEY}) and paste as the value of
LuisSubscriptionKey in the App.config file.

    c. For the LuisRegion configuration setting in the App.config file,
use the text segment immediately following the https:// in the
resource endpoint URL (westus in this case).

      After setting up the configuration values, we can write code to
perform the steps outlined in the sequence diagram earlier.

40. Right-click the **MySchedulerConsoleApp** project in Solution
Explorer and go to **Add ➤ Class...** from the context menu.

41. Enter *MyScheduler.cs* as the class name and click the **Add** button.

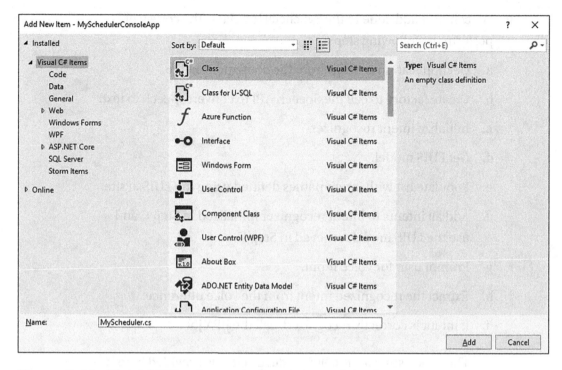

Figure 5-19. *The Add New Item window in Visual Studio 2017*

42. Change the namespace to **CognitiveRecipes** and add using
statements so that the code in the MySchedule.cs file looks like this:

```
using System;
using System.Collections.Generic;
using System.Linq;
using System.Text;
using System.Configuration;
using System.Threading.Tasks;
using Microsoft.CognitiveServices.Speech;
using Microsoft.CognitiveServices.Speech.Intent;

namespace CognitiveRecipes
{
    class MyScheduler
    {
    }
}
```

43. We can now add code to the MyScheduler class. The code will
      perform the following steps:

   a. Get application settings from the configuration file.

   b. Create factory to call the Speech API to convert speech to text.

   c. Initialize intent recognizer.

   d. Get LUIS model.

   e. Populate list with intent names defined using the LUIS.ai site.

   f. Add all intents to intent recognizer initialized in Step C and
       use the LUIS model retrieved in Step D.

   g. Prompt user for voice input.

   h. Extract the recognized intent from the voice utterance.

   i. If intent is correctly recognized, call the RPA job.

      The code listing for the MyScheduler class is provided here
      (formatted for readability) with the preceding steps included
      in the code as comments:

```
class MyScheduler
{
    public static async Task ExtractIntents()
    {
        // ------------------------------------------------------------
        // a) Get application settings from the configuration file
        // ------------------------------------------------------------

        var luisAppId = ConfigurationSettings.
AppSettings["LuisAppId"].ToString();
        var luisSubscriptionKey =
                    ConfigurationSettings.AppSettings["LuisSubscr
iptionKey"].ToString();
```

```csharp
var luisRegion = ConfigurationSettings.AppSettings
["LuisRegion"].ToString(); ;
var speechRegion = ConfigurationSettings.AppSettings
["speechAPIRegion"].ToString();

// ----------------------------------------------------------
// b) Create factory to call the Speech API to convert
//    speech to text
// ----------------------------------------------------------
var speechFactory = SpeechFactory.FromSubscription
(luisSubscriptionKey, speechRegion);

// ----------------------------------------------------------
// c) Initialize intent recognizer
// ----------------------------------------------------------
using (var intentRecognizer = speechFactory.
CreateIntentRecognizer())
{
    // ----------------------------------------------------
    // d) Get LUIS model from subscription
    // ----------------------------------------------------
    var luisModel = LanguageUnderstandingModel.FromSubscript
    ion(luisSubscriptionKey,luisAppId,luisRegion);

    // ----------------------------------------------------
    // e) Populate list with intent names defined using the
    //    LUIS.ai site
    // ----------------------------------------------------
        List<string> intentNamesList = new
        List<string>(new string[]
                        { "None",
                          "Schedule.SetOutOfOffice"
                        });
```

```csharp
// ------------------------------------------------------------
// f) Add all intents to intent recognizer initialized in Step C
//    and use the LUIS model retrieved in Step D
// ------------------------------------------------------------
foreach (string intentName in intentNamesList)
{
    intentRecognizer.AddIntent(intentName, luisModel,
    intentName);
}

// ------------------------------------------------------------
// g) Prompt user for voice input
// ------------------------------------------------------------
Console.WriteLine("Please tell us the calendar event you
want to schedule?");
Console.WriteLine("(Waiting for speech input...)");

// ------------------------------------------------------------
// h) Extract the recognized intent from the voice utterance
// ------------------------------------------------------------
var result = await intentRecognizer.RecognizeAsync().
ConfigureAwait(false);

// ------------------------------------------------------------
// i) If intent is correctly recognized, call the RPA job
// ------------------------------------------------------------
if (result.RecognitionStatus == RecognitionStatus.Recognized)
{
    Console.WriteLine($"{result.ToString()}");
}
else
{
    Console.WriteLine("Invalid or unrecognized input
    received...");
```

```
        }
      }
    }
}
```

44. In order to call the preceding class, we add code to our `Main` program. The code listing is provided here:

```
class Program
    {
        static void Main(string[] args)
        {
            Console.WriteLine("0 - Exit");
            Console.WriteLine("1 - Recognize LUIS Intent...");

            Console.Write("Enter either 0 or 1: ");

            ConsoleKeyInfo consoleInput;
            do
            {
                consoleInput = Console.ReadKey();
                Console.WriteLine("");
                switch (consoleInput.Key)
                {
                    case ConsoleKey.D1:
                        Console.WriteLine("LUIS Intent Recognition
                        selected...");
                        MyScheduler.ExtractIntents().Wait();
                        break;
                    case ConsoleKey.D0:
                        Console.WriteLine("Exiting console
                        application...");
                        break;
                    default:
                        Console.WriteLine("Invalid input.");
                        break;
                }
```

```
                    Console.WriteLine("\n\nEnter either 0 or 1: ");
                } while (consoleInput.Key != ConsoleKey.D0);
            }
        }
```

45. Before you can build and execute the console application, make sure that your project's targeted platform is set to **x64**. Right-click the project name in **Solution Explorer** and select **Properties** from the context menu.

46. Click the **Build** tab and select **x64** as the **Platform target** from the drop-down.

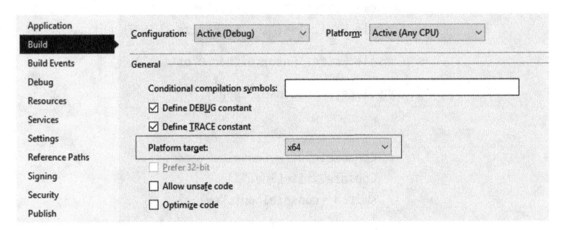

Figure 5-20. *The Build properties tab for the project in Visual Studio 2017*

47. Build and run the console application from Visual Studio by clicking **Start** from the top menu bar.

    When prompted, speak into your microphone (e.g., "I will be on vacation between October 14, 2018, and October 19, 2018").

    The application will correctly identify the intent and display the entity value extracted from the utterance.

    A text listing of the application output is included here:

    ```
    ResultId:5d7296fe112f42fca6bdb30e3ca433f5 Status:Recognized
    IntentId:<Schedule.SetOutOfOffice> Recognized text:<Will be on
    vacation between October 14 2018 and October 19 2018?> Recognized
    ```

Json:{**"DisplayText":"Will be on vacation between October 14 2018 and October 19 2018?"**,"Duration":56100000,"Offset":10200000,"Recog nitionStatus":"Success"}. LanguageUnderstandingJson:{
  "query": "will be on vacation between October 14 2018 and
  October 19 2018",
  "topScoringIntent": {
    "intent": "Schedule.SetOutOfOffice",
    "score": 0.5438184
  },
  "entities": [
    {
      "entity": "between october 14 2018 and october 19 2018",
      "type": "builtin.datetimeV2.daterange",
      "startIndex": 20,
      "endIndex": 62,
      "resolution": {
        "values": [
          {
            "timex": "(2018-10-14,2018-10-19,P5D)",
            "type": "daterange",
            "start": "2018-10-14",
            "end": "2018-10-19"
          }
        ]
      }
    }
  ]
}

You can further increase the intent recognition confidence score
by training the LUIS model for more utterances.

For this particular use case, once the entities and intents have
been extracted, the application can make a call to an automation
job to set an out of office message for email and voice, fill out
the timesheet for the specified vacation period, and/or send out
emails or calendar events to other team members.

5-2. Email Classification and Triage for Automated Support-Ticket Generation

Problem

In large enterprise settings, support emails can become high volume, and therefore processing and distribution can become a constant battle. Sending emails to the right mailbox and applying automation for easily automatable tasks can provide much-needed relief to the IT support desk. A real-world technical case study of this problem is published as "Applying the power of Azure Machine Learning to improve SAP incident management."[1]

Solution

A typical email triage can be achieved via naïve Bayes and a simple Python script. However, in this solution we will show how you can visually create a workflow in Azure ML. This email triage solution will address training a model that can do automated triage and help accelerate this process by preprocessing and feature hashing.

This is very similar to how a typical email spam detector works, but in this case we create different buckets (categories) based on where the email should be routed. We build upon an existing Azure solution to showcase the power of Azure ML studio here.

How It Works

Let's start by training the model:

1. Visit `https://studio.azureml.net/` and sign in.

2. Click on the **New** button and select **Blank Experiment**.

---

[1]`https://www.microsoft.com/itshowcase/Article/Content/1044/`
`Applying-the-power-of-Azure-Machine-Learning-to-improve-SAP-incident-management`

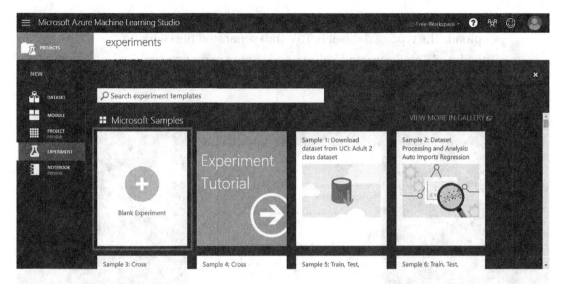

Figure 5-21. Create a new experiment using the Azure Machine Learning Studio

3. Click on the **New** button, then **Dataset**, and then **From Local File**.

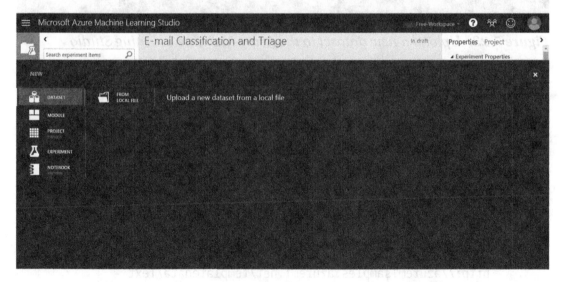

Figure 5-22. Upload a new dataset to the Azure Machine Learning Studio

4. Choose the dataset file, choose the type of dataset, and then upload. The type of dataset is TSV (tab separated file) with no header ⁄ Tab-Separated Values, and there are no headers. Choose this as per your dataset.

Figure 5-23. *Upload a new dataset to the Azure Machine Learning Studio*

5. Once the upload is completed, drag and drop the dataset to add it to the flow.

6. We need to preprocess the data to remove stop words, remove duplicate characters, replace numbers, and so on. For that, we need to import another small dataset of stop words. Add the **Import Data** module.

7. Select **Web URL via HTTP** from the list and enter this URL. This dataset is provided as part of the Azure ML studio samples:

    `http://azuremlsamples.azureml.net/templatedata/Text -`
    `Sentiment Stopwords.tsv`

8. Set **Data format** to **TSV**.

9. Add the **Preprocess Text** module and connect it with other modules, then click **Launch Column Selector**.

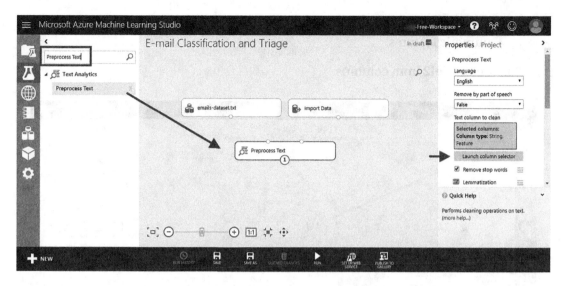

Figure 5-24. *Drag the Preprocess Text module to the design surface*

10.   Select **Col2** and save.

11.   Add the **Edit Metadata** module to remove unnecessary meta
data. Select **Col2** from the list, **String** as data type, **Make non-
categorical**, and in the fields, select **Clear feature**.

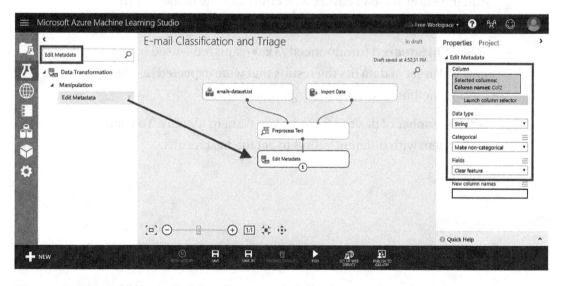

Figure 5-25. *Add the Edit Metadata module to the machine learning
experiment*

12. Add the **Feature Hashing** module to convert text data into numeric features.

13. Select **Col2** from columns.

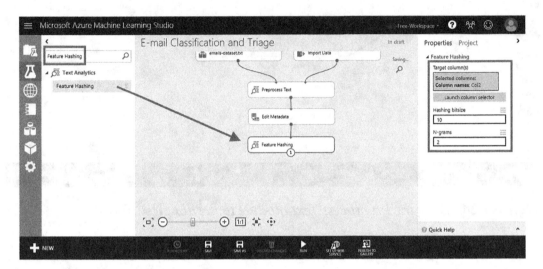

Figure 5-26. *Add the Feature Hashing module to the machine learning experiment*

14. Add the **Filter Based Feature Selection** module to identify the features.

15. Select **Chi Squared** (pronounced /•ka•/ squared—used to test how well a set of data fits the results that were expected) as the scoring method and **Col1** in Target Columns.

16. Set the number of desired features you want to identify. You can experiment with different values to get the best results.

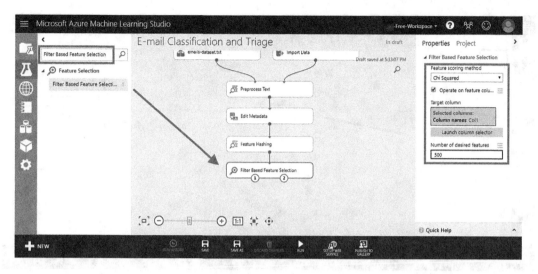

Figure 5-27. *Add the Filter Based Feature Selection module to the machine learning experiment*

17. Add a **Split Data** module to split the dataset. Set the fraction to .7—70 percent of the data will be used for training and a random number will be used as seed data.

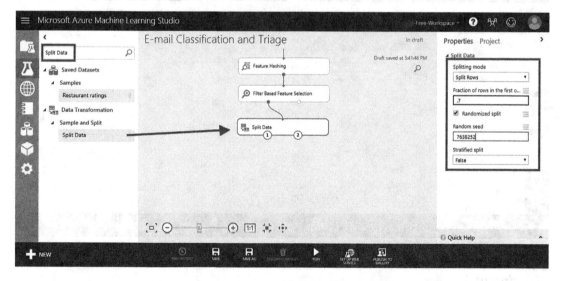

Figure 5-28. *Add the Split Data module to the machine learning experiment*

18. Add another **Split Data** module to further split the data. Fifty percent of data (of the 30 percent) will be used for tuning the model and 50 percent will be used for testing.

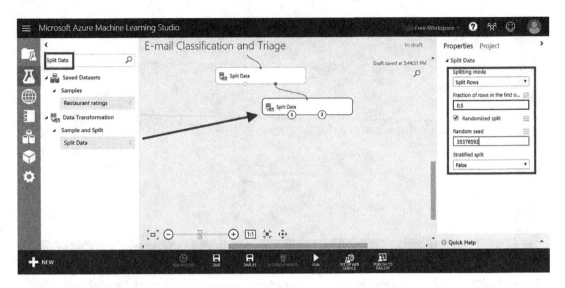

Figure 5-29. *Add another Split Data module to the machine learning experiment*

19. Add a Multiclass Neural Network module to the flow. You can
    configure the parameters to meet your specific requirements.

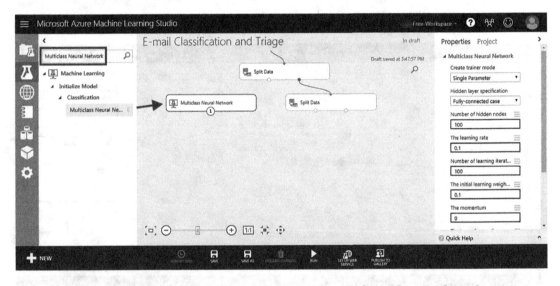

Figure 5-30. *Add a Multiclass Neural Network module to the machine learning*
experiment

20. Add a **Tune Model Hyperparameters** module to find the
    optimum parameters for the model. Select **Col1** as the **Label**
    column and **AUC** as the metric for measuring performance.

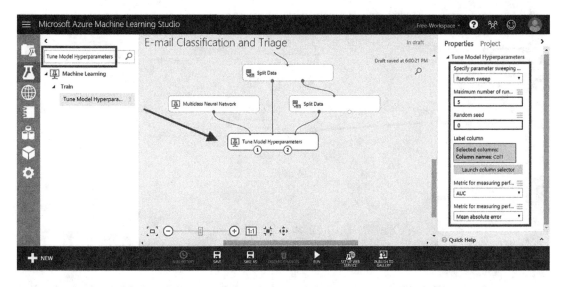

Figure 5-31. *Add the Tune Model Hyper-parameters module to the machine learning experiment*

21. Add the **Score Model** module to score the classification result.

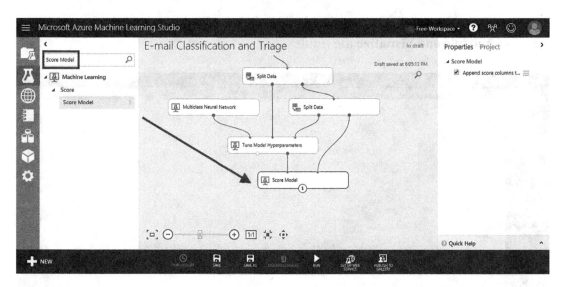

Figure 5-32. *Add the Score Model module to the machine learning experiment*

22. Add the **Evaluate Model** module to evaluate the scored results.

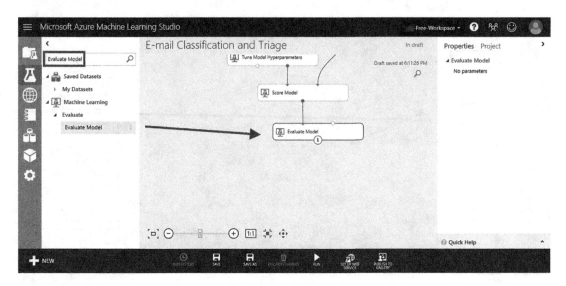

Figure 5-33. *Add the Evaluate Model module to the machine learning experiment*

23.   Click on the **Run** button to run the experiment.

24.   Once the training is completed, right-click the **Evaluate Model** module and **Visualize** the result.

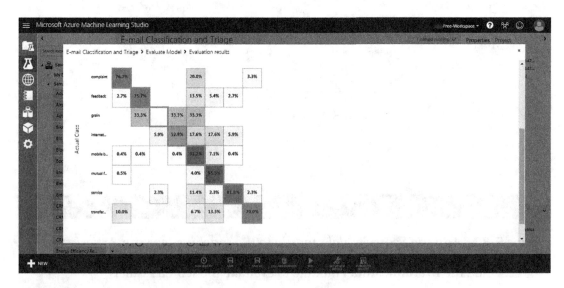

Figure 5-34. *Visualize the result for model evaluation*

The summary of prediction results for this classification problem show the actual case and the predicted class in the form of a confusion matrix. The matrix literally shows the ways in which your classification model is confused when it makes predictions—i.e., the actual versus predicted instances for all the classes—to describe the performance of the classification model. In this case, you can see great results for mutual funds (with higher accuracy). Other examples of comparison matrices can be found at `https://docs.microsoft.com/en-us/azure/machine-learning/studio/evaluate-model-performance`.

Saving the Trained Model

Now we can save the model:

1. Right-click on "Tune Model Hyperparameters," hover over "Trained best model," and then select "Save as Trained Model."

2. Enter the model name and save.

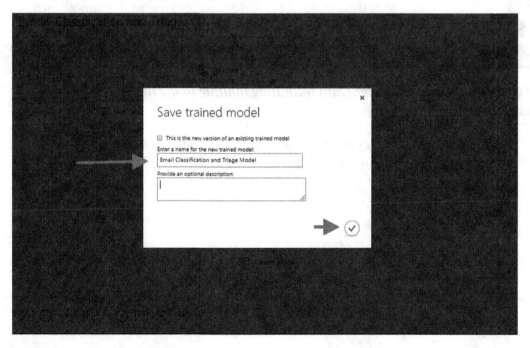

Figure 5-35. *Save the trained machine learning model*

Creating an Experiment to Use the Model

Let's use the model:

1. Create a new blank experiment.

2. Add the **Enter Data Manually** module and enter label and text (separated by a comma) to test.

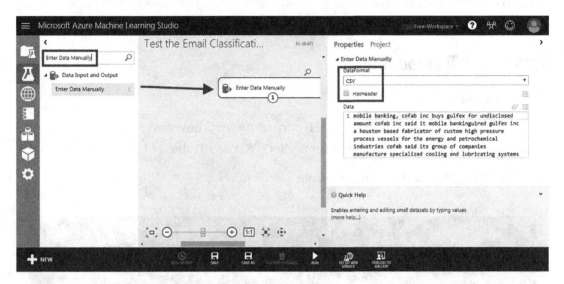

Figure 5-36. *Add the Enter Data Manually module to the machine learning experiment*

3. We need to preprocess the data as we did for training. Add the **Preprocess Text** module and select **Col2** from column selector.

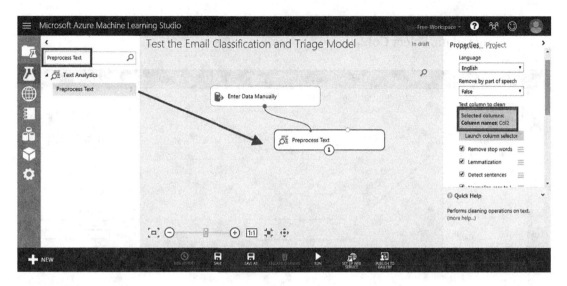

Figure 5-37. *Add the Preprocess Text module to the machine learning experiment*

4. We also need a dataset of stop words. Add an **Import Data** module and import the stop word data using this link:

    ```
    http://azuremlsamples.azureml.net/templatedata/Text -
    Sentiment Stopwords.tsv
    ```

    (This is the same data that we used earlier.)

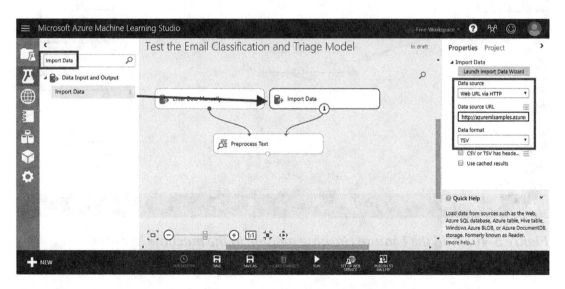

Figure 5-38. *Add the Import Data module to the machine learning experiment*

5. Add the **Edit Metadata** module to remove any unnecessary metadata. Select **Col2**.

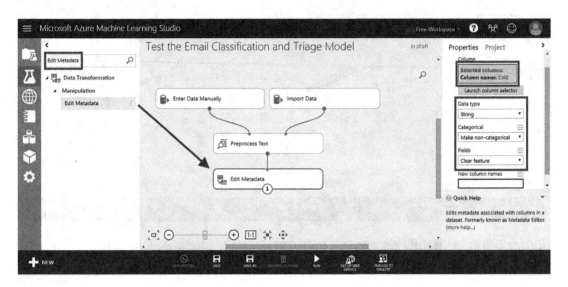

Figure 5-39. *Add the Edit Metadata module to the machine learning experiment*

6. Add the **Feature Hashing** module to convert text into numeric features, then select **Col2** from columns.

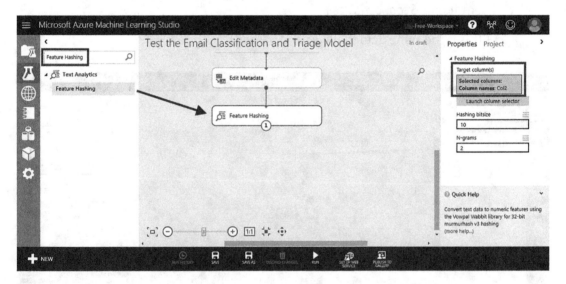

Figure 5-40. *Add the Feature Hashing module to the machine learning experiment*

7. Now load the trained module that we saved earlier. Write the name of the model in the search box and add it to the flow.

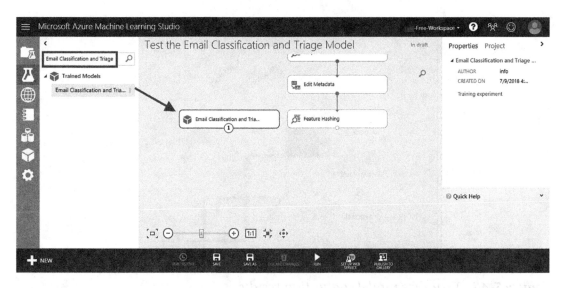

Figure 5-41. *Add the previously trained machine learning model to the flow*

8. Add the **Score Model** and **Evaluate Model** modules and run the experiment.

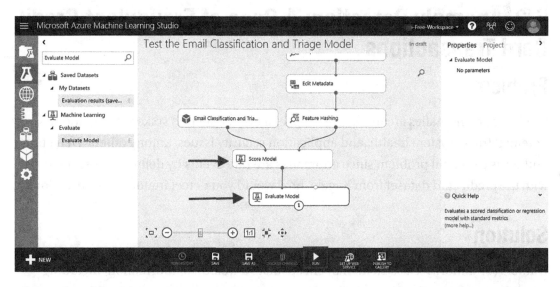

Figure 5-42. *Add the Score Model and Evaluate Model modules to the machine learning experiment*

9. Once the experiment is finished, right-click on the **Evaluate Model** module and select **Visualize**.

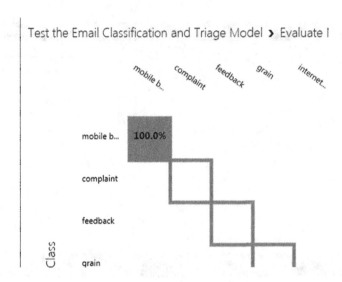

Figure 5-43. *Visualize model evaluation results*

The model detected the text with 100 percent accuracy.

5-3. Anomaly Detection: A Case of Fraudulent Credit Card Transactions

Problem

Outliers and anomalies are indicative of special events, such as spikes in demand, potential fraud, system health, and application security issues, among others. Detecting outliers is a difficult problem since anomalies are rare events by definition. Provided with the credit card dataset from Kaggle, how would you detect fraudulent transactions?

Solution

Outliers (or minority-class elements) encapsulate a wealth of information, including fraudulent activities that do not adhere to typical spending patterns. It is critical for financial institutions to recognize and stop fraudulent credit card activities to protect customers.

In this example we will use the Kaggle dataset, available at `https://www.kaggle.com/mlg-ulb/creditcardfraud/home`.

The dataset contains transactions made by credit cards in September 2013 by European cardholders. This dataset presents transactions that occurred over two days and includes 492 frauds out of 284,807 transactions. The dataset is highly unbalanced, as the positive class (frauds) accounts for 0.172% of all transactions.

How It Works

Let's get started:

1. Create an empty directory on your computer where the whole project will be kept. In our case it is on the desktop.

Figure 5-44. *The Jupyter browser-based UI*

2. Start the jupyter notebook server from the command line using the following command:

    `jupyter notebook`

    This command will open the jupyter dashboard in the browser using the `localhost` server at port 8888.

3. Navigate to the directory created in the first step, click on the **New** tab, then click on Python 3 to create a new jupyter notebook.

    This will open a new tab in your browser with jupyter notebook, where we will write the code.

4. Rename the file by clicking on **Untitled**, then enter a desired file name and click on the **Rename** button.

5. Start writing code in the code cell.

Figure 5-45. *Write and execute code for a Jupyter notebook*

6. Import the required dependencies. We will use the following
    libraries in our project:

```
pandas as pd
from sklearn.preprocessing import StandardScaler
from sklearn.model_selection import train_test_split
keras
from keras.models import Sequential
from keras.layers import Dense
from keras.layers import Dropout
```

In case of error (Module Not Found), install required
dependencies by using the following command:

```
pip install <dependency-name>
```

```
import pandas as pd
from sklearn.preprocessing import Standardscaler
from sklearn.model_selection import train_test_split
import keras
keras.models import Sequential
keras . layers import Dense
keras. layers import Dropout
```

7. Validate that either the environment is accepting the input or
    there is an error by using **Shift+Enter**, which will execute the code
    and create a new code cell in the case of no error; otherwise, it will
    display an error message under the code cell.

8. Load the data that will be used to detect fraud.

```
In [8]:   1  df = pd.read_csv('creditcard.csv')
          2  df.head(1)
```

Figure 5-46. *Load CSV data using Python code*

```
df = pd.read_csv('creditcard.csv')
df.head(1)
```

head(n): Return the first *n* rows, which in this case is the first row of the CSV file.

9. Assign unique values to the object by using the unique() method of the Python Pandas library: 0 = no fraud, 1 = fraudulent.

```
In [6]:   1  df['Class'].unique()
```

Figure 5-47. *Calling the unique() method*

```
df['Class'].unique()
```

10. We will split our data for the training and testing of our model by using the following:

```
X_train, X_test, Y_train, Y_test = train_test_split(X, y, test_
size=0.1, random_state=1)
```

The model will be trained on 90 percent of the data, and we have reserved 10 percent of our data for testing.

```
In [7]:   1  X = df.iloc[:, :-1].values
          2  y = df.iloc[:, -1].values
          3  X_train, X_test, Y_train, Y_test = train_test_split(X, y, test_size=0.1, random_state=1)
          4  sc = StandardScaler()
          5  X_train = sc.fit_transform(X_train)
          6  X_test = sc.transform(X_test)
```

Figure 5-48. *Split the data for training and testing using Python code*

```
X = df.iloc[:, :-1]-values
y = df.iloc[:, -1].values
X_train, X_test, Y_train, Y_test = train_test_split(X, y, test_
size=0.1, random_state=1)
sc = StandardScaler()
X_train = sc.fit_transform(X_train)
X_test = sc.transform(X_test)
```

11. We will use a sequential model for making the prediction. A sequential model is a deep-learning model in Keras, which is used to make predictions on new data. We can create a sequential model by passing a list of layer instances to the constructor (in our case, the constructor is `clf`). The summary of the sequential model can be seen by using `clf.summary()`.

```
In [8]:   1  clf = Sequential([
          2      Dense(units=16, kernel_initializer='uniform', input_dim=30, activation='relu'),
          3      Dense(units=18, kernel_initializer='uniform', activation='relu'),
          4      Dropout(0.25),
          5      Dense(20, kernel_initializer='uniform', activation='relu'),
          6      Dense(24, kernel_initializer='uniform', activation='relu'),
          7      Dense(1, kernel_initializer='uniform', activation='sigmoid')
          8  ])
```

Figure 5-49. *Use sequential model for making prediction*

```
clf = Sequential([
    Dense(units=16, kernel_initializer='uniform', input_dim=30,
activation='relu'),
    Dense(units=18, kernel_initializer='uniform',  activation='relu'),
    Dropout(0.25),
    Dense(20, kernel_initializer='uniform', activation='relu'),
    Dense(24, kernel_initializer='uniform activation='relu'),
    Dense(1, kernel_initializer='uniform', activation='sigmoid')
])
```

12. Now we will fit our sequential model on the training data and set epochs (iterations on a dataset). The `Fit` function is used for training the model.

```
In [11]:  1  tbCallBack = keras.callbacks.TensorBoard(log_dir='./Graph', histogram_freq=0, # for tensorboard
          2              write_graph=True, write_images=True)
          3  clf.fit(X_train, Y_train, batch_size=15, epochs=5, callbacks=[tbCallBack])

Epoch 1/5
256326/256326 [==============================] - 13s 49us/step - loss: 0.0069 - acc: 0.9991
Epoch 2/5
256326/256326 [==============================] - 12s 47us/step - loss: 0.0037 - acc: 0.9994
Epoch 3/5
256326/256326 [==============================] - 12s 46us/step - loss: 0.0034 - acc: 0.9994
Epoch 4/5
256326/256326 [==============================] - 12s 49us/step - loss: 0.0033 - acc: 0.9994
Epoch 5/5
256326/256326 [==============================] - 12s 46us/step - loss: 0.0032 - acc: 0.9994

Out[11]: <keras.callbacks.History at 0x18a000139588>
```

Figure 5-50. *Train the model using the fit(...) method*

```
tbCallBack = keras.callbacks.TensorBoard(log_dir='./Graph',
histogram_freq=0, # for tensorboard
    write_graph=True, write_images=True)
clf.fit(X_train, Y_train, batch_size=15, epochs=5,
callbacks=[tbCallBack])
```

13. Evaluate the accuracy of the constructor (classifier) by using
     evaluate().

```
In [12]:   1  score = clf.evaluate(X_test, Y_test, batch_size=128)
           2  print('\nAnd the Score is ', score[1] * 100, '%')
```

Figure 5-51. *Evaluate the model by calling the evaluate(...) method*

```
Score = clf.evaluate(X_test, Y_test, batch_size=128)
Print('\nAnd the Score is ', score[1] * 100, '%')
```

14. Finally, now we can store the result of our model. The following
     code will create a file in our directory (with a .h5 extension)
     containing the predicted values of our model.

```
In [13]:   1  model_json = clf.to_json()
           2  with open("model.json", "w") as json_file:
           3      json_file.write(model_json)
           4  # serialize weights to HDF5
           5  clf.save_weights("model.h5")
           6  print("Saved model to disk")
```

Figure 5-52. *Store the trained model*

```
model_json = clf.to_json( )
with open("model. json", "w") as json_file:
    json_file.write(model_json)
# serialize weights to HDFS
clf.save_weights("model.h5")
print("Saved model to disk")
```

Based on the given dataset, we know the following:

```
Fraud Cases: 49
Valid Cases: 28432
```

And the dataset is highly unbalanced, as the positive class (frauds) accounts for
0.172% of all transactions. As seen in the output, the loss function has decreased and
evaluation accuracy is 0.9992.

```
In [35]:   1  score = clf.evaluate(X_test, Y_test, batch_size=128)
           2  print('\nAnd the Score is ', score[1] * 100, '%')

28481/28481 [==============================] - 0s 6us/step

And the Score is  99.92626663389628 %
```

```
Score = clf.evaluate(X_test, Y_test, batch_size=128)
Print('\nAnd the Score is ', score[1] * 100, '%')
```

5-4. Finding Needles: Cross-Correlation in Time Series

Problem

In distributed applications across large enterprise systems, events happen in multiple places, and application telemetry does not always have a unique correlation ID to corroborate with. This also is happens in real-life scenarios when sensors capture events that later need to be correlated to find a pattern. Given two time series, how do you correlate sampled time-series data? The basic problem we're considering is the description and modeling of the relationship between two time series.

Solution

There are multiple ways within the cognitive services landscape to address the time-series problem. This includes Azure Time Series Insights,[2] which supports scenarios like storing time-series data in a scalable way, doing root-cause analysis and anomaly detection within time-series data, and providing a global view of time-series data streaming from disparate locations for multi-asset/site comparison. You can also use the Time Series Anomaly Detection module in Azure Machine Learning Studio to detect anomalies in time-series data.[3] In this recipe, however, we use DCF, the underlying algorithm, and its use to showcase how a simple bespoke implementation can be done.

---

[2]https://docs.microsoft.com/en-us/azure/time-series-insights/
time-series-insights-overview

[3]https://docs.microsoft.com/en-us/azure/machine-learning/studio-module-reference/
time-series-anomaly-detection

To solve the multiple-time-series correlation problem, we use the DCF (discrete correlation function) implementation in Python here. PyDCF is a Python cross-correlation command-line tool for unevenly sampled time series. It is available on GitHub at `https://github.com/astronomerdamo/pydcf`. Traditional timing analysis or CCF (cross-correlation function) assumes that a time series is sampled evenly in the time domain.

As just described, several real-world applications vary in their perfectly timed samples; a timing analysis tool like PyDCF helps perform correlation in such cases.

How It Works

Let's see it in action:

1. Visit this link and select "Data Science Virtual Machine for Linux (Ubuntu)" from the list: `https://azure.microsoft.com/en-us/services/virtual-machines/data-science-virtual-machines/`.

2. Click on the **Test Drive** button to get DSVM for free for eight hours.

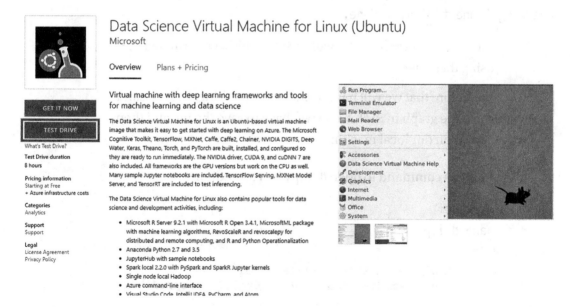

Figure 5-53. *Test-drive the Azure Data Science Virtual Machine for Linux*

3. Enter your login details to log in.

4. Connect to the server using PuTTY or any other SSH client and clone this repository:

    git clone https://github.com/astronomerdamo/pydcf.git

```
dsvm@                    :~$ git clone https://github.com/astronomerdamo/pydcf.git
Cloning into 'pydcf'...
remote: Counting objects: 265, done.
remote: Compressing objects: 100% (45/45), done.
remote: Total 265 (delta 27), reused 59 (delta 18), pack-reused 195
Receiving objects: 100% (265/265), 286.65 KiB | 0 bytes/s, done.
Resolving deltas: 100% (112/112), done.
Checking connectivity... done.
```

Figure 5-54. *The cloning results of the GitHub Repo*

```
dsvm@ **********:~$ git clone https://github.com/astronomerdamo/pydcf.git
Cloning into 'pydcf'...
remote: Counting objects: 265, done.
remote: Compressing objects: 100% (45/45), done.
remote: Total 265 (delta 27), reused 59 (delta 18), pack-reused 195
Receiving objects: 100* (265/265), 286.65 KiB | 0 bytes/s, done.
Resolving deltas: 100* (112/112), done.
Checking connectivity... done.
```

There is an Example folder with two CSV files. Let's run pyDCF using these files.

But before that we will have to change something. PyDCF can't show the graph in SSH, so we will have to save the file and then copy it on our local machine.

5. Run this command to open dcf.py in a text editor:

    cd pydcf
    nano dcf.py

```
dsvm@dsvmtdy475pvioj4y7a:~$ cd pydcf
dsvm@dsvmtdy475pvioj4y7a:~/pydcf$ nano dcf.py
```

Figure 5-55. *Open the dcf.py file in a text editor*

6. Scroll to the bottom of the file. Add `plt.switch_backend('agg')` after `import matplotlib.pyplot as plt` and `plt.savefig('graph.png')` instead of `plt.show()`.

```
if OPTS.noplot :

  try:
      import matplotlib . pyplot as plt
      plt.switch backend('agg')
  except ImportError:
      print("Matplotlib not installed, try - pip install matplotlib")
      import sys
      sys.exit()

  plt.figure(0)
  plt.errorbar(T, DCF, DCFERR, color='k', 1s='-', Capsize=0)
  plt.xlabel("Lag")
  plt.ylabel("Correlation Coefficient")
  plt.xlim(OPTS.1gl[0], OPTS.1gh[0])

  plt.savefig('graph.png')
```

7. Press **CTRL + O**, then the **Enter** key, and then **CTRL + X** to save the file and exit from the editor.

8. Now, run the following command to correlate the two example CSV files over a time range of +/- 100 days with a bin width of 1.5 days:

    python dcf.py example/ts1.csv example/ts2.csv -100 100 1.5

```
dsvm@dsvmtdy475pvioj4y7a:~/pydcf$ python dcf.py example/ts1.csv example/ts2.csv -100 100 1.5

   A simple implementation of the discrete correlation function (DCF)
   Author: Damien Robertson - robertsondamien@gmail.com

   Usage:
     $ python dcf.py -h for help and basic instruction
```

Figure 5-56. *Execute the dcf.py file*

```
dsvm@dsvmtdy475pvioj4y7a:~/pydcf$ python dcf.py example/tsl.cav example/
ts2.cav -100 100 1.5
```

```
    A simple implementation of the discrete correlation function (DCF)
    Author: Damien Robertson - robertsondamien@gmail.com
```

```
Usage :
        $ python def.py -h for help and basic instruction
```

9. To copy the graph, we will need to use the secure copy (scp) command. Open a git bash session and enter the following line of code:

```
    scp <username>@<server address>:~/pydcf/graph.png E:/
```

Note   Copying the file in C:/ may throw a permission error. Make sure you have admin privileges.

```
$ scp dsvm@▨                    .westcentralus.cloudapp.azure.com:~/pydcf/graph.png E:/
dsvm@▨                    .westcentralus.cloudapp.azure.com's password:
graph.png
```

Figure 5-57. *Execute the Secure Copy (scp) command*

```
$ scp dsvm@*************.westcentralus.cloudapp.azure.com:~/pydcf/graph.
4png E:/
dsvm@*************.westcentralus.cloudapp.azure.com's password:
graph.png
```

10. Open the file to see the graph.

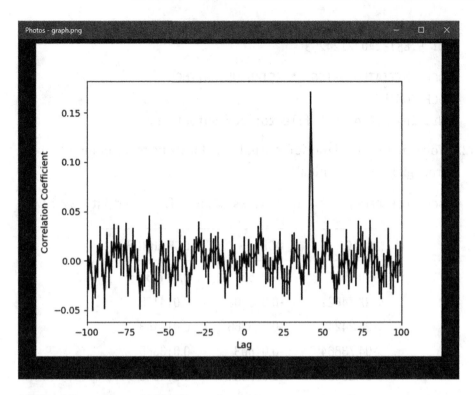

Figure 5-58. *View the generated graph*

11. You can also run the following command to get more information. It
     subtracts a linear fit from the input data, uses a Gaussian weighting for
     bin pairs, and writes dcf_output.csv in the current working directory:

```
python dcf.py example/ts1.csv example/ts2.csv -100 100 1.5 -v
-w=gauss -p=1 -o

PYTHON SCRIPT : dcf3

INPUT TIMESERIES 1: example/tsl.csv
INPUT TIMESERIES 2: example/ts2.csv
LAG RANGE PROBED : -100 .0 : 100 . 0
LAG BIN WIDTH : 1.5

Time series preparation
Linear De-trend Coefficients [a*x + b]
a: -7.279895942398102e-05
b: 5.846585155581444
Linear De-trend Coefficients [a*x + b]
```

```
a: -6.970931411465984e-05
b: 5.851324032124263

DCF INITIATED USING GAUSSIAN WEIGHTING
DCF COMPLETE
Writing DCF output file to: dcf output.csv
```

12. You can download the `dcf_output.csv` file using this command from git bash or terminal:

```
scp <username>@<server address>:~/pydcf/dcf_output.csv E:/
```

# LAG	DCF	DCF ERROR
-99.25	-0.0158	0.014134
-97.74621	-0.005308	0.014178
-96.24242	-0.016368	0.014183
-94.73864	-0.01503	0.013365
-93.23485	-0.007524	0.013348
-91.73106	0.012541	0.013567
-90.22727	0.017252	0.013371
-88.72349	-0.001564	0.01328
-87.2197	-0.013837	0.013102
-85.71591	-0.005997	0.012989
-84.21212	0.007061	0.013148
-82.70833	0.019557	0.0131
-81.20455	0.012169	0.012936
-79.70076	0.006193	0.012985
-78.19697	0.009875	0.012577
-76.69318	-0.006394	0.012586
-75.18939	-0.001397	0.012828
-73.68561	0.003778	0.012448
-72.18182	0.00635	0.012435
-70.67803	0.012826	0.012178
-69.17424	0.006401	0.012511

The verbose output and the reported correlation relates lag in time series; i.e., how the first time series should be shifted to match the second (i.e., ts2 = ts1 - correlation. Positive correlation is ts1 leading ts2, while negative correlation is ts1 lagging ts2. This helps connect the events together to build temporal consistency across different events required for analysis of events.

5-5. Understanding Traffic Patterns: Demand Forecasting for Energy

Problem

Forecasting demand is a problem in a variety of sectors: retail, energy, hospitality, e-commerce, and even healthcare would like to know how their traffic unfolds. From an energy-sector perspective, worldwide electricity demand and consumption is increasing every year.

This recipe focuses on demand forecasting within the energy sector. Storing energy is not cost-effective, so utilities and power generators need to forecast future power consumption so that they can efficiently balance the supply with the demand.

Solution

The solution is based on the Azure AI gallery solution,[4] which applies a demand forecasting model, and will showcase how to use prebuilt models. The solution described here can be automatically deployed through the Cortana Intelligence Gallery.[5] This solution combines several Azure services, including Event Hubs, Stream Analytics, Power BI, Data Factory, Azure SQL, and Machine Learning forecasting models.

If you are interested in implementing this solution in Python or R, AI residential electricity-bill prediction[6] would be helpful.

The solution involves the following features:

- **Data Collection:** Event Hubs collects real-time consumption data.

- **Data Aggregator:** Stream Analytics aggregates the streaming data.

---

[4]https://gallery.azure.ai/Solution/Demand-Forecasting-3
[5]https://gallery.azure.ai/Solution/Energy-Demand-Forecasting-4
[6]https://github.com/nivmukka/AI-residential-electricity-bill-prediction

- **Storage:** Azure SQL stores and transforms the consumption data.

- **Forecasting:** Machine Learning implements and executes the forecasting model.

- **Visualization:** Power BI visualizes the real-time energy consumption as well as the forecast results.

- **Orchestrator:** Data Factory orchestrates and schedules the entire data flow.

A high-level solution architecture for forecasting energy demand is illustrated in the diagram and explained (using numbered labels) here:

1 – Weather data along with data on energy consumption is continually produced and staged for consumption by the solution.

2a – Data for energy consumption and weather is ingested through Azure Event Hubs.

2b – Azure Data Factory extracts the energy-consumption and weather data from its source and stores it in Azure SQL.

3a – Data ingested using Azure Event Hubs is streamed through Azure Stream Analytics for aggregation.

3b – Stream Analytics makes sure of geographical data stored in Azure blob storage to aggregate and transform streaming data.

4a – Energy consumption and weather data, along with previous energy-demand forecast data, is used for creation and/or improvement of the machine-learning model for energy-demand forecast.

4b – The energy-demand forecasts done using the machine-learning model are written to Azure SQL using Azure Data Factory to orchestrate the scheduled updates.

5a (dotted line) – The data streamed and aggregated in Step 3a is consumed by Power BI dashboards for continual forecast of energy demand.

5b – Source data stored in Azure SQL is also surfaced on Power BI dashboard for visualization.

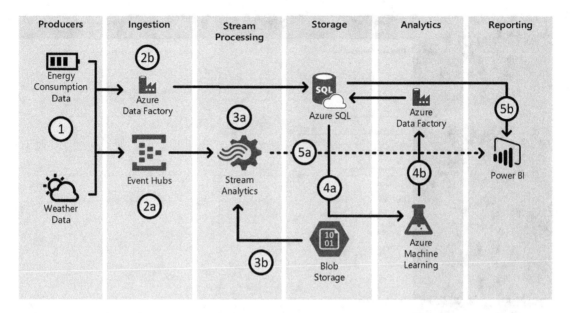

Figure 5-59. *A high-level view of the solution using Microsoft Azure services*

How It Works

Let's get started:

1. Go to `https://goo.gl/KhxVYU` and click on any one of two
    buttons on the right side of the document. Click **Deploy** to directly
    deploy the solution, or click on **Try It Now** to view the summary
    of Demand Forecasting (the deployment button is also available
    inside the Try It Now page at the top of the page).

    An end-to-end demand forecast for the energy solution is
    available for users to explore and try Cortana Intelligence Suite.

    Demand forecasting requires an SQL server; we will soon go
    through some steps for creating this. This may charge $6.85 daily.
    Please refer to the pricing to get the exact information as it may
    change.

2. Set name and other required parameters and go to the next step
    by clicking on **Create**.

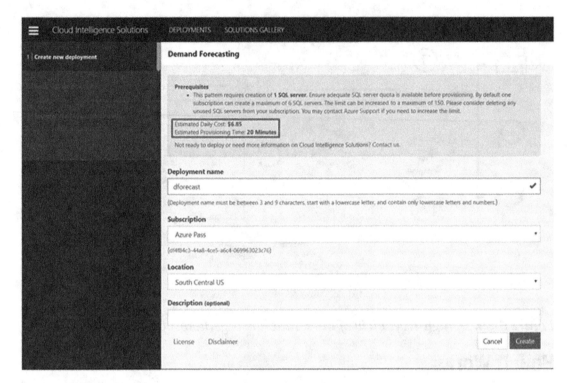

Figure 5-60. *Deploy the Demand Forecasting solution from the Cortana Intelligence Solutions Gallery*

Set up the SQL server account (set SQL name and password) and go to **Next**.

The system will start provisioning the resources, which will be done by an automated process. There is nothing to do here; we just have to sit back and let the process complete, which takes around 20 minutes.

3. Once the process has completed successfully, the following screen will be appear with "ready" status.

Figure 5-61. *Successful deployment of the Demand Forecasting solution*

4. Once the solution is deployed to the subscription, you can see the services deployed by clicking the resource-group name on the final deployment screen in the CIS.

    Azure SQL database is used to save the data and forecast results, while the Power BI dashboard is used to visualize the real-time energy-consumption data as well as the updated forecast results.

    After deploying the solution, it is recommended to wait a couple of hours before doing the next step since you will have more data points to visualize.

    In this visualization step, the prerequisite is to download and install the free Power BI Desktop software from the following link: https://powerbi.microsoft.com/en-us/desktop/.

    Once the download completes, open and install Power BI.

5. Get the database credentials.

    You can find your database and server name on the page when you finish your deployment. The SQL username and password will be the ones you chose at the beginning of the deployment.

6. Update the data source of the Power BI file.

    In this GitHub repository, you can download the EnergyDemandForecastSolution.pbix file under the folder Power BI and then open it.

    If you see an error message, please make sure you have installed the latest version of Power BI Desktop.

7. On the top of the file, click the **Edit Queries** drop-down menu, then choose **Data Source Settings**.

8. In the pop-out window, click **Change Source**, then replace the server and database with your own server and database names and click **OK**. For the server name, make sure you specify port 1433 in the end of the server string (YourSolutionName.database. windows.net, 1433).

9. After you finish editing, close the Data Source Settings window.

    On the top of the screen, you will see a message. Click **Apply Changes**. A new window will pop out and ask for database credentials. Click **Database** on the left of the window, enter your SQL credentials, then click **Connect**.

Figure 5-62. *Enter the SQL Server database credentials to connect to the data source*

    Now the dashboard is updated to connect to your database. In the backend, the model is scheduled to be refreshed every hour. You can click the **Refresh** button at the top to get the latest visualization as time moves forward.

    The Machine Learning service is used to make forecasts on the energy demand of particular region given the inputs received. Azure SQL Database is used to store the prediction results received from the Azure Machine Learning service. These results are then consumed in the Power BI dashboard.

10. Browse to Azure Dashboard and click on **dforecastmlwk**.

11. On the very next page, click on **Launch Machine Learning Studio**.

12. Click on **My Experiment** on the next page, and then click on **Energy Demand Forecast Solution—Machine Learning Model** on the experiment page.

13. On the following page, the model is already created; we just have to run the model by clicking the **Run** button at the bottom. This will evaluate and validate every step of the model. You can see each step is used, from reading to executing the R script, and then applying the boosted decision tree visually.

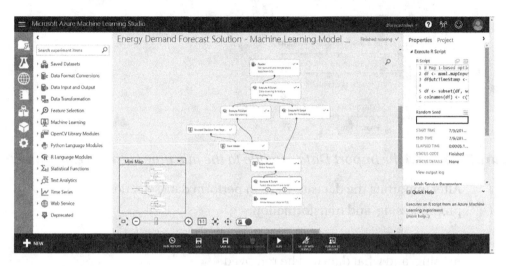

Figure 5-63. *The Energy Demand Forecast Solution in the Azure Machine Learning Studio*

This recipe can be easily duplicated on the dataset of your choice. From the import data option provided within the Data Input and Output section, you can import data that will be used to perform training on the model.

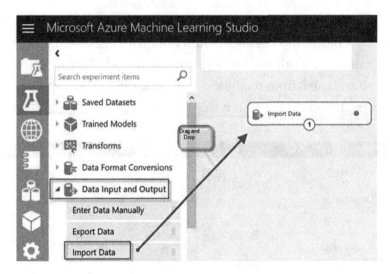

Figure 5-64. *Add the Import Data module to the machine learning experiment*

After importing the dataset, you can perform data selection, preprocessing, and transformation.

14. Data Selection: Consider what data is available, what data is missing, and what data can be removed.

15. Data Preprocessing: Organize your selected data by formatting, cleaning, and sampling from it.

16. Data Transformation: Transform preprocessed data ready for machine learning by engineering features using scaling, attribute decomposition, and attribute aggregation.

The following figure shows the Power BI dashboard visualizing the results of the energy-demand forecast.

Data will be split into two parts for the purpose of training and testing; usually 80 percent of data is kept for training, and the remaining 20 percent is used for testing in machine learning.

In this case, we are using Boosted Decision Tree Regression. This regression method is a supervised learning method and therefore requires a *labeled dataset*. The label column must contain numerical values. Further details about Boosted Decision Tree Regression or other regression models such as Bayesian Linear Regression, Decision Forest Regression, Fast Forest Quantile Regression, Linear Regression, Neural Network

Regression, Ordinal Regression, and Poisson Regression can be found as part of Azure ML Studio documentation.[7]

Now the model will be trained by providing the training data and algorithm.

After completing the training, the model will be tested on test data, which will confirm whether the model is performing well.

Final output (predictions) will be stored in Azure SQL Database. These results are then consumed in the Power BI dashboard.

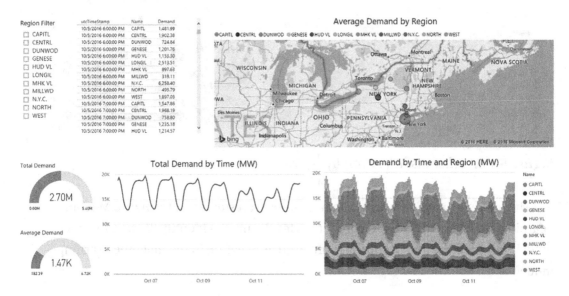

Figure 5-65.   *The visualizations in the Power BI Dashboard*

The following shows the overall status of the energy demand of each region. Select a single region by clicking the filter on the left to investigate each region's status.

---

[7]https://docs.microsoft.com/en-us/azure/machine-learning/studio-module-reference/
machine-learning-initialize-model-regression

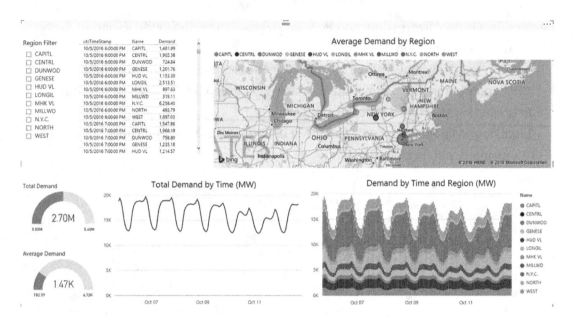

Figure 5-66. *Filter visualization by region*

The following page shows the demand forecast results from the Azure Machine Learning model and different error metrics for the user to identify the quality of the model. Temperature and its forecasts are used as a feature in the machine-learning model.

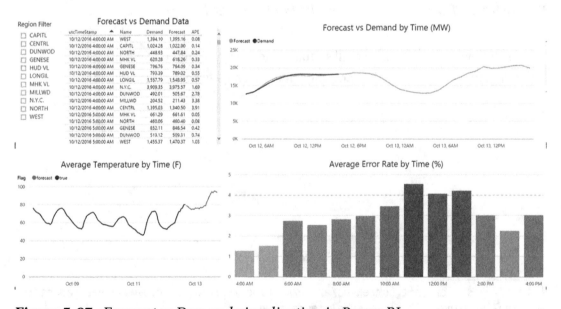

Figure 5-67. *Forecast vs Demand visualization in Power BI*

References & Further Reading

Azure—Demand Forecasting and Energy: `https://github.com/Azure/cortana-intelligence-energy-demand-forecasting`

Machine Learning and Power BI Visualization: `https://powerbi.microsoft.com/en-us/industries/energy/`

CHAPTER 6

Knowledge Management & Intelligent Search

"Knowledge Management is expensive—but so is stupidity!"

—Thomas Davenport, Distinguished Professor of Information
Technology and Management

"Connection, not collection: That's the essence of knowledge management."

—Tom Stewart, *The Wealth of Knowledge*

Knowledge management is a rather large and formidable discipline that deals with identifying, capturing, storing, retrieving, archiving, and sharing information, both inside and outside an organization. Imagine working as a helpdesk representative and receiving a ticket that requires you to address a certain issue within an application. Now consider getting all the information that is automatically associated with this ticket, such as similar tickets and their fixes, application telemetry data and logs, standard operating procedures, and other knowledge-base items associated with the application, such as wiki articles. The knowledge graph associated with this application even recommends a potential fix and provides information about the associate who last worked on a similar issue, or the same application.

If you get all this information as part of your ticket, and don't have to go around hunting for it, it will not only make your life much easier but also more productive. This is the core purpose of a good knowledge-management system—to provide seamless access to information and help increase worker productivity and efficiency in making intelligent data-driven decisions.

© Adnan Masood, Adnan Hashmi 2019
A. Masood and A. Hashmi, *Cognitive Computing Recipes*, https://doi.org/10.1007/978-1-4842-4106-6_6

To put this in a larger context, knowledge management helps build capabilities around comprehension, which constitutes human-style cognitive capabilities such as being able to perform intelligent search, answer questions, correlate facts, build dynamic taxonomies, build concept hierarchies and topic models, and summarize the ideas in a concise manner. Even though keyword-based search has been around for a long time, for most enterprise use cases a more elegant solution is necessary that can address real-world demands of usability. Keyword search has evolved to semantic search, where indexing is performed as part of natural-language processing. Semantic search is further refined into contextual search, which applies machine-learning algorithms to first determine the context before searching through the data. For instance, if your query is to find the SLA of service A, it makes no sense to explore the splunk logs of service B or to scour through the knowledge base for auditing policies for service A. Next, the natural progression of contextual search is cognitive search, where we use the human-interaction construct to increase usability and business value at the same time. This approach of search provides results that are much more relevant to the specific user or application.

Forrester defines cognitive search and knowledge discovery solutions as follows:

> *"A new generation of enterprise search solutions that employ AI technologies such as natural language processing and machine learning to ingest, understand, organize, and query digital content from multiple data sources."*

There are a few factors that separate "classical" search and knowledge-management solutions from their cognitive counterparts. The first one is the ability to ingest multiple data sources and build correlations. The data sources may belong to different modalities—i.e., structured versus unstructured data, or dark data items such as PDFs, tables, and graphs; Excel worksheets; images; audio and video data; and sensory data from IoT devices. Combining these multiple data feeds, applying natural-language processing and entity detection, and improving the relevancy of results over time is what distinguishes typical search from cognitive search. Cognitive search does not look for specific keywords, but rather the intent. A user can ask what my vacation balance is, or can I take ten days off, or what is our vacation policy, and the intent is quite similar. It requires making a call to the HR knowledge base to find the right vacation balance and report it to the user.

From an enterprise knowledge-management perspective, cognitive search queries provide a wealth of information around a user's intents and knowledge-consumption behaviors. Cognitive services also rely on the modern ecosystem of digital assistants and contextual, geotargeted search results.

A knowledge-management system truly serves its purpose when it helps in assisting with making the right decisions—i.e., by providing the right type of information, in the correct format—at the right time. When done correctly, an intelligent knowledge-management system helps improve collaboration across information silos and enables the entire enterprise to access different facets of knowledge that span across a multitude of business units. This not only leads to more streamlined and efficient business processes for the workers, but also results in increased customer satisfaction.

Artificial intelligence and machine learning are very data-hungry fields where data scientists are always looking for clean, relevant, useful data to train their models. Contrary to typical datasets used in machine-learning problems, the knowledge within an enterprise can typically be divided into three categories, namely explicit, tacit (tribal) and embedded or process-ingrained knowledge. When building a knowledge-management model for the enterprise, we need to work with all of these different forms to get the desired results.

Explicit knowledge is the one we are most used to, the information that exists in document-management systems as records and is stored in easily usable formats. Contrary to explicit sources of knowledge, tacit knowledge is kept by humans and is not so easy to mine. This tribal knowledge is based on the innate understanding humans have regarding processes based on their experiences. This organizational knowledge is typically the hardest to acquire; extracted through interviews and surveys, this kind of knowledge acquisition opens up room for intelligent process mining by looking at the data of organizational activities, including but not limited to meeting minutes, actionable insights from call transcripts, and message exchange. Organizational culture drives the need for tacit knowledge, which in our experience is one of the most critical components in building a knowledge-management system. The third information source is embedded knowledge, which includes information from application telemetries, processes, and logs of inter-process communication. This knowledge is not only limited to applications and services, but also includes the automation processes with a human-in-the-loop element that helps expand beyond what is immediate and apparent.

Cognitive computing plays a major role in knowledge management by providing correlation capabilities between these knowledge sources. All three types of knowledge sources—explicit, tacit, and embedded—can be subclassified into dynamic and static information sources. A dynamic source is one that changes and updates automatically based on the passage of time; for instance, the real SLA (service-level agreement) of an application (however, the documented SLA that is part of some agreement would be static and remains unchanged until both parties decide to agree on a new number). A cognitive knowledge-management system doesn't merely report these numbers but also provides predictive insight into their past, current, and future values. In our SLA example, a cognitive knowledge-management system will simulate the human thought process by not only reporting the current SLA of the application in real-time, but also performing predictive analytics on the future SLA and potential cascading failure issues. This is the key value proposition of cognitive processes: using AI and machine learning to simulate the valuable insight human intuition brings by looking at the knowledge and making better decisions.

Cognitive search follows the same paradigm as knowledge management; by mining and correlating structured and unstructured data, it goes beyond search and into the realm of insight engine. With guided search and natural-language capabilities, an insight engine operates on an enterprise knowledge graph and continuously improves itself by connecting the queries with the intent behind these questions.

An AI-driven cognitive search caters to the industry. In legal or patent processing, for instance, it can help with automatic contract analysis by analyzing massive amounts of legal documents, such as contracts, NDAs, leases, and filings. This information can then be used by knowledge workers to perform natural-language queries such as "find me all NDAs that have a two year limit and IP clause."

Subject-matter experts provide immense value in business processes because of their insights. A cognitive search searches through intranet and employee portal to build a skill knowledge graph and recommend the right person for the job based on their organizational affiliation, previous work on the specific problem, and corresponding skill entity.

With cognitive search and knowledge management, usability plays an important role. An organization can publish intelligent search endpoints to be utilized by cognitive digital assistants, which can then use the knowledge repository to query the problem description and provide the relevant answer with a higher degree of confidence. The high-quality answer is powered by enriched annotations and helps in easier decision making.

Building cognitive knowledge-base systems requires a variety of AI and machine-learning components to come together; this includes building dynamic taxonomies to keep up with changing content and providing features like smart content verification, natural-language query and intent detection, dynamically generated pages from new data sources, smart-knowledge blocks, annotation engine, and smart templates. Knowledge-management features like versioning, analytics, integration with systems such as Microsoft teams or Slack, single sign-on, content import and export, admin controls, and custom integrations come standard.

We briefly touched upon it earlier, but one core piece of intelligent search is the knowledge graph. The knowledge graph connects several pieces of data to fill in the blanks and portray a complete enterprise system. There are a variety of graph databases around that can help with building knowledge graphs, including CosmoDB, GRAKN, and Neo4j. These graph database systems provide the capability of role-based relationship modeling from datasets. A typical approach is to build the knowledge graph using a graph database schema and run predefined or known rules to establish inferred rules. While building a knowledge graph, you must be cognizant of the potential challenges due to the volume of data and complexity of running the rules.

With this brief introduction to the very large field of knowledge management, let's dive into some of the recipes, where we will see the individual components of a knowledge-management system and how to apply techniques like OCR, graph search, natural-language queries, entity search, and linking to build an intelligent knowledge engine.

6-1. Explore the Azure Search Indexing Process

Problem

Many organizations still maintain and house large repositories or record centers comprising scanned documents. While stored and viewed as PDFs or images, most of the content is not searchable unless the scanned documents go through an OCR (Optical Character Recognition) process to extract text from images. This mostly involves utilizing third-party solutions deployed to the on-premises data center and requires additional hardware resources to be provisioned.

In the JFK files scenario, the U.S. government declassified a treasure trove of documents, going through which presents a huge challenge for anyone wanting to explore the released dataset.

The JFK files demo is developed, maintained, and owned by Microsoft and is presented here to showcase the use of Microsoft Azure Search and Cognitive Services to explore, crawl, and index a fairly large corpus of the CIA's JFK papers. You can learn more about the solution by following these links:

- JFK Assassination Records: `https://www.archives.gov/research/jfk`

- GitHub Repo: `https://github.com/Microsoft/AzureSearch_JFK_Files`

- Solution Overview: `https://azure-scenarios-experience.azurewebsites.net/search-ai.html`

- Demo: `https://jfk-demo.azurewebsites.net/`

Solution

The solution to the preceding articulated problem uses a combination of the following services offered by Microsoft Azure:

- Azure Storage

- Cosmos DB

- Cognitive Services

- Azure Search

- Azure Functions

At a high level, the solution involves extracting text from scanned documents by performing OCR. Once extracted, the text is stored and crawled to build a search index. As part of creating the index, the content is enriched by extracting and linking the entities in the text and annotating text in the scanned documents. The Azure Search service crawling the content is enhanced with a custom skillset to fit the problem domain. The custom search skills pertain to linking cryptonyms (code words used by the CIA) with the text and extracting OCR metadata using the hOCR standard. Lastly, a UI is created to allow users to submit search queries and visually view the search results.

A detailed view of the solution is presented in the sequence diagram shown in Figures 6-1a and 6-1b (split into two separate diagrams for clarity).

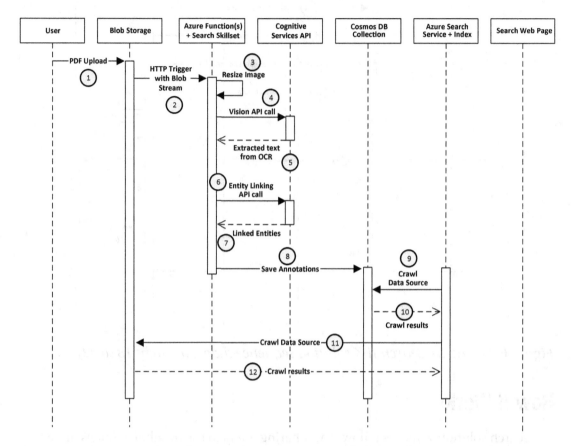

Figure 6-1a. *Azure Search JFK solution sequence diagram (steps 1 to 12)*

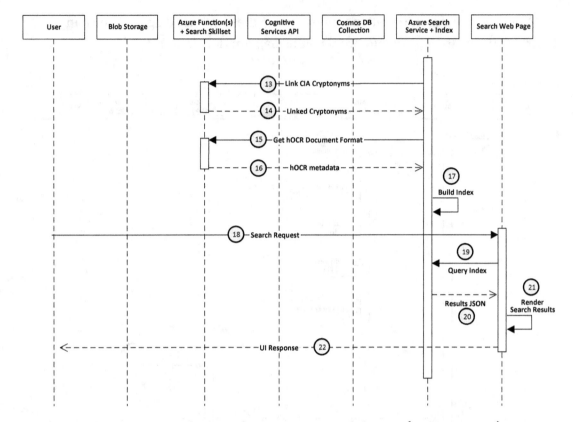

Figure 6-1b. *Azure Search JFK solution sequence diagram (steps 13 to 22)*

How It Works

The search solution works as follows (numbering refers to the numbered labels in the sequence diagram):

1. A user uploads one or more PDF files containing scanned images of documents and handwritten notes.

2. An HTTP trigger instantly fires to call logic contained in an Azure function.

3. The Azure function code resizes the image and stores it in Azure Storage for further processing.

4. The function makes a call to the Microsoft Cognitive Services Vision API, passing the image as a blob stream.

5. The Vision API returns the OCR results for the image back to the Azure function code.

6. The function now makes a call to the Microsoft Cognitive Services Entity Linking API.

7. The Entity Linking API returns a set of linked entities from the text extracted from the OCR operation from Step 5.

8. The Azure function generates annotations from the linked entities and stores them in an Azure Cosmos DB database collection.

Note   Steps 9 to 16 occur concurrently, whereby Steps 9, 11, 13, and 15 crawl the content and call the custom skills, and steps 10, 12, 14, and 16 return the results back to the Azure Search Service for creation of the search index.

---

9. The Azure Search instance crawls the annotations.

10. Crawl results are returned to the Azure Search instance to build the search index.

11. The Azure Search instance crawls the blob storage.

12. Crawl results are returned to the Azure Search instance to build the search index.

13. The Azure Search instance uses the custom cryptonyms skillset to link indexed terms with CIA cryptonyms.

14. The linked cryptonyms are returned to the Azure Search service.

15. The Azure Search instance uses the custom hOCR formatting skillset to extract hOCR metadata.

16. The hOCR metadata is returned back to the Azure Search service instance.

17. The Azure Search Service Indexer builds the search index using results from the crawled content (retrieved in Steps 10, 12, 14, and 16).

18. A user submits a search request from the UI, hosted on `https://jfk-demo.azurewebsites.net/` and generated using `AzSearch.js` (explained later in this chapter; see Step 20 of Recipe 6-2, Natural-Language Search with LUIS).

19. A query to the search index is sent by the UI.

20. JSON results are sent back to the UI.

21. The returned JSON results are rendered in the UI.

22. The search results are displayed to the user.

6-2. Natural-Language Search with LUIS

Problem

For any organization that houses content in a host of data stores, such as relational or NoSQL databases, content-management systems, or simply fileshares, providing a consistent search experience to all users can be a daunting task. In a majority of cases, searches are performed using just a keyword that can return hundreds of results, sifting through which can be tedious.

Solution

Building a natural-language interface on top of existing search can greatly enhance the user experience by allowing search queries to be framed using natural language as opposed to just using the traditional keyword-search approach.

Figure 6-2 illustrates the solution we will be building using the Consumer Complaint Database, a CSV file available from the U.S. government's open data site. An explanation of the numbered arrows in the illustration is provided in the "How It Works" section.

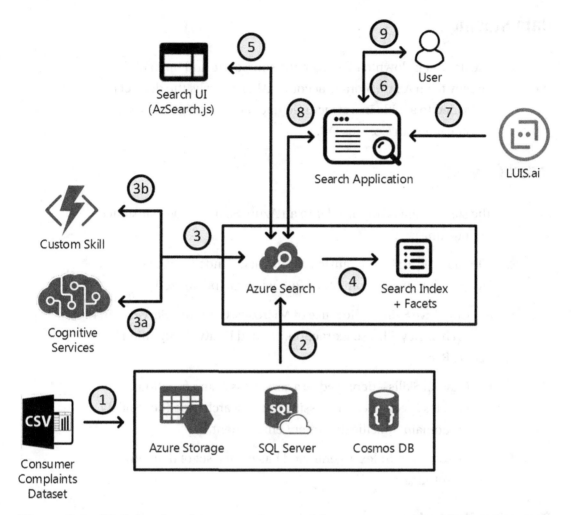

Figure 6-2. *High-level architecture of natural-language search with LUIS solution*

How It Works

The events and/or actions in the preceding illustration can be broadly classified into three categories: data staging, index creation, and querying the index. Let's look at each with respect to the numbered labels in the diagram.

Data Staging

1. The dataset is downloaded from the source site and uploaded directly to an Azure Storage account. Alternatively, the dataset can be loaded to a table in a structured database such as SQL Server or to a collection in Cosmos DB.

Index Creation

2. The staged data is imported into an Azure Search service instance for indexing.

3. [OPTIONAL] To further enrich the extracted index and search facets, either one or both of the following can be utilized:

    a. Cognitive Skills – allow use of Microsoft Cognitive Service APIs such as Key-Phrase Extraction, Named Entity Recognition, OCR, etc.

    b. Custom Skills – deployed as a serverless Azure function; enables specialized processing in the search pipeline to allow for domain-specific document enrichment.

4. A named search index is generated based on a set of defined search settings.

Querying the Index

5. [OPTIONAL] To quickly test the search index, generate a prototype UI using AzSearch.js (covered a little later in this section) and perform some search and filter queries.

6. A chatbot or custom search application allows a user to submit a search query to the Azure Search service endpoint using natural language.

7. The search application or chatbot uses LUIS.ai to determine and extract the intent and entities from the user utterance.

8. Based on the intent and entities extracted from the utterance, a search query is generated and submitted to the Azure Search service endpoint, which returns the search results back to the calling application.

9. The search results are formatted and presented to the user.

Now that we have looked at a high-level view of the solution, let's see how the solution can be built. To allow for a clearer understanding, the steps in the next section are classified under the same three categories as the solution explanation.

Data Staging - Steps by step instructions

1. Download the CSV data file from the following URL: `https://catalog.data.gov/dataset/consumer-complaint-database`.

    Alternatively, you can also go to the `data.gov` site and search the term *Consumer Complaints* to get to the dataset page.

2. In order for the downloaded CSV file to be crawled, it would need to be split into smaller, more manageable files, since crawling a large file is not recommended from a performance and service-threshold standpoint.

    a. Open up a bash command line and navigate to the drive and folder that contains the downloaded CSV file using a command similar to the following (the folder structure on your system might differ):

    `cd /mnt/d/Datasets/ConsumerComplaints`

    b. Split the file using the following command, specifying 100 as the number of rows per CSV file:

    `split -l 100 Consumer_Complaints.csv`

    On my system, the preceding command generated over 15,000 files.

    Splitting one large CSV file into smaller ones is beneficial if you plan to upload the CSV content to a blob storage account, because of service and tier limits.

    c.   The generated files will be missing the file extension. Use the following command to set the file extension to `.csv`:

```
for i in *; do mv "$i" "$i.csv"; done
```

At this point, the files can be uploaded to a data store of choice for the content to be crawled.

For this example, we will load the data into a SQL Server database table.

3.   Open SQL Server Management Studio and connect to the database where you want to load the Consumer Complaints data.

4.   In the **Object Explorer**, right-click the database and go to **Tasks ➤ Import Flat File...**

5.   Click the **Next** button on the **Introduction** screen.

6.   Select the CSV file you want to load into the database. For this recipe, I will simply pick the first CSV file generated after splitting the large file from Step 2b.

Enter *Consumer_Complaints* (or any name of your choice) as the table name.

Click the **Next** button when done (Figure 6-3).

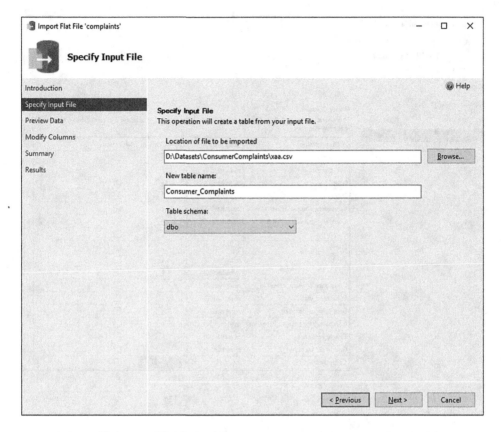

Figure 6-3. *Specify input file to import*

7. Click **Next** on the **Preview Data** screen after you make sure that all CSV data is being read correctly.

8. On the **Modify Columns** screen, scroll down and check the **Primary Key** box for the **Complaint_ID** column. Click the **Next** button when done (Figure 6-4).

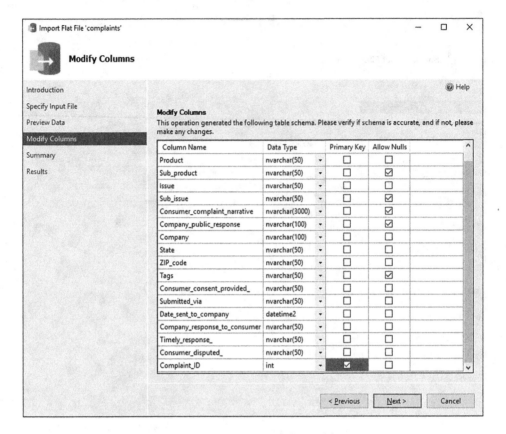

Figure 6-4. *Modify imported dataset schema if need be*

9. Click the **Finish** button on the **Summary** screen.

    You will see the **Operation Complete** message once CSV data has
    been inserted into the table.

    For simplicity purposes, I chose to only load one CSV file to the
    SQL Server database table.

    Alternatively, you can upload the large CSV file in its entirety,
    which, in turn, will take longer to load and also take a while for the
    Search index to be created.

Index Creation - Steps by step instructions

10. Log in to Azure Portal, click **Create a resource** in the top-left corner, type *Azure Search* in the search text box, hit Enter, and click **Azure Search** from the search results (Figure 6-5).

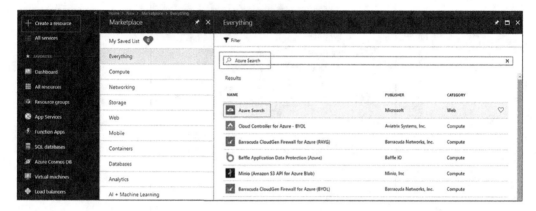

Figure 6-5. *Create an Azure Search service instance using Azure Portal*

11. Click **Create** on the **Azure Search** blade.

12. Specify the **Search Service** properties in the **New Search Service** blade and click **Create** when done (Figure 6-6).

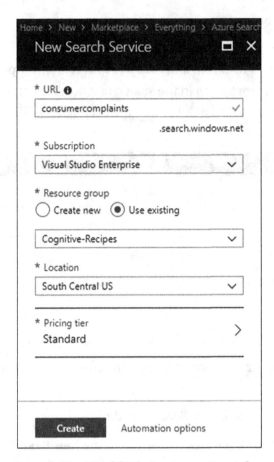

Figure 6-6. *The New Search Service blade in Azure Portal*

13. After it is provisioned, navigate to the Search Service and click the
     Import data link from the top toolbar in the **Overview** blade (Figure 6-7).

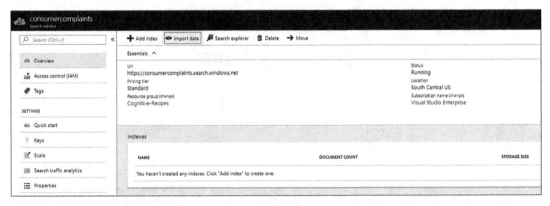

Figure 6-7. *Import data to create a search index*

14. In the **Import data** blade, click the **Data Source – Connect to your data** option, select **Azure SQL Database** as the data source, specify a name of your choice as the data-source name, and click the **Input a connection string** link (Figure 6-8).

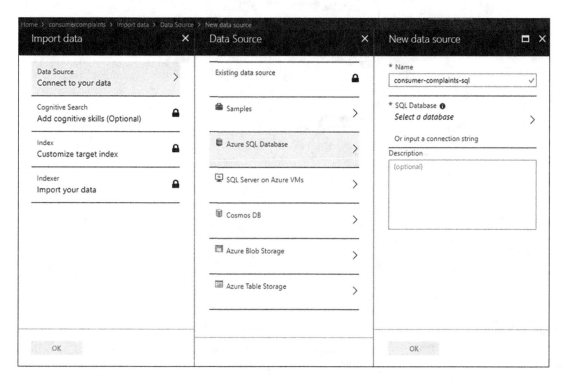

Figure 6-8. *Specify an Azure SQL data source to crawl*

Paste the connection string for the SQL database, then click the **Test Connection** button to validate the entered connection details.

Select the table **Consumer_Complaints** from the **Table/View** drop-down and click the **OK** button (Figure 6-9).

Figure 6-9. *Specify connection string and login credentials for the data source*

15. [OPTIONAL] While optional, you can use the settings in the
    Cognitive Search blade to extract additional information from a
    column in the table.

    In this case, we will specify settings to use Microsoft Cognitive
    Services to extract information from the **Consumer_complaint_
    narrative** column, which contains text of the actual complaint
    made by a consumer.

    Enter a skillset name of your choice and select the **Consumer_
    complaint_narrative** column from the **Source data field**
    drop-down.

Check all the **Cognitive Skills** checkboxes except **Detect language** since we already know that all the complaint narratives are in English.

Click the **OK** button when done (Figure 6-10).

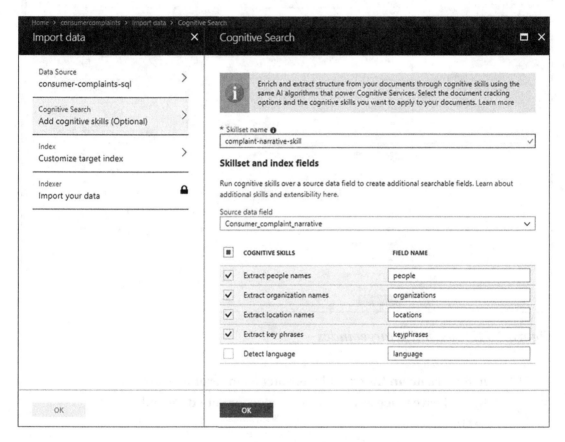

Figure 6-10. *Select cognitive skills to use for individual columns*

16. On the **Index** blade, enter an **Index name** and make sure that **Complaint_ID** (the primary key for the table) is selected in the **Key** drop-down.

    Make all the fields Retrievable, Filterable, Facetable (pronounced facet-able and NOT face-table), and Searchable by checking the boxes in the header.

    Click the **OK** button when done (Figure 6-11).

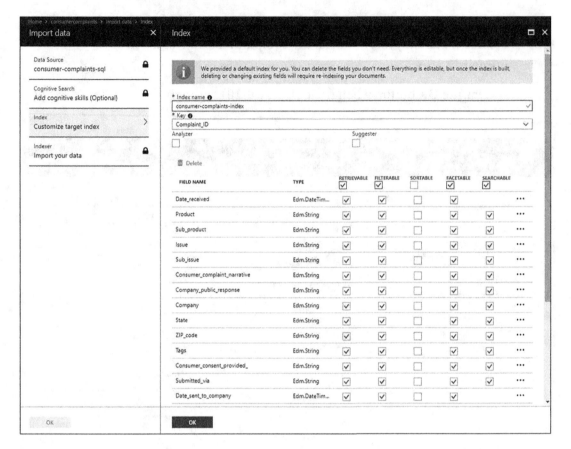

Figure 6-11. *Customize target index*

17. On the **Create an Indexer** blade, enter an indexer name of your choice. Leave **Once** as the selected value for **Schedule** and click the **OK** button.

Depending on the frequency with which a data source is updated, you can specify an hourly or daily schedule for the content to be indexed (Figure 6-12).

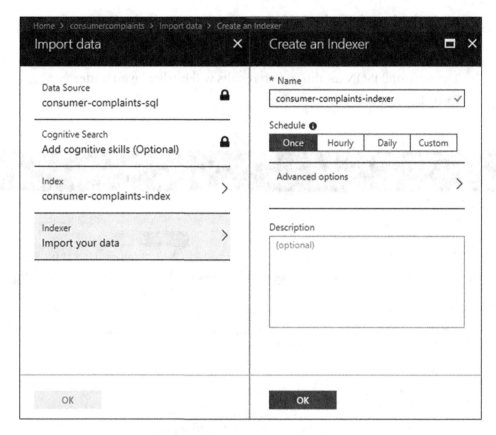

Figure 6-12. *Set schedule for crawling content*

18. Click the **OK** button on the **Import data** dialog after all the sections have been completed.

Depending on the size of the data to be indexed, it may take a while for the index to be created.

Querying the Index - Steps by step instructions

19. [OPTIONAL] You can query the search index using Azure Portal to make sure the Azure Search service is working correctly by following these steps:

a. Click on the **Search Explorer** link in the top toolbar of the **Overview** blade.

    b.   In the **Search Explorer** blade, enter some text in the **Query string** text box and click the **Search** button.

    The returned JSON for the search results will be displayed under **Results** (Figure 6-13).

Figure 6-13. *JSON results inspected in the Search Explorer blade*

20. [OPTIONAL] To generate a quick UI that calls the Search service and displays the results, follow the following steps:

    a. Navigate to the AzSearch Generator page at the following URL:

```
http://azsearchstore.azurewebsites.net/
azsearchgenerator
```

    We will need to fill in the details on this page to generate an HTML UI file to query our Search service.

    b. Click on the **Keys** link on the Search service's main navigation blade (Figure 6-14).

Figure 6-14. *The Keys link in the main Search service blade*

    c. Copy the **primary** or **secondary admin keys** and paste it in the **Query Key** text box of the AzSearch Generator page.

    The primary and secondary keys allow for both read and write. You can alternatively click the **Manage query keys** link on the **Keys** blade to copy the read-only key (Figure 6-15).

Figure 6-15. *The Keys blade for the Search service (admin keys intentionally hidden)*

    d.   To get the Azure Search index JSON value for the AzSearch Generator:

         i.   Navigate to the **Search Explorer** blade (see Step 19a).

        ii.   Select and copy the **Request URL** value, starting from **https**, all the way to the index name, ending right before / **docs** (Figure 6-16).

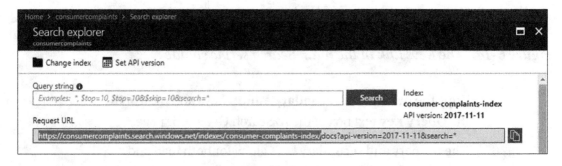

Figure 6-16. *The search index Request URL in the Search Explorer blade*

        iii.   Open the Postman application, select **GET** as the verb, and paste the copied URL into the **Enter request URL** text box.

In our case, the pasted URL would be as follows:

```
https://consumercomplaints.search.windows.net/
indexes/consumer-complaints-index
```

iv. Append the pasted URL in Postman with the api-version
     query string from the **Search Explorer** window shown
     earlier.

     After adding the query string, the pasted URL in Postman
     would be as follows:

```
https://consumercomplaints.search.windows.
net/indexes/consumer-complaints-index?api-
version=2017-11-11
```

v.   Click the Postman **Send** button to retrieve the JSON from
     the Search service (Figure 6-17).

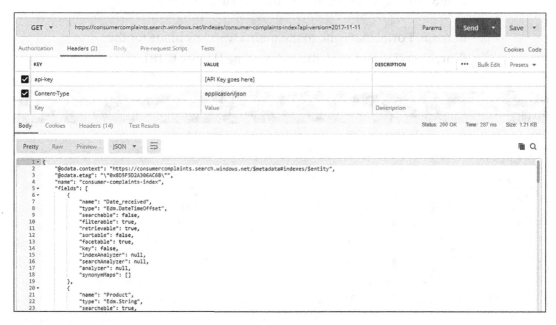

Figure 6-17. *JSON results from the Search service displayed in Postman*

vi. Click the **Raw** tab in Postman and select + to copy
the JSON.

Paste the copied JSON text into the **Azure Search index
JSON** text box in the **AzSearch Generator** page.

e. Type the name of the Search service (**consumercomplaints**
in our case) in the Service Name text box of the **AzSearch
Generator** page.

f. Now that you have specified all the values in the **AzSearch
Generator**, click the **Generate App** button at the bottom.

An HTML file (`azsearchjsApp.html`) will be downloaded to
your computer.

If you open the generated HTML file in your browser and click
the Search icon at the top, you will not see any results since
CORS is not enabled on the Search service endpoint.

g. In Azure Portal, navigate to the main Overview blade for the
Search service and click the index name (Figure 6-18).

Figure 6-18. *The Search service index*

h. Once you are on the index's blade, click the **Edit CORS options** link in the top bar, select **All** as the value for **Allowed origin type**, and click the **Save** icon (Figure 6-19).

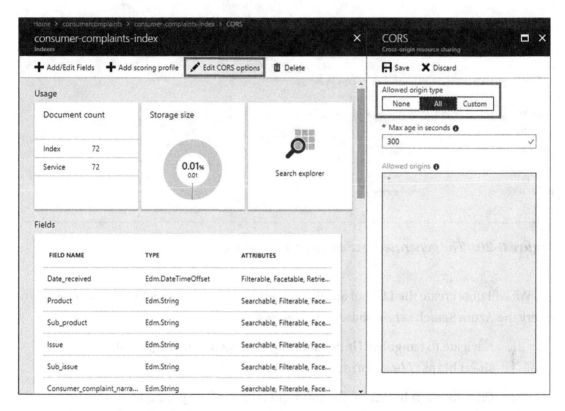

Figure 6-19. *The Edit CORS options in the Indexes blade*

i. If you open the `azsearchjsApp.html` file in your browser, type a search term (e.g., *mortgage*) in the search text box, and click the search icon, you'll be able to see the results on the page.

Notice that all fields specified as filterable appear as filters on the left side of the screen (Figure 6-20).

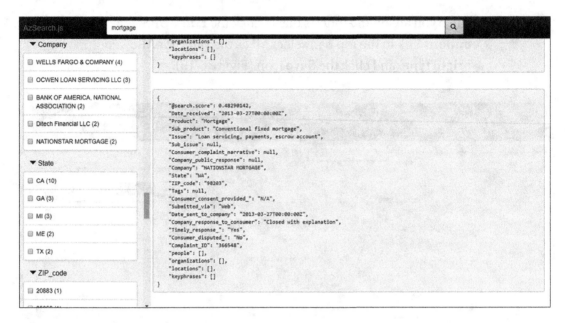

Figure 6-20. *The generated AzSearch.js application*

We will now create the LUIS.ai application and write code using Visual Studio 2017 to query the Azure Search service based on user intent.

21. Navigate to Language Understanding Intelligent Service (LUIS) site at `https://www.luis.ai`.

22. Click the **Sign In** link on the top-right corner of the page and log in using the same account credentials you used to sign into Azure Portal.

23. Click on the **Create new app** button under **My Apps**.

24. In the **Create New App** dialog, enter *ConsumerComplaints* in the **Name** field and click **Done** (Figure 6-21).

Figure 6-21. *The Create New App dialog on the LUIS.ai website*

Once the app is created, the browser will automatically navigate to
the **Intents** screen.

25. Click the **Create new intent** button, enter *Complaints.*
    SearchByCompany in the **Intent name** text box, and click **Done**
    (Figure 6-22).

Figure 6-22. *The Create New Intent dialog on the LUIS.ai website*

26. On the Intent screen, type *Get complaints filed for Company X* in the text box and hit Enter on the keyboard.

    The entered text will be added to the utterances list below the text box.

27. Repeat Step 26 and add the following utterances:

    i.   List all complaints for Company X.

    ii. What complaints were made against X?

    iii. Company X Complaints

    iv. Search complaints for X.

    v.   Search complaints for Company X (Figure 6-23).

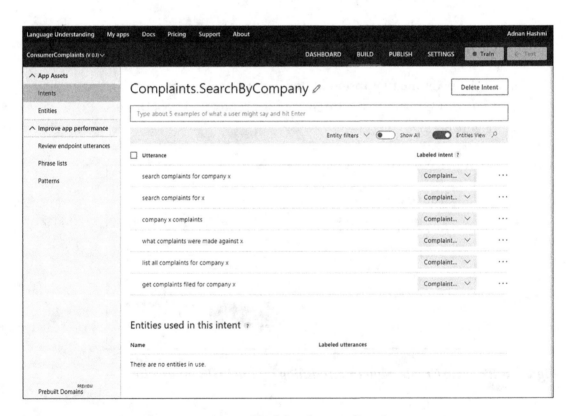

Figure 6-23. *List of utterances specified for the application*

28. Click on the **Entities** link in the left navigation.

29. On the **Entities** screen, click the **Create new entity** button under the **Entities** heading.

30. Enter *Company* as the **Entity Name**, select **List** as the **Entity type**, and click **Done** (Figure 6-24).

Figure 6-24. *Select an entity type for a created entity*

31. On the **Company Entity** screen, enter *Wells Fargo and Company* in the text box under **Values**.

32. Type *Wells Fargo* as the **Synonym** for entered value from Step 31 and hit Enter.

33. Repeat Steps 31 and 32 for the following values and synonyms:

Normalized Values	Synonyms
US Bancorp	Bancorp
Equifax Inc	Equifax, Equifax Incorporated
American Express Company	Amex, American Express
First National Bank of Omaha	First National, First National Bank, Omaha First National

For values with multiple synonyms, hit the Enter key or type a comma character after you enter a synonym to commit and add another one (Figure 6-25).

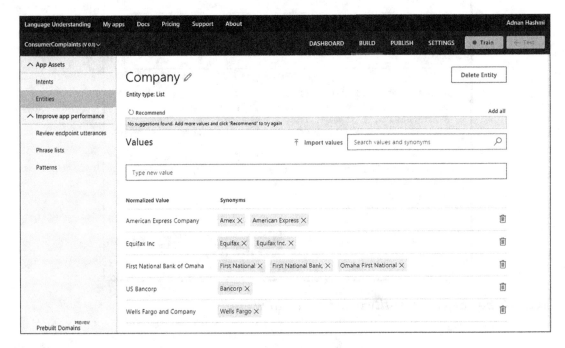

Figure 6-25. *Specify synonyms for sample entity values*

34. Click the **Intents** link in the left navigation.

35. Click the **Complaints.SearchByCompany** intent to view the utterances for the intent.

36. Hover your mouse over the **"x"** in the text for any of the utterances (which will put bar brackets around it), click, go to **Company ➤ Set as synonym**, then select a random company name from the popup menu (Figure 6-26).

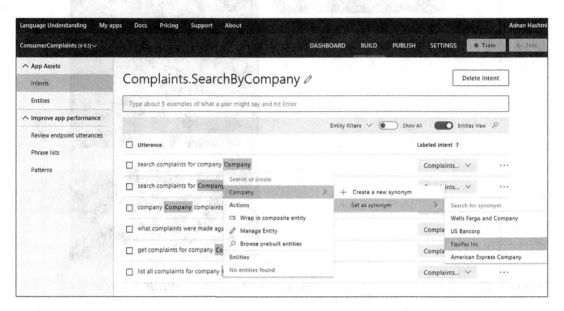

Figure 6-26. *Specify synonyms for entity values*

37. Repeat Step 36 for all utterances listed under the **Complaints. SearchByCompany** intent.

38. Click the **Train** button at the top right-hand corner of the screen.

    Once complete, the red icon on the **Train** button will turn green.

39. Click the **Test** button in the top right-hand corner of the screen to display the **Test** pane.

40. Type *Wells Fargo complaints* in the test utterance text box and hit Enter.

    LUIS will identify **Complaints.SearchByCompany** as the recognized intent, and the company name as the entity (Figure 6-27).

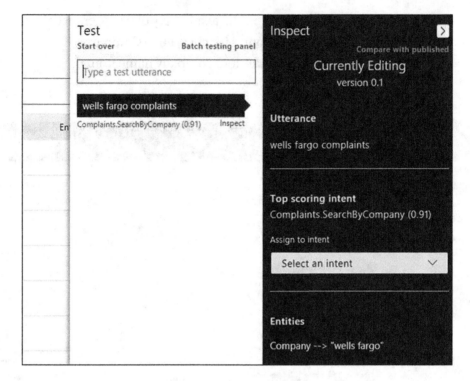

Figure 6-27. *Test pane to inspect intent extraction for a sample utterance*

Over time, you will have to retrain the model to identify more company names and their synonyms.

41. Repeat Steps 39 and 40 and enter *get complaints for Capital One* as the test utterance.

You will notice that while LUIS was able to identify the intent correctly, it could not extract the entity.

42. In the Inspect pane, select **Complaints.SearchByCompany** in the **Assign to intent** drop-down (Figure 6-28).

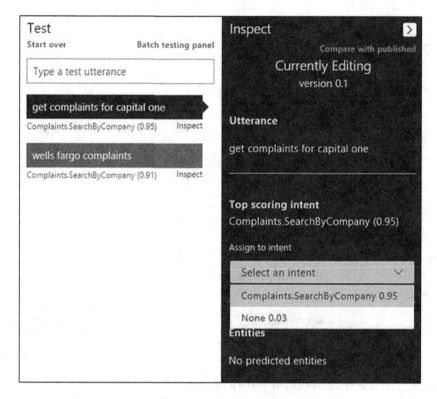

Figure 6-28. *Manually assign intent for an utterance*

The test utterance **get complaints for Capital One** will be added to the **Utterance** list without the entity being tagged.

43. Since the entity comprises multiple words (**Capital** and **One**), in the Utterance list hover over the first word in the entity value, click (to display the popup menu), and move the mouse cursor over the other words in the entity value and click.

The entire entity value will now be surrounded with the bar brackets.

44. Go to **Company ➤ Create a new synonym** in the popup menu to add the company name as a new value for the List Entity (Figure 6-29).

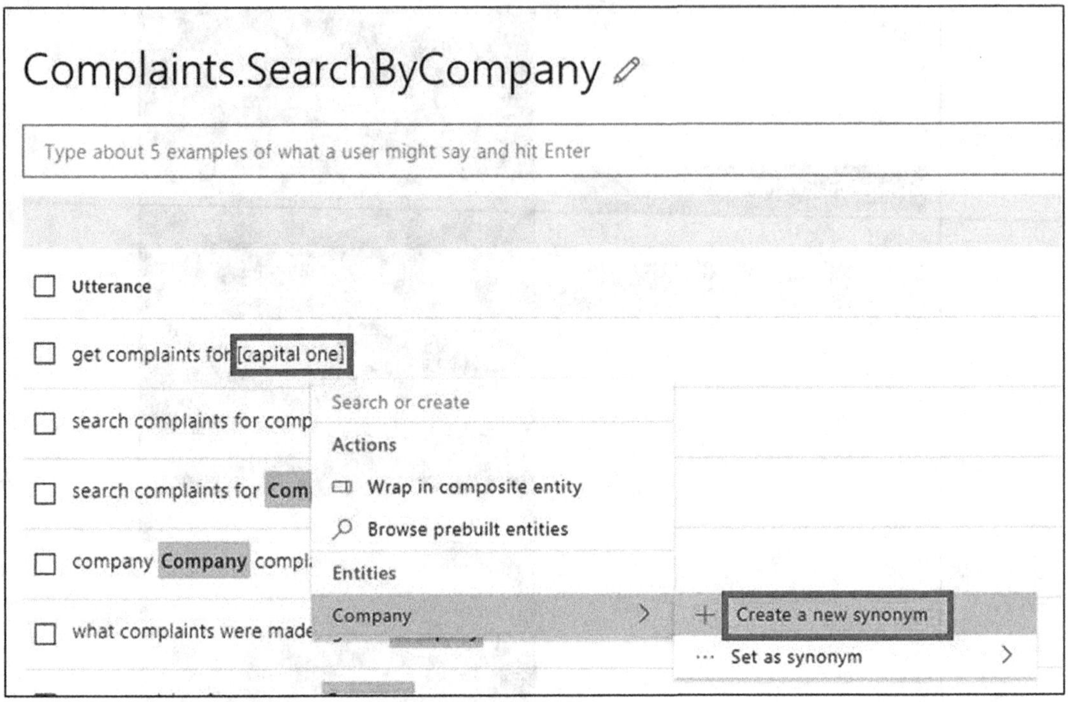

Figure 6-29. *Create synonyms for entity values*

You can also see the newly added value on the **Company** entity
screen.

45. Click the **Train** button to retrain the model for the newly added
value for the List Entity type.

The last set of steps brings together the provisioned Search service
(Steps 10 to 18) and the trained LUIS.ai model (Steps 21 to 45)
using custom code developed in Visual Studio.

To avoid repeating all the steps covered earlier in the book, we will
be referring to the steps from the **Data Center Health Monitor
Bot** recipe from Chapter 2 and the **Extract Intent from Audio**
recipe from Chapter 5.

46. Go to Azure Portal and create a **Web App Bot** and name it
ComplaintsBot (Figure 6-30).

(See Steps 1 to 6 in "Data Center Health Monitor Bot," Chapter 2.)

Figure 6-30. *The Create blade for the LUIS service*

Download the generated source code for the **ComplaintsBot** from the Build section of the bot service.

(See Steps 38 to 41 in "Data Center Health Monitor Bot," Chapter 2.)

47. Open the Web.config file for the downloaded ComplaintsBot Visual Studio project and add the following configuration settings:

```
<appSettings>
    <add key="LuisAppId" value="" />
    <add key="LuisAPIKey" value="" />
    <add key="LuisAPIHostName" value="" /
</appSettings>
```

48. Specify values for the added configuration settings.

    (See Steps 25 to 30 and Step 39 in "Extract Intent from Audio," Chapter 5.)

49. Add the following four application configuration settings in the appSettings section:

```
<add key="SearchServiceName" value="consumercomplaints" />
<add key="SearchIndexName" value="consumer-complaints-index" />
<add key="SearchServiceAdminApiKey" value="" />
<add key="SearchServiceQueryApiKey" value=" " />
```

    We get the values for the SearchServiceName and SearchIndexName settings from the names we specified for the Search service and the Index in Steps 12 and 16 earlier.

50. Navigate to the Search service we provisioned in Step 12 in Azure Portal and click the **Keys** link under **Settings** to view the **Primary** and **Secondary Admin keys**.

    Copy either one of the keys as the value for SearchServiceAdminKey in the Web.config file.

51. Click the **Manage query keys** link on the **Keys** page for the Search service to view the Query API key.

    Copy and paste the Query API key value as the value for the SearchServiceQueryApiKey setting in the Web.config file for the project.

52. In Visual Studio 2017, open the Global.asax.cs file and modify the Application_Start method so that it looks like this:

```
// Code Listing
protected void Application_Start()
{
    GlobalConfiguration.Configure(WebApiConfig.Register);
}
```

Since we will not be using any storage to store state in this recipe, we essentially removed the code that specified the data-store settings.

53. Add a new class file to the project, name it **ConsumerComplaint. cs**, and add code as follows:

(This is similar to Step 42 in "Extract Intent from Audio," Chapter 5.)

```
namespace Microsoft.Bot.Sample.LuisBot
{
    public class ConsumerComplaint
    {
        public DateTime Date_received { get; set; }
        public string Product { get; set; }
        public string Sub_product { get; set; }
        public string Issue { get; set; }
        public string Sub_issue { get; set; }
        public string Consumer_complaint_narrative { get; set; }
        public string Company_public_response { get; set; }
        public string Company { get; set; }
        public string State { get; set; }
        public string ZIP_code { get; set; }
        public string Tags { get; set; }
        public string Consumer_consent_provided_ { get; set; }
        public string Submitted_via { get; set; }
        public DateTime Date_sent_to_company { get; set; }
        public string Company_response_to_consumer { get; set; }
        public string Timely_response_ { get; set; }
        public string Consumer_disputed_ { get; set; }
        public int Complaint_ID { get; set; }
    }
}
```

54. Open the BasicLuisDialog.cs file and paste the following method code below the auto-generated code for all the intents.

```
[LuisIntent("Complaints.SearchByCompany")]
public async Task SearchByCompanyIntent(IDialogContext context,
                                               LuisResult result)

{

}
```

The code to handle the user's Search intent will go in this method.

55. Using the **Nuget Package Manager**, add the **Microsoft.Azure. Search** package to your project.

56. Add the following using statements at the top of the BasicLuisDialog.cs file:

```
using Microsoft.Azure.Search;
using Microsoft.Azure.Search.Models;
```

57. Add the following code to the SearchByCompanyIntent stub added in Step 55. (Code formatted for readability only.)

```
[LuisIntent("Complaints.SearchByCompany")]
public async Task SearchByCompanyIntent(IDialogContext context,
LuisResult result)
{
        // ------------------------------------------------------------
        // Get Entity value extracted from Utterance
        // ------------------------------------------------------------
        string entityValue = result.Entities[0].Entity;

        // ------------------------------------------------------------
        // Get Search Service Configuration Settings
        // ------------------------------------------------------------
        string searchServiceName =
                ConfigurationManager.AppSettings["SearchService
                Name"].ToString();
        string adminApiKey =
                ConfigurationManager.AppSettings["SearchServiceAdmin
                ApiKey"].ToString();
```

```
string queryApiKey =
    ConfigurationManager.AppSettings["SearchServiceQuery
    ApiKey"].ToString();
string searchIndexName =
    ConfigurationManager.AppSettings["SearchIndexName"].
    ToString();

// ------------------------------------------------------------
// Initialize client objects to reference the Search
   Service, Index, and Results
// ------------------------------------------------------------
SearchServiceClient serviceClient = new
SearchServiceClient(
                                    searchServiceName,
                                    new SearchCredentials
                                    (adminApiKey)
                                    );
ISearchIndexClient indexClient = new SearchIndexClient(
                                    searchServiceName,
                                    searchIndexName,
                                    new SearchCredentials
                                    (queryApiKey)
                                    );
DocumentSearchResult<ConsumerComplaint> searchResults;

// ------------------------------------------------------------
// Specify fields to return from the search results
// ------------------------------------------------------------
SearchParameters parameters = new SearchParameters()
{
    Select = new[] { "Company", "Product", "Issue" },
    IncludeTotalResultCount = true
};

// ------------------------------------------------------------
// Call the search service and pass the extracted entity
   value
```

```csharp
// ------------------------------------------------------------
searchResults = indexClient.Documents.Search<Consumer
Complaint>(
                                entityValue,
                                parameters
                                );
// ------------------------------------------------------------
// Format the returned results to display a response to the
   user
// ------------------------------------------------------------
const string strSummary = "I found {0} complaints for {1}.
\nHere is a quick summary:{2}";
long totalCount = searchResults.Count.GetValueOrDefault();

string summary = "";
if (totalCount > 0)
        foreach (SearchResult<ConsumerComplaint> complaint
        in searchResults.Results)
    summary += String.Format( "\n - {0} filed for {1}",
                        complaint.Document.Issue,
complaint.Document.Product
                        );

string responseText = (totalCount > 0) ?
                                String.Format(strSummary,
                                totalCount.ToString(),
                                entityValue.ToUpper(),
                                summary) : "I cannot find
                                any complaints in the
                                system.";
// ------------------------------------------------------------
// Display the response
// ------------------------------------------------------------
await context.PostAsync(responseText);
}
```

58. Build and run the Visual Studio project by clicking the Run icon in the toolbar.

59. Open the Bot Emulator, type an utterance, and hit Enter.

    You will see a response from the bot allowing you to see the search results (Figure 6-31).

Figure 6-31.   *Test the bot in the Bot Framework Emulator*

6-3. Implement Entity Search

Problem

Named-entity recognition or finding out entities in a given body of text is a challenging problem due to idiosyncrasies in spoken language. As humans, we can easily distinguish between apple (fruit) and Apple (AAPL) due to the context, but machines can't; therefore, context-sensitive entity linking of search queries in enterprise knowledge graphs is an area of interest for both academia and enterprise.

Businesses these days must deal with enormous amounts of textual data in the form of government and industrial reports, legal and contractual documentation, customer correspondence, and social media feeds. To enable deeper insights about the general sentiment, perception of, and online chatter about its brands and products, an organization must ingest large amounts of data from a host of data sources, both external and internal. Because of the sheer size of the data ingested, a large part of which may not be pertinent to the use case or context, the business needs a way to allow a search for the named entities contained within the text.

Solution

In this recipe, we will use the Bing entity search to determine fast and accurate named-entity recognition in search queries, which helps map information. Custom building of such capability requires analyzing search logs and creating knowledge bases for entities. Modern techniques apply probabilistic entity-linking algorithms from domain-specific knowledge graphs. With Bing entity search, all this work is taken care of by the APIs, and you can get started quickly. Having said that, building custom models with a domain-specific knowledge graph may still provide higher accuracy and value for specialized domains.

How It Works

At a high level, developing the entity search solution involves the following steps:

1. Download and install Node.js prerequisites and dependencies.

2. Create code stub to get user input and display message.

3. Get Cognitive Services API key and endpoint and add references in code.

4. Update code stub to call API endpoint using the user input, then display the results.

Download and Install Node.js Prerequisites and Dependencies

1. Go to the Node.js website at `https://nodejs.org` and download the installation package that pertains to the operating system platform you are using.

2. Execute the downloaded package and specify the installation preferences in the installation wizard.

3. Create a new directory with the name **BingEntity** or any other name and open it in your favorite editor. This recipe makes use of Microsoft Visual Studio Code.

4. Open the terminal using the **CTRL + ~** shortcut and type
    the following commands to initialize the project and install
    dependencies. We will be making use of **axios** and **readline**
    libraries in this recipe. A description of the 2 is provided below:

```
npm init -y
npm install axios
```

axios makes it easier to make HTTP requests.

readline is a built-in module to read a stream, one line at a time.
We will use it to read user input.

Create Code Stub to Get User Input and Display Message

5. Create a new file with the name index.js and write the following
    lines of code to include dependencies:

```
const axios = require('axios');
const readline = require('readline');
```

6. Add the following lines of code to create an interface using the
    readline module:

```
const rl = readline.createInterface({
  input: process.stdin,
  output: process.stdout
});
```

7. Now, add the following lines of code to print the user a message
    and show the input:

```
rl.question('Enter a search term: ', (answer) => {
  console.log('Search term entered: ${answer}');
  rl.close();
});
```

This will print the text on the console, wait for the user to enter the answer, and then
show the answer back to the user. To test the application so far you can run node index
in the console (Figure 6-32).

```
$ node index
Enter a search term: Karachi
Search term entered: Karachi
```

Figure 6-32. *Code stub execution results*

Get Cognitive Services API Key and Endpoint and Add References in Code

8. Before we continue, we need to get a Bing Entity Search API key. Visit the Cognitive Services site at the following URL:

   https://azure.microsoft.com/en-us/try/cognitive-services/

   Create an account if required, and you will get free keys for seven days.

9. Now that we have the API keys, we add the following lines of code in the index.js file:

```
const subscriptionKey = '<Your API Key>';
const endpoint = 'https://api.cognitive.microsoft.com/
bing/v7.0/entities';
const market = 'en-US';
```

In the preceding code listing:

- subscriptionKey is the API key.

- endpoint is the address of the Bing Entity Search API.

- market is to get the best results for a market.

  You can find a list of available market codes at the following URL: https://docs.microsoft.com/en-us/rest/api/cognitiveservices/bing-entities-api-v7-reference#market-codes

10. Update the code stub to call the API endpoint using the user input and display the results.

Now, replace this code:

```
console.log('Search term entered: ${answer}');
```

with this one:

```
console.log('Searching for: ${answer}');
const params = '?mkt=' + market + '&q=' + encodeURI(answer);

axios({
    method: 'get',
    url: endpoint + params,
    headers: { 'Ocp-Apim-Subscription-Key': subscriptionKey },
})
.then(response => {
    response.data.places.value.forEach(place => {
      if(place._type === 'Restaurant'){
        console.log('
          Name: ${place.name}
          Location: ${place.address.addressLocality}, ${place.
          address.addressRegion}, ${place.address.postalCode}
          Telephone: ${place.telephone}
        ')
      }
    });
})
.catch(err => {
    console.log('ERROR');
})
rl.close();
```

Here is the explanation of the code:

- The parameters are created and stored in the params variable.

- Axios configuration to send a GET request with the key in the header.

- When the response is received, it will loop over the response, filter the restaurants, and print their names, addresses, and phone numbers.

11. Our application is ready. Run the code by entering *node index* in the console, and then search for something (Figure 6-33).

```
$ node index
Enter search term: halal foods near 33617
Searching for: halal foods near 33617

        Name: Petra Restaurant
        Location: Tampa, FL, 33617
        Telephone: (813) 984-9800


        Name: Rana Halal Meat & Deli
        Location: Tampa, FL, 33612
        Telephone: (813) 972-1550
```

Figure 6-33. *Entity Search program output*

6-4. Get Paper Abstracts

Problem

There is a treasure trove of knowledge hidden in research publications from prestigious, peer-reviewed sources, just waiting to be explored and utilized. However, finding the right information within the context of an enterprise search can be hard. How do we find recommended papers, preferably ones with some gist or blurb that correlates with the organizational problem at hand.

Solution

Manually building a knowledge base of publications and searching through this dataset and APIs provided by third-party publishers is not an easy task. There are paywalls and a variety of different formats to work through before we can provide meaningful results.

Luckily, Bing academic APIs can help. In this recipe, we will see the use of Bing academic APIs to search and return topics of interest from academic resources. This recipe uses one of the APIs of the Microsoft Academic Graph to demonstrate how easy it is to get the abstract of a research paper by just entering its title.

How It Works

At a high level, developing the solution involves the following steps:

1. Download and install Node.js prerequisites and dependencies.

2. Get the Microsoft Academic Graph API key from the Cognitive Services Labs website.

3. Write code to call the API endpoint and display the results.

Download and Install Node.js Prerequisites and Dependencies

1. Go to the Node.js website at `https://nodejs.org` and download the installation package that pertains to the operating system platform you are using.

2. Execute the downloaded package and specify the installation preferences in the installation wizard.

3. Create a new folder with the name **AcademicGraph** (or any other name of your choice) and open the folder in Visual Studio Code (or any other editor).

4. Open the console using **CTRL + ~** and write the following commands to initialize the project and install **axios**:

    ```
    npm init -y
    npm install axios
    ```

    axios is a module to make HTTP requests easily. We will use it to make the HTTP request to the API.

    readline is a built-in module to read a stream, one line at a time. We will use it to read user input.

Get the Microsoft Academic Graph API Key from the Cognitive Services Labs Website

5. Before starting to code, we need to get the API key for the Microsoft Academic Graph.

    Visit the following link and click the **Subscribe** button:

    https://labs.cognitive.microsoft.com/en-us/project-academic-knowledge

6. Sign up using any one of the available options.

7. It will ask for permission. If you agree to the terms, click **Yes** to continue.

8. Once you are logged in (automatically after signup), you will see the keys for the API (Figure 6-34).

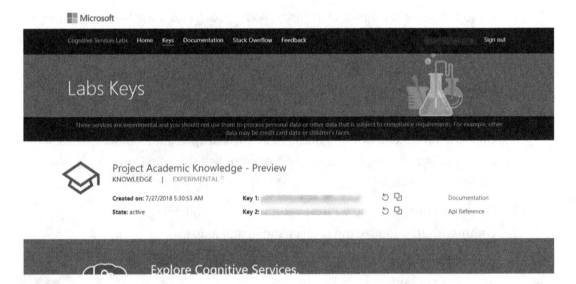

Figure 6-34. *Keys listed for Academic Graph API*

9. Create a new file with the name index.js (or any other name) and add the following lines of code to include dependencies:

```
const axios = require('axios');
const readline = require('readline');
```

10. Add the following lines of code to make variables that will store some constants:

```
const subscriptionKey = '<Your API Key>';
const endpoint = 'https://api.labs.cognitive.microsoft.com/
academic/v1.0/evaluate';
```

Replace <Your API Key> with your API key.

11. Add the following lines of code to create an interface that uses **readline** to get input from the user:

```
const rl = readline.createInterface({
  input: process.stdin,
  output: process.stdout
});
```

12. Add the following lines of code to the file:

```
rl.question('Enter something to search: ', (answer) => {
  console.log(`Searching...`);
  const params = `?expr=Ti='${answer}'&attributes=Ti,E`;
  axios({
    method: 'get',
    url: endpoint + params,
    headers: { 'Ocp-Apim-Subscription-Key': subscriptionKey },
  })
    .then(response => {
if(response.data.entities.length === 0) return console.log('No
results.');
      console.log(JSON.parse(response.data.entities[0].E).
      IA.InvertedIndex);
    })
    .catch(err => {
      console.log('ERROR', err);
    })
  rl.close();
});
```

The important parts of the code are as follows:

- The interface we created will print a question in the console and wait for the user to enter input.

- Once the user has entered something, it will print "Searching..." in the console.

- Creating parameters. We are searching using Title (Ti), and we want Title and Extended metadata in results (Ti and E).

- API call is made using axios.

- If the API call is successful but there is no result, it will print "No results."

- If there is a result, it will print the **InvertedIndex**.

- If there is an error in making the API request, it will print the error to the console.

- As soon as the user enters the text, it will close the interface.

13. Let's run this app by running node index in the console and entering a title (Figure 6-35):

   personalizing search via automated analysis of interests and activities

```
$ node index
Enter something to search: personalizing search via automated analysis of interests and activities
Searching...
{ We: [ 0, 66, 138 ],
  formulate: [ 1 ],
  and: [ 2, 83, 88, 97, 103, 114, 130 ],
  study: [ 3 ],
  search: [ 4, 59 ],
  algorithms: [ 5, 134, 143 ],
  that: [ 6, 20, 32, 44, 108, 122, 140 ],
  consider: [ 7 ],
  a: [ 8, 13, 62 ],
  'user\'s': [ 9, 21, 50 ],
```

Figure 6-35. *Program output*

This is not human-friendly. Let's modify our code to construct the text version of the abstract from it.

14. Add the following lines of code at the bottom of the file:

```
function constructAbstract(InvertedAbstract) {
  const abstract = [];
  for (word of Object.entries(InvertedAbstract)) {
    word[1].forEach(index => {
      abstract[index] = word[0];
    });
  }
  console.log(abstract.join(' '));
}
```

This will create a new function that will receive the inverted abstract as the argument, loop through it, and create another array with the words in order.

Then, it will join the array to create a string version of the abstract and print to the console.

15. Now, call this function by replacing line 22 with this code:

```
constructAbstract(JSON.parse(response.data.entities[0].E).
IA.InvertedIndex);
```

16. Now, run the code again. You should see the abstract as the output shown in Figure 6-36.

Enter something to search: personalizing search via automated analysis of interests and activities
Searching...
We formulate and study search algorithms that consider a user's prior interactions with a wide variety of content to personalize that user's current Web search. Rather than relying on the unrealistic assumption that people will precisely specify their intent when searching, we pursue techniques that leverage implicit information about the user's interests. This information is used to re-rank Web search results within a relevance feedback framework. We explore rich models of user interests, built from both search-related information, such as previously issued queries and previously visited Web pages, and other information about the user such as documents and email the user has read and created. Our research suggests that rich representations of the user and the corpus are important for personalization, but that it is possible to approximate these representations and provide efficient client-side algorithms for personalizing search. We show that such personalization algorithms can significantly improve on current Web search.

Figure 6-36. *Abstract displayed as output in console*

6-5. Identify Linked Entities in Text Analytics

Problem

One of the difficult problems in machine learning is to identify the identity of an entity found in text. This process requires the presence of a knowledge base to which recognized entities are linked. In an enterprise context, when a large corpus of textual data is processed and entities are extracted, the next logical step to derive additional insights is to link related entities. This enables a more-detailed view of each extracted named identify as it relates to other named entities. Additionally, the frequent appearance of certain linked entity names alongside other linked named entities can help to identify patterns over a period of time. For example, if a certain accounting firm's name repeatedly appears alongside (linked to) publicly traded companies that are being investigated for flawed accounting practices, it can be inferred that the accounting firm's ethical standards need to be re-evaluated and/or investigated.

Solution

The Text Analytics API, which is part of Microsoft Cognitive Services, offers a simple solution for linking entities without having to implement and maintain a huge database of linked entity names from which to ascertain and identify relationships.

How It Works

1. The first thing we need is the data (text). This document uses texts from this dataset. However, you can use any text:

   https://github.com/philipperemy/financial-news-dataset

2. We need the Text Analytics API key to make requests to the API endpoint. You can get an API key for free using this link:

   https://azure.microsoft.com/en-us/try/cognitive-services/

3. We will be using Postman to make requests to the API. Download and install Postman from this link:

   https://www.getpostman.com/

4. Open **Postman**, select **POST** from the list of methods, paste your API endpoint in the box, and open the **Headers** tab. Then, enter the following key/value pairs in the Headers (Figure 6-37):

- Ocp-Apim-Subscription-Key: <Your API key>

- Content-Type: application/json

- Accept: application/json

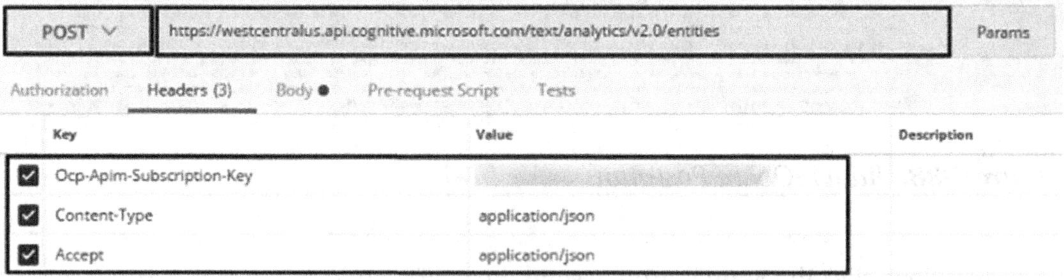

Figure 6-37. *HTTP headers displayed in Postman*

5. Now, open the **Body** tab, select **raw**, and add your document. The document format must be as follows (Figure 6-38):

```
{
    "documents":[
      {
        "id":"1",
        "language":"en",
        "text": "Text"
      }
    ]
}
```

Figure 6-38. Raw JSON in Postman

6. Now, click the **Send** button to send the POST request.

Figure 6-39 shows that the API was able to identify the entities and provide the links to the Wikipedia URLs.

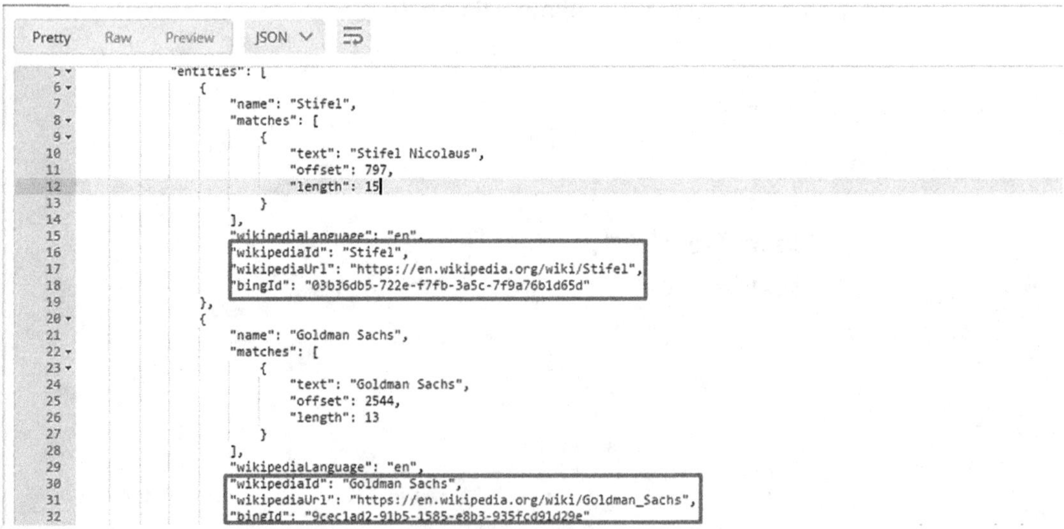

Figure 6-39. JSON result in Postman

6-6. Apply Cognitive Search

Problem

Cognitive search is the capability of performing a natural language–style search on data, both structured and unstructured. Provided a corpus of news stories, how can we quickly apply cognitive search on the Daily Mail corpus?

Solution

Azure Cognitive Search provides the perfect solution for such searches. In this recipe, we will see how Azure Search can be quickly engaged to perform the cognitive search on a large text corpus such as the CNN/Daily Mail dataset.

Set Up Azure Search

1. Log into Azure Portal using your account credentials and click on **Create a resource**.

2. Search for Azure Search and click on it (Figure 6-40).

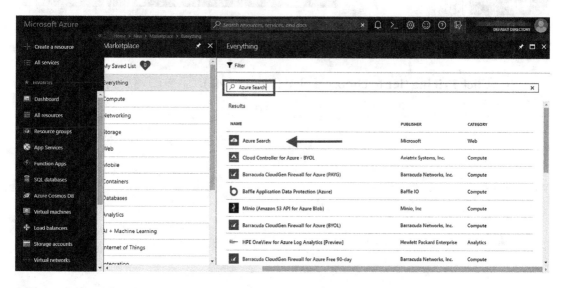

Figure 6-40.   *Create an Azure Search instance in Azure Portal*

3. Click on the **Create** button.

4. Enter the required details (Figure 6-41):

    - The URL can be used to access the service.

    - In Location, choose either South Central or West Europe, as this
      service is only available in these two regions.

    - Pin to dashboard if you like.

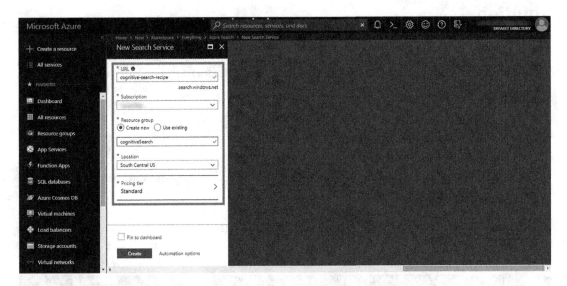

Figure 6-41. *The New Search Service blade in Azure Portal*

5. Click **Pricing tier** to choose a plan (Figure 6-42).

Figure 6-42. *Select a pricing tier for the Azure Search service*

6.   Click the ***Create*** button to continue.

Create a Storage

7.   Once the deployment is successful, click **Storage Accounts**.

8.   Click the **Add** button to create a storage account.

9.   Enter a name for the storage account and select the resource group we created earlier. Then, click the **Create** button to create the storage (Figure 6-43).

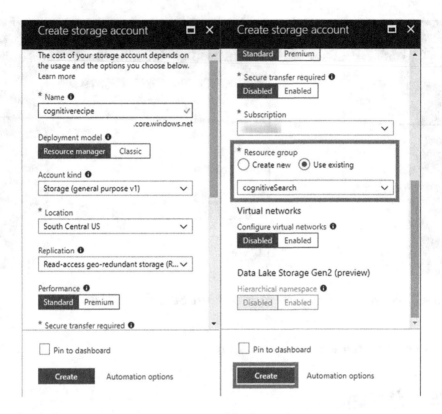

Figure 6-43. *The Create Storage Account blade*

10. Once the storage account is created, click **Blobs** (Figure 6-44).

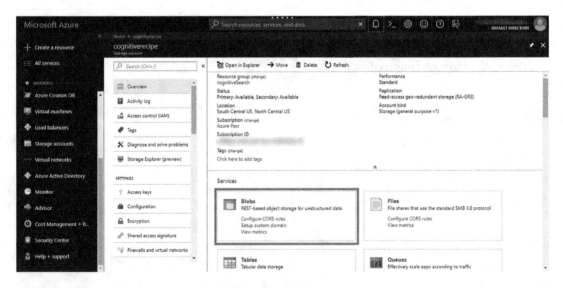

Figure 6-44. *The Blobs link for the resource group*

11.   Click the **Container** button to create a new container, enter the
       name, and click the **OK** button (Figure 6-45).

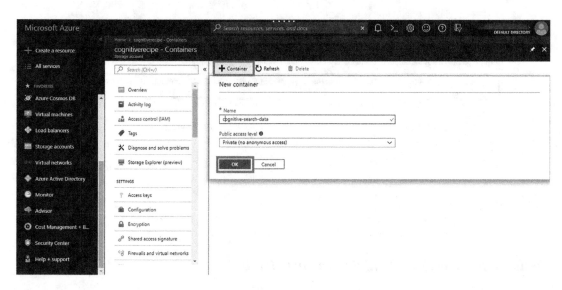

Figure 6-45.   *The Containers blade for the Storage Account*

Click on the container to access it.

Upload the Dataset

12.   Before we proceed further, we have to download a dataset. Use the
       following link to get the dataset:

```
https://github.com/JafferWilson/Process-Data-of-CNN-
DailyMail
```

Extract the dataset (92,579 files) to your computer. Uploading this
amount of files is not a convenient option. So, we will only use 500
stories (you can use more; Figure 6-46).

Figure 6-46. *The Daily Mail dataset on GitHub*

13. Click the **Upload** button to start uploading files (50 at a time).

    You can also install Storage Explorer to upload using a installed client application if you prefer:

    ```
    https://azure.microsoft.com/en-us/features/storage-
    explorer/
    ```

Create the Enrichment Pipeline

14. Once all the files are uploaded, go to the Search service and click **Import Data** (Figure 6-47).

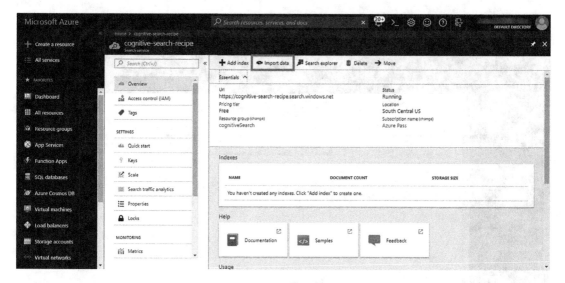

Figure 6-47. *Import data into the Search service*

15. Click **Data Source**, then **Azure Blob Storage**, then enter a name.

    Click **Storage container** (Figure 6-48).

Figure 6-48. *Specify data source to crawl*

16. Select the container we created earlier (Figure 6-49).

Figure 6-49. *Specify storage account and container to crawl*

17. Enter the skillset name, enable **OCR and merge all text**, and select
the skills you want. Finally, click the **OK** button (Figure 6-50).

Figure 6-50. *Select cognitive skills to use for individual columns.*

18.   Leave everything the way it is on the **Index** blade (Figure 6-51).

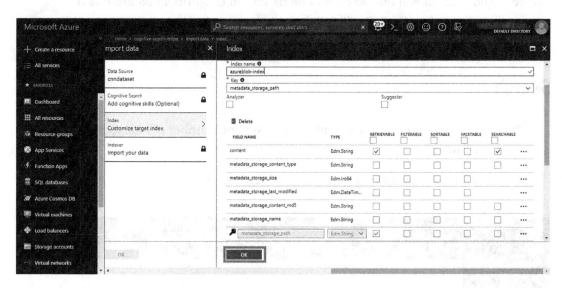

Figure 6-51.   *The Index blade*

19.   Enter a name for the index and click ***OK***. Indexing will start
      immediately (Figure 6-52).

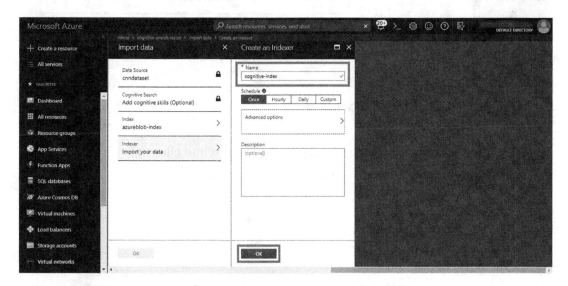

Figure 6-52.   *The Create an Indexer blade*

Note   The indexer will not be able to index all the documents as there is a ten-minute execution limit. It will fail, but we can use the indexed document.

Search

20.   Open the Search service, and you can see the number of indexed documents.

Click on "Search explorer" to search (Figure 6-53).

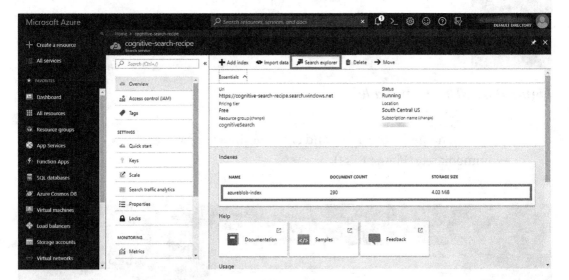

Figure 6-53.   *The Search Service blade*

21.   Type a search term in the *Query string* text box and click the *Search* button (Figure 6-54).

Figure 6-54. *The Search Explorer blade*

You will see the search results along with people and organizations' names (Figure 6-55).

Figure 6-55. *Search results displayed as JSON*

References & Further Reading

Named Entity Recognition: https://docs.microsoft.com/en-us/azure/machine-learning/studio-module-reference/named-entity-recognition

Knowledge Graphs for Enhanced Machine Reasoning: https://www.forge.ai/blog/knowledge-graphs-for-enhanced-machine-reasoning-at-forge.ai

Microsoft Research Open Data BETA: https://msropendata.com

## CHAPTER 7

AIOps: Predictive Analytics & Machine Learning in Operations

"By 2022, 40% of all large enterprises will combine big data and machine learning functionality to support and partially replace monitoring, service desk and automation processes and tasks, up from 5% today."

—Gartner Report: Market Guide for AIOps Platforms

"Machine learning for IT operations.... Class of methods to analyze data—iteratively learn from the data—and find hidden insights without being explicitly told where to look, in real-time and at scale.... What's created AIOps is we've gone past the point where you can anticipate a priori how things are going to break and what they will do when they break.... [We] need to move beyond building rules to manually search for the failure conditions, to starting to use the data that you get to define the logic that is used to look for the failure conditions. When we talk about AIOps, we talk about operations enabled with essentially the full suite of machine learning, data science, and AI techniques."

—Philip Tee, CEO Moogsoft Inc.

"AIOps is for us a solution to react to the real critical events and not [to] the thousands of events which are coming up from our monitoring tools."

—Rüdiger Schmid, IT Management, Diagnostics & Connected Vehicle Data, Daimler AG

© Adnan Masood, Adnan Hashmi 2019
A. Masood and A. Hashmi, *Cognitive Computing Recipes*, https://doi.org/10.1007/978-1-4842-4106-6_7

The operations landscape today is more complex than ever. IT Ops teams have to fight an uphill battle managing the massive amounts of data that is being generated by modern IT systems. They are expected to handle more incidents than ever before with shorter service-level agreements (SLAs), respond to these incidents more quickly, and improve on key metrics, such as mean time to detect (MTTD), mean time to failure (MTTF), mean time between failures (MTBF), and mean time to repair (MTTR). This is not because of lack of tools. Digital enterprise journal research suggests that 41 percent of enterprises use ten or more tools for IT performance monitoring, and downtime can get expensive when companies lose a whopping $5.6 million per outage and MTTR averages 4.2 hours and wastes precious resources. With a hybrid multi-cloud, multi-tenant environment, organizations need even more tools to manage the multiple facets of capacity planning, resource utilization, storage management, anomaly detection, and threat detection and analysis, to name a few.

It is evident that to correlate millions of data points across a variety of IT domains and analyze that data to detect patterns and to visualize information so the operations team can see their systems in real-time we need to use AI and machine-learning capabilities. Artificial intelligence for IT operations (AIOps) has emerged as a solution to ever-increasing IT complexity. This emerging new discipline of AIOps targets automation, correlation, visualization, auto discovery, and data ingestion to support today's operational needs.

Defining AIOps, Forrester, a leading market research company based in Cambridge - Massachusetts, published a vendor landscape cognitive operations paper which states that "AIOps primarily focuses on applying machine learning algorithms to create self-learning—and potentially self-healing—applications and infrastructure. A key to analytics, especially predictive analytics, is knowing what insights you're after." In this chapter, we will discuss some recipes that showcase the benefits of AIOps, such as event coverage and correlation, outlier analysis and detection, new correlation and new monitoring strategy, identifying dependencies between services, and speeding up root-cause analysis.

To be fair, it is virtually impossible to cover the breadth of machine-learning capabilities for AIOps in this chapter. Anomaly detection, dynamic thresholding, event clustering, and prediction are fairly large areas to be covered and probably would require volumes of their own. The purpose of this chapter is to showcase the value and art of the possible for key concepts like threshold adaption in real-time; detecting and highlighting trends and alerting about anomalous behavior; preventing service degradation; event prioritization; self-healing with alerts triggered automatically by anomalous activity; predicting outages and anomalies before they occur; and providing incident responders with the capability to see across IT silos that your services are not affected.

7-1. Building Knowledge Graph Using Grakn

Knowledge graphs are ubiquitous in modern knowledge-management and information-retrieval applications, including search applications and knowledge bases. Knowledge graphs are a data structure, typically a directed acyclic graph, where nodes and edges signify relationships between entities. In a real-world application, this helps to combine documents that contain heavy amounts of text and unstructured data.

In an AIOps use case, this applies to ticket data, application telemetry, logs, and other related information that can be used to create word embeddings where the distance between terms signals relationships. These terms could be application or service names, process identifiers, or other entities helping to correlate and establish meaningful relationships between diverse data sources.

Problem

How to build a knowledge graph using Grakn that can correlate elements.

Solution

Grakn is an open source intelligent database. More precisely, it is a knowledge-graph system that can be used to model relationships between complex data. A knowledge graph is used to convert data into information and then information into knowledge. It is the ideal tool for both effectively exploring large datasets and building AI-based applications.

In this example, we will use the MySQL World database. The database portrays statistics surrounding the world and relevant information such as cities, population, head of state, and so forth. It's a bit dated though.

Before we start, let's explain a couple of key concepts regarding knowledge graphs: taxonomies and ontologies. Taxonomies are a way to organize knowledge as a hierarchical classification system. It can be defined as a tree that starts from a universal root concept and progressively divides it into more-specific child concepts. Each node of the taxonomy represents a concept, and an edge directs the root node toward the leaf nodes.

When taxonomies represent a collection of topics with "is-a" relationships, ontologies are more complex taxonomies. Ontologies are used to express objects and relationships, such as "has-a" and "use-a," etc.

How It Works

Now, let's get building.

Get a Virtual Machine

1. Get a DSVM Test Drive machine from this link:

    ```
    https://azure.microsoft.com/en-us/services/virtual-
    machines/data-science-virtual-machines/
    ```

    Select **Data Science Virtual Machine for Linux (Ubuntu)** and
    then **TEST DRIVE** (Figure 7-1).

Apps > Data Science Virtual Machine for Linux (Ubuntu) > Test Drive

Test Drive
Data Science Virtual Machine for Linux (Ubuntu)
by Microsoft

Your Test Drive is ready (7 hours 53 minutes remaining)

Your test drive is available. Access your server at
cloudapp.azure.com with username dsvm and password

You can login to the test drive VM with an SSH client, like PuTTY or X2Go. X2Go uses XFCE as the
desktop environment.

Test Drive details

The Linux Data Science Virtual Machine is a custom Azure virtual machine image purposely built for data science.
It contains many of the popular data science tools pre-installed and pre-configured to jump-start advanced
analytics. It also has several Azure tools and libraries installed to allow working with various Azure data and
analytics products in the cloud. This virtual machine improves data scientist productivity and enables users to try
our products, run analytics modeling workloads, and replace their analytics desktop with a cloud-hosted data-
science machine for a significant part of their work.

Documentation
Test Drive User Manual

Figure 7-1. *Data Science Virtual Machine for Linux (Ubuntu)*

2. Once you get the credential, connect to the server using SSH.

Install MySQL

We need to install MySQL database for GRAKN.

1. Run the following commands to install the MySQL database:

```
sudo apt-get update
sudo apt-get install mysql-server
```

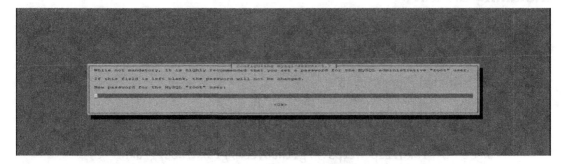

Figure 7-2. *MySQL installation on the Data Science Virtual Machine*

Choose a password when asked.

2. Run the following command to start MySQL:

```
systemctl start mysql
```

Get Sample Database

As discussed earlier, for the purpose of demonstration we will use a sample MySQL database, World, that portrays information and attributes associated with world statistics.

1. Use this command to download the file and unzip it:

```
wget -O world.zip http://downloads.mysql.com/docs/world.sql.zip
unzip world.zip
```

2. Load the data to the MySQL database by running the following command:

```
mysql -u root -p <your password>
```

It will open the MySQL shell; run this command to load the data:

```
SOURCE ./world.sql;
exit;
```

Installing GRAKN

GRAKN requires Java 8, but it is already installed in the DSVM. You can install Java using this command:

```
sudo apt-get install openjdk-8-jre
```

1. Run this command to download GRAKN and unzip it:

```
wget -O grakn.zip https://github.com/graknlabs/grakn/
releases/download/v1.3.0/grakn-dist-1.3.0.zip

unzip grakn.zip
```

2. Start GRAKN using this command:

```
./grakn-dist-1.3.0/grakn server start
```

Figure 7-3. *GRAKN server starting*

3. Open the nano editor and copy–paste the following text to create the ontology for some fields of the data. As defined earlier, the ontology here defines the relationship between the country and its sub-elements.

```
define

country sub entity
  has countrycode
  has name
  has surfacearea
  has indepyear
  has population
  has lifeexpectancy
  has gnp
  has gnpold
  has localname
  has governmentform
  has headofstate
  plays speaks-language
  plays contains-city;

city sub entity
  has population
  has name
  plays in-country;

language sub entity
  has name
  plays language-spoken;

name sub attribute datatype string;
countrycode sub attribute datatype string;
surfacearea sub attribute datatype double;
indepyear sub attribute datatype long;
population sub attribute datatype long;
lifeexpectancy sub attribute datatype double;
gnp sub attribute datatype double;
```

```
gnpold sub attribute datatype double;
localname sub attribute datatype string;
governmentform sub attribute datatype string;
headofstate sub attribute datatype string;
iscapital sub attribute datatype boolean;
isofficial sub attribute datatype boolean;
percentage sub attribute datatype double;

speaks sub relationship
  relates speaks-language
  relates language-spoken
  has percentage
  has isofficial;
has-city sub relationship
  relates contains-city
  relates in-country
  has iscapital;

speaks-language sub role;
language-spoken sub role;
contains-city sub role;
in-country sub role;
```

Then, press **CTRL + O** to save the file. Give it the name ontology.
gql or anything you prefer.

Press **CTRL + X** to exit.

4. Now, load the ontology using this command:

    ```
    ./grakn-dist-1.3.0/graql console  --file ./ontology.gql
    ```

    Open your favorite browser and visit the following:

    ```
    <IP or domain name of your server>:4567
    ```

    You will see a web page for GRAKN. In the Graph tab, select **All**
    from the **Types** list to visualize the ontology.

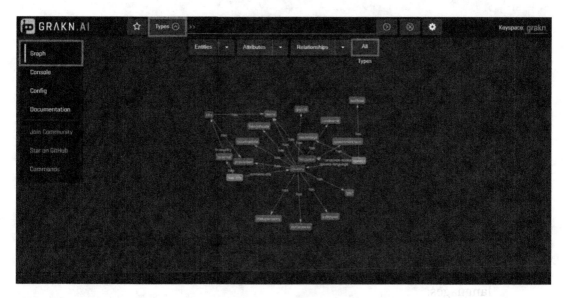

Figure 7-4. *Ontology graph visualization in GRAKN*

Creating Templates for Data Migration

To migrate the data from MySQL to GRAKN, we will need to create templates.

1. Create a new directory using this command and add templates:

```
mkdir templates
cd templates
```

2. Let's start with the countries template:

```
nano ./countries.gql
```

Copy and paste this template; save using **CTRL + O** and exit using **CTRL + X**.

```
insert $country isa country
  has name <Name>
  has countrycode <Code>
  if(<IndepYear> != null) do { has indepyear <IndepYear> }
  if(<Population> != null) do { has population <Population> }
  if(<LifeExpectancy> != null) do { has lifeexpectancy
<LifeExpectancy> }
  if(<GNP> != null) do { has gnp <GNP> }
  if(<GNPold> != null) do { has gnpold <GNPold> }
```

```
    if(<LocalName> != null) do { has localname <LocalName>  }
    if(<GovernmentForm> != null) do { has governmentform
<GovernmentForm> }
    if(<HeadOfState> != null) do { has headofstate <HeadOfState> };
```

3. Next, it's the languages template:

   `nano ./languages.gql`

   Copy and paste the this template; save using **CTRL + O** and exit using **CTRL + X**.

   `insert $language isa language has name <language>;`

4. Now it's the template for the relationship between countries and languages:

   `nano ./relation-countries-languages.gql`

   Copy and paste this template; save using **CTRL + O** and exit using **CTRL + X**.

```
match
  $language isa language has name <Language>;
  $country isa country has countrycode <CountryCode>;
insert
  $relation (speaks-language: $country, language-spoken:
  $language) isa speaks
  has isofficial if(<IsOfficial> = "F") do { false } else { true }
  has percentage <Percentage>;
```

5. And the cities template:

   `nano ./cities.gql`

   Copy and paste this template; save using **CTRL + O** and exit using **CTRL + X**.

```
match
  $country isa country has countrycode <CountryCode>;
insert
  $city isa city
```

```
has name <Name>
has population <Population>;
(contains-city: $country, in-country: $city) isa has-city;
```

6. Finally, we have the template to determine if the city is the capital city:

```
nano ./is-capital-city.gql
```

Copy and paste this template; save using **CTRL + O** and exit using **CTRL + X**.

```
if(<capital> != null) do {
match
  $country isa country has countrycode <code>;
  $city isa city has name <capital>;
  $rel (in-country: $country, contains-city: $city) isa has-city;
insert
  $rel has iscapital true;}
```

7. Now run this command to go back to the home directory:

```
cd ..
```

Get JDBC Driver

Before we start migrating data, we will have to download the JDBC driver for MySQL. Run these commands to download the JDBC driver and move it to the GRAKN lib directory:

```
wget -O jdbc.zip https://cdn.mysql.com//Downloads/Connector-J/mysql-
connector-java-8.0.12.zip
unzip jdbc
mv ./mysql-connector-java-8.0.12/mysql-connector-java-8.0.12.jar
./grakn-dist-1.3.0/services/lib/
```

Migrate Data to GRAKN

1. GRAKN has built-in scripts to migrate data. Run these scripts to migrate data.

   - Countries:

     ```
     ./grakn-dist-1.3.0/graql migrate sql -q "SELECT *
     FROM country;" -location jdbc:mysql://localhost:3306/
     world -user root -pass <password> -t ./templates/
     countries.gql -k grakn
     ```

   - Languages:

     ```
     ./grakn-dist-1.3.0/graql migrate sql -q "SELECT
     DISTINCT language FROM countrylanguage;" -location
     jdbc:mysql://localhost:3306/world -user root -pass
     <password> -t ./templates/languages.gql -k grakn
     ```

   - Relationship between countries and languages:

     ```
     ./grakn-dist-1.3.0/graql migrate sql -q "SELECT
     * FROM countrylanguage;" -location jdbc:mysql://
     localhost:3306/world -user root -pass <password> -t
     ./templates/relation-countries-languages.gql -k grakn
     ```

   - Cities:

     ```
     ./grakn-dist-1.3.0/graql migrate sql -q "SELECT *
     FROM city;" -location jdbc:mysql://localhost:3306/
     world -user root -pass <password> -t ./templates/
     cities.gql -k grakn
     ```

   - Determine if the city is the capital city:

     ```
     ./grakn-dist-1.3.0/graql migrate sql -q "SELECT
     code, capital FROM country;" -location jdbc:mysql://
     localhost:3306/world -user root -pass <password> -t
     ./templates/is-capital-city.gql -k grakn
     ```

Let's Test

1. Open the GRAKN web interface by opening `<server ip or domain name>:4567` and enter the following query in the console:

    `match $x isa city, has name "Toronto"; offset 0; limit 30; get;`

    It will return the city with the name "Toronto" (see Figure 7-5).

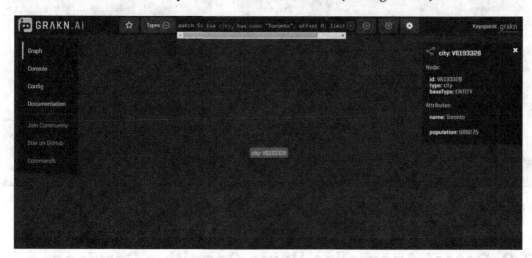

Figure 7-5. *Query result displayed in the GRAKN web interface*

Double-click on the city, and it will return the country the city belongs to (see Figure 7-6).

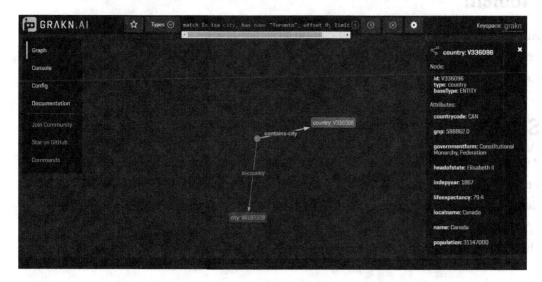

Figure 7-6. *Expand city node to view country*

Now, double-click on the country, and it will return all the cities and languages of that country (see Figure 7-7).

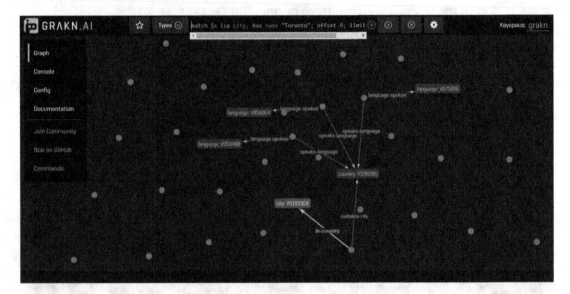

Figure 7-7. *View all cities by expanding country*

7-2. Detect Anomalies Using Cognitive Services Labs Project Anomaly Finder

Problem

Anomaly detection from a dataset can be a challenge due to a variety of different approaches and algorithms. How can we detect and predict anomalies in a dataset using Cognitive Services, specifically the Labs Project Anomaly Finder?

Solution

Anomalies are deviations from the usual trend of data. Anomalies and outliers can be just noise or values that provide valuable information, such as a spike in product demand, a fraudulent transaction, a security breach, or a CPU/memory-hogging application. In the AIOps landscape, anomalies are highly useful, and this recipe will showcase how to detect these outliers using Cognitive Services.

In this solution, we will use the Anomaly Finder API, which helps monitor data over time and detect anomalies while adapting to the specific dataset. Using a time series as input, the API returns whether a data point is detected as an anomaly, determines the expected value, and measures deviation.

How It Works

As a prebuilt AI service, Project Anomaly Finder doesn't require any machine-learning expertise beyond understanding how to use a RESTful API, which makes development simple and versatile since it works with any time-series data and can also be built into streaming data systems.

Let's do a deep dive to look into prerequisites and how to get started.

Prerequisites

There are some prerequisites for this task, as follows:

- The example has been developed for .NET Framework using Visual Studio 2017.

- Before developing, you must subscribe to the Anomaly Finder API, which is part of Microsoft Cognitive Services. To subscribe, follow this link:

  https://labs.cognitive.microsoft.com/en-us/project-anomaly-finder

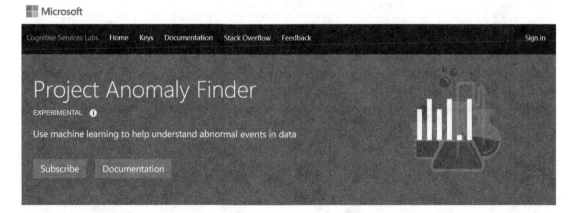

Figure 7-8. *Anomaly Finder API*

- Click the **Subscribe** button, then log in with your Microsoft account to subscribe to the API. Then you will find your free subscription key.

Figure 7-9. *Sign into Cognitive Services Labs*

- Clone the Anomaly Detection example application to your computer from GitHub by following this link: `https://github.com/ MicrosoftAnomalyDetection/csharp-sample`.

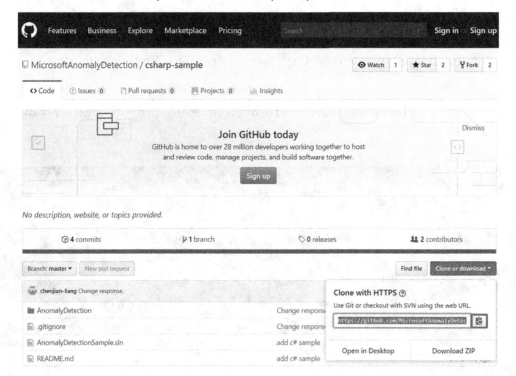

Figure 7-10. *Microsoft Anomaly Detection GitHub Repo*

- Under the repository name, click **Clone or download**.

- In the Clone with HTTPs section, click to copy the clone URL for the repository.

- Open Git Bash in your PC. Change the current working directory to the location where you want the cloned directory to be made.

- Type the following:

  ```
  git clone https://github.com/MicrosoftAnomalyDetection/csharp-
  sample.git
  ```

- Now, open the cloned directory (`csharp-sample`). The folder structure will be like Figure 7-11.

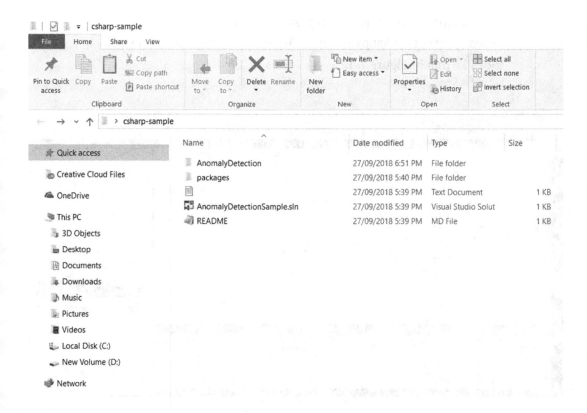

Figure 7-11. *Cloned project's directory structure on local drive*

- Here is a description of the files in the cloned directory (`csharp-sample`):

  - `AnomalyDetection` folder contains the files related to building the task.

  - `Packages` folder contains packages details used in this app.

  - The text document file with no name is a gitignore file, which is automatically created by Microsoft Visual Studio.

  - The `AnomalyDetectionSample.sln` file will be used to build and run the Anomaly Detection app in data.

  - The `README.md` file contains installation and running instructions for this project.

- In your cloned directory (`csharp-sample`), open `AnomalyDetectionSample.sln` in Visual Studio 2017; the code will look like that in Figure 7-12.

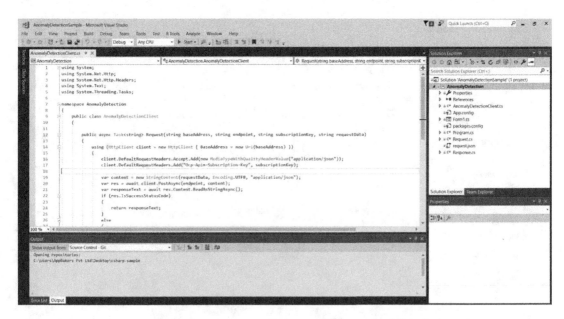

Figure 7-12. *Anomaly Detection Sample project in Visual Studio 2017*

- Press **Ctrl+Shift+B**, which will create the build of the project. After the build is successfully completed, the output should look like Figure 7-13.

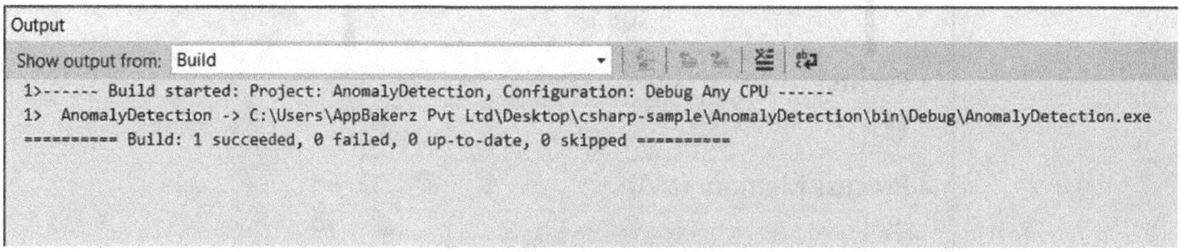

Figure 7-13. *Project build success messages in the Visual Studio Output pane*

- After the build is completed, press **F5** to run the code. Data for detecting anomalies is present in the request.json file, which is inside the AnomalyDetection folder.

- After running successfully, "Diagnostic Tools" will appear on the right side of the IDE, and an Anomaly Detection user interface window with a text-edit box with the title Form1 will open.

- Diagnostic tools will indicate session time, memory used in process, and usage of CPU in percentage (%).

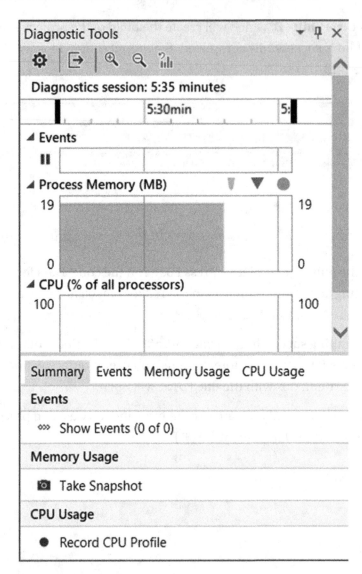

Figure 7-14. *Diagnostic Tools pane in Visual Studio 2017*

- The Anomaly Detection user interface window with the text-edit box will show the preview of the request with the response according to the request.

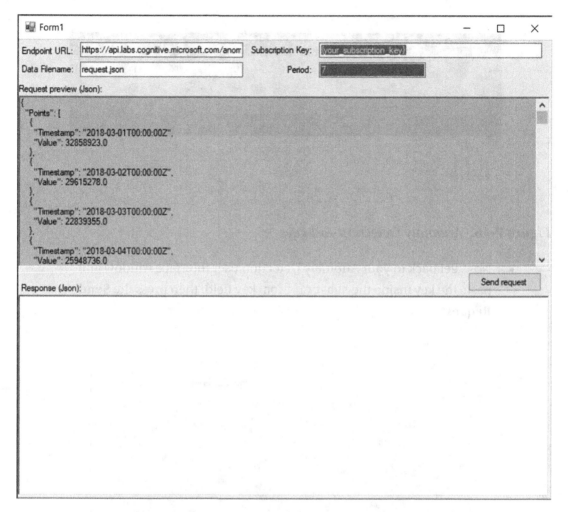

Figure 7-15. *JSON Request and Response displayed in the Anomaly Detection project's user interface*

- Here we need to insert the API key we got by registering on the Anomaly Finder API.

- Go to the Anomaly Finder API link, log in with your credentials, and copy any of the keys from the site.

Note   Both Key 1 and Key 2 can be used.

Figure 7-16. *Anomaly Detection API keys*

- Now, get back to your Anomaly Detection user interface window and paste the key inside the subscription_key field, then press the **Send Request** button.

Figure 7-17. *Paste API Subscription Key in the Anomaly Detection project's user interface window*

- After clicking the button, you can see the anomaly value in the **Response (json)** window by scrolling through the window. The following picture collage shows the readings collected by scrolling through the Response(json) window.

Response (Json):	Response (Json):	Response (Json):
1306439.3896211728,	false	false,
1767212.2210928784	],	false
],	"IsAnomaly_Neg": [	],
"IsAnomaly": [	false,	"IsAnomaly_Pos": [
false,	false,	false,
false,	false,	false,
false,	false,	false,
false,	false,	false,
false,	false,	false,
false,	false,	false,
false,	false,	false,
false,	false,	false,
false,	false,	false,
false,	false,	false,
false,[	false,	false,
false,	false,	false,
false,	false,	false,
false,	false,	false,
false,	false,	false,
false,	false,	false,
false,	false,	false,
false,	false,	false,
false,	false	false,

Figure 7-18. JSON API Response

- To perform the anomaly detection on your custom data, replace the request.json file with your own data, create build, and press **F5**. In the Anomaly Detection user interface window, enter your key in the subscription_key field then click the **Send** button.

- Cognitive Services receives the data you upload and uses them to detect any anomaly points among them, and then shows the response in the Response(json) window.

- If the data is good, you will find the anomaly-detection result in the **Response** field. If any error occurs, the error information will be shown in the Response field as well.

In this preview of AIOps, we have discussed a variety of different cases that can easily be accomplished using Cognitive Services or custom-built bespoke models. Whether you decide to use a commercial system like Moogsoft, SmartOps, or BigPanda or to build your own, the use of AI and machine learning in operations is here to stay, and being in the forefront of this cognitive revolution will certainly pay off.

References & Further Reading

Getting a Handle on AIOps: `http://fixstream.com/blog/getting-a-handle-on-aiops/`

What Is AIOps?: `http://www.bmc.com/blogs/what-is-aiops/`

What Will AIOps and Machine Learning Mean It?: `https://www.lakesidesoftware.com/blog/what-will-aiops-and-machine-learning-mean-it`

Gartner AIOps Market Guide: `https://www.moogsoft.com/resources/aiops/guide/gartner-2017-aiops-market-guide/`

Ways to Start with an AIOps Solution: `https://www.splunk.com/blog/2018/03/09/3-ways-to-get-started-with-an-aiops-solution.html`

## CHAPTER 8

AI Use Cases in the Industry

In the final chapter of this book, we want to show the art of the possible, connecting technology to real-world use cases and business scenarios. We are going to use the same problem–solution format in this chapter as in the rest of the book. However, we will not get into detailed discussion on the implementation details of the potential solutions at this point.

Financial Services

Early adopters of machine learning, banks and insurance companies mostly employ AI solutions for credit and risk assessment. However, with the sheer amount of data points and customer channels, AI can be applied in a host of ways to financial services. We present a few use cases here.

8-1. Mobile Fraud Detection

Problem

With the rapid rise in bank customers' interacting with their checking accounts using apps on their mobile devices, mobile bank fraud is on the rise as well. Phishing, vishing, and smishing are the most common ways hackers try to get unsuspecting customers to divulge personal information like login credentials, account numbers, etc., which are subsequently used to defraud the bank and/or the customer. By the time a hack is detected or reported, the damage has already been done, costing the bank millions of dollars as a result.

© Adnan Masood, Adnan Hashmi 2019
A. Masood and A. Hashmi, *Cognitive Computing Recipes*, https://doi.org/10.1007/978-1-4842-4106-6_8

Solution

To effectively create a machine-learning model to detect anomalies in customer behavior, login location, or money transfers, all telemetry data for each mobile channel engagement must be streamed and stored in a central location for analysis. Figure 8-1 presents a high-level architecture of what a cloud landscape would look like for a mobile fraud analysis solution.

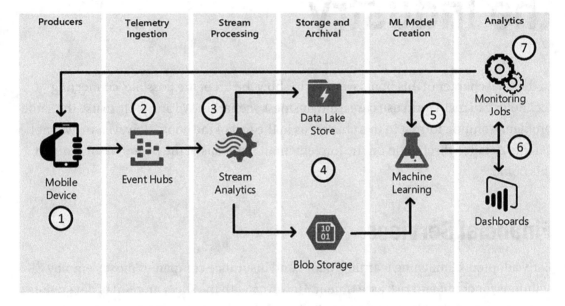

Figure 8-1. *High-level architecture of a mobile fraud detection solution*

1. Messages containing information about customer authentication, transactions, geographic location, activities, etc. are generated.

2. The generated messages are streamed through event hubs, which partition messages based on topics or categories.

3. Information is extracted from the partitioned messages by a Stream Analytics instance. Information from the messages can also be aggregated at this stage with data from other streams depending on requirements for reporting and machine-learning model training.

4. Data is stored in a data-lake store or archived in blob storage.

5. The stored/archived data is used to train, test, and build machine-learning models and is published for consumption. Model training and publishing can be done using a host of different tools such as Azure Machine Learning or TensorFlow.

6. Power BI dashboards consume the machine-learning models to provide predictive analytics to end users.

7. Automated monitoring jobs keep track of user activity in real-time, and if any anomalies are detected, they send out alerts or notifications to the affected users.

8-2. Float Optimization

Problem

One of the ways a bank makes money is through the issuance of short- and long-term loans to individuals and businesses. The amount of cash held by a bank determines how much is available to loan out. However, banks also have to maintain cash in their ATMs across many geographic locations. Unwithdrawn cash that sits in ATMs cannot be put to any use and negatively affects the bank's float, or ability to loan out money.

Solution

A solution I came across was developed by Capax Global (https://www.capaxglobal.com). To enable the bank to increase their float, and in turn increase their lending ability, the bank would need an accurate measure of exactly how much cash needs to be stored at each ATM location. Banks can take the historical cash-withdrawal time-series data from all ATM locations and apply machine-learning models to predict how much cash an ATM is expected to dispense on any day of the week. This would allow the bank to only store the needed amount of cash in each ATM without having to leave extra cash that can otherwise be used for lending to customers and generating a profit.

8-3. Accident Propensity Prediction (Insurance)

Problem

Auto insurance companies typically base their quotes on a number of factors, including the daily commute, the driving record, the general condition of the vehicle, the geographic location, and so on. There is no way to track the regular driving habits of the drivers or vehicle operators until it's too late and an accident claim is filed. Insurance companies want to be able to track how the insured asset is handled on a day-to-day basis and to also accurately predict a claim before one is filed to allow the insurer to provision for cash needed to service the claim.

Solution

The solution to the above-mentioned problem overlaps with the IoT-based AI discussed later in this chapter in the "Automotive and Manufacturing" section and entails streaming telemetry information from the vehicle, including adherence to traffic rules and speed limits, overuse of the vehicle, reckless driving, and so on. IoT devices in vehicles can transmit the data to a central data store for the training of AI models that can then predict the accident propensity of a driver or vehicle well in advance of an accident claim.

Healthcare

Healthcare AI solutions rely heavily on near real-time patient data streamed from bedside or point-of-care peripheral devices, which is combined with historical patient data to create and continuously update machine-learning models or accurately predict patient outcomes.

Like other sectors, healthcare has been challenged with the collection, aggregation, storage, and processing of data from disparate and dispersed sources. Public clouds such as Microsoft Azure have enabled these challenges, typically associated with on-premises or private clouds, to be addressed.

A high-level view and explanation of how data is generated, ingested, and subsequently used for AI using Microsoft Azure services is provided in Figure 8-2.

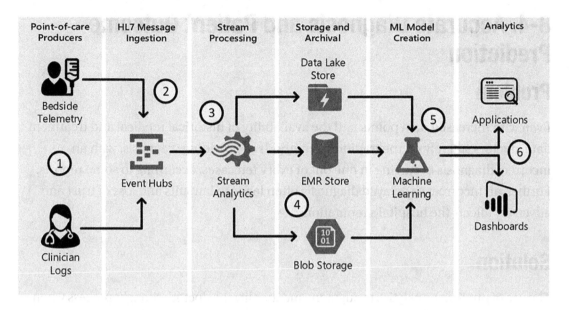

Figure 8-2. *High-level architecture of a healthcare analytics solution*

1. Messages are generated in the HL7 format by bedside peripheral devices as well as through mobile devices or tablets used by clinicians or caregivers to log patient care information.

2. The messages are streamed through event hubs, which partition messages based on topics or categories.

3. Information is extracted from the partitioned messages by a Stream Analytics instance using HL7QL (HL7 Query Language). Information can also be aggregated at this stage with data from other streams depending on requirements for reporting and machine-learning model training.

4. Data is stored in a data-lake store or blob storage, and the electronic medical record (EMR) for the patient is also updated if needed.

5. The stored/archived data is used to train, test, and build machine-learning models and is published for consumption. Model training and publishing can be done using a host of different tools such as Azure Machine Learning or TensorFlow.

6. Applications or Power BI dashboards consume the machine-learning models to provide predictive analytics to end users.

8-4. Accurate Diagnosis and Patient Outcome Prediction

Problem

Even with increased data points and the availability of historical medical and treatment data, doctors still rely on the traditional methods of providing diagnosis, with an incorrect diagnosis occurring in one out of every ten cases, according to some reports. Further, an incorrect or delayed diagnosis often leads to lawsuits and loss of trust and adversely affects the hospital's reputation.

Solution

The use of predictive analytics to augment and amplify the doctor's thought process when diagnosing a patient can greatly reduce and possibly eliminate diagnostic errors. Using data collected over longer periods of time to continually update the resulting machine-learning models used for diagnosis, combined with health data at the population level (the general population being served), can also drastically improve outcome prediction for inpatients.

8-5. Hospital Readmission Prediction and Prevention

Problem

The future of the Affordable Care Act (Obamacare) notwithstanding, both payers and providers are adversely affected when a previously discharged patient is readmitted to the hospital within a certain time period for the same ailment. Payers (health insurance companies) have to subsequently pay for the same treatment administered to the patient previously, whereas the providers' (hospitals') reputation is affected and their quality of care questioned for every readmission instance.

Solution

The solution to the preceding problem lies in generating machine-learning models based on data collected on previous readmissions along with patient data collected during the course of treatment. Once a model is finalized that accurately predicts a patient outcome and probability of readmission, clinicians can be alerted early on to allow them to rectify or course correct medications and/or treatment before the patient is discharged.

Automotive & Manufacturing

AI use cases in the automotive and manufacturing space revolve around using real-time device telemetry data for analytics and predictive maintenance from either an automobile or machinery or equipment.

The solution in almost all IoT use cases involves ingesting sensor data in the form of messages from a large number of IoT devices, storing the data for a particular length of time to generate predictive models, and finally providing analytics from the generated ML models.

A high-level logical diagram of an AI solution in the Azure cloud based on IoT sensor data is provided in Figure 8-3.

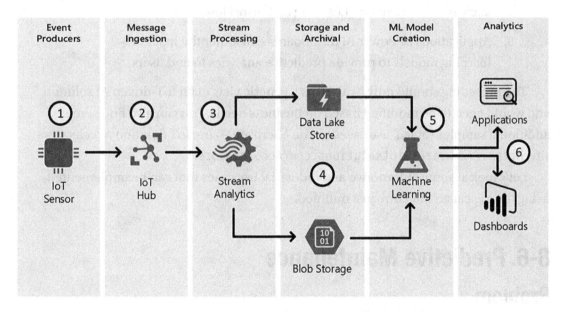

Figure 8-3. *High-level architecture of an IoT analytics solution*

An explanation of the logical flow is provided here:

1. IoT sensors attached to an automobile or piece of industrial equipment produce telemetry data.

2. Telemetry data from IoT sensors is received as messages by an IoT hub, which transmits the data to one or more consumer groups, each of which represents a set of consumers for a data stream.

3. An Azure Stream Analytics instance receives the data streamed from its consumer group and applies a set of predefined operations or calculations for the data in motion.

4. The resulting data is stored in a data-lake store or archived in blob storage.

5. The stored/archived data is used to train, test, and build machine-learning models and is published for consumption. Model training and publishing can be done using a host of different tools such as Azure Machine Learning or TensorFlow.

6. Applications or Power BI dashboards consumer the machine-learning models to provide predictive analytics to end users.

The preceding should only be used as a generic view of an IoT-driven AI solution and would need to be modified based on business needs. You can also find some additional samples for IoT use cases on the Microsoft Azure IoT Solution Accelerators site: `https://www.azureiotsolutions.com/Accelerators`.

Let's look at some automotive and industrial use cases that can be implemented using the logical architecture just outlined.

8-6. Predictive Maintenance
Problem

Periodic inspection of machinery in industrial units is carried out to identify equipment issues or damage before they become problematic, causing the entire unit or plant. The same care applies to the constant monitoring required for passenger and transport aircraft, both of which need to be given a detailed inspection after a certain number of hours of flying time. Manual inspections take a long time, potentially placing the machinery or aircraft out of commission while the inspection happens. Also, manual inspections are not entirely error-proof. Case in point is the engine failure on Southwest Flight 1380 in April 2018, reportedly caused by a fatigued section of the engine blade that was not visible to the human inspectors, causing the physical damage to go un-noticed and un-reported, leading to the mid-air disaster.

Solution

IoT sensors installed inside machinery or aircraft monitor and report the condition of each monitored unit to a central store for analysis and AI model creation. With the aggregated data combined with historical maintenance data, machine learning or AI models can be constructed to predict when maintenance might be required, thus giving operators the exact picture of when to anticipate maintenance.

Retail

Online retailers have traditionally used AI to recommend products or customize online experiences for shoppers based on previous shopping history and interests. However, the use of AI in traditional retail storefronts is also witnessing a rapid adoption. The following sections present a couple of use cases for use of artificial intelligence in traditional retail scenarios.

8-7. Personalized Storefront Experiences
Problem

Shoppers have been moving in droves from traditional retail stores to online e-commerce websites for over a decade. Traditional retailers, grocery stores, and warehouse clubs are finding it hard to build a strong customer base and retain customers over time since most customers choose to shop online because of the convenience and the customized experience offered by online shopping.

Solution

As competition between traditional brick-and-mortar retailers and online shopping sites heats up, retail businesses want to introduce technologies and experiences to draw the customer into the physical store.

To allow for a customized experience for each shopper, and without having to store a lot of information on individual shoppers and/or members, grocery stores or warehouse clubs can use facial recognition to identify a shopper when she is physically in the store so as to generate a personalized experience, using shelf-based monitors to display recommended brands or accompanying products based on the shopper's prior buying patterns.

The sequence diagram illustrated in Figure 8-4 and the explanation that follows captures a typical flow for the generation of a personalized experience for an individual shopper.

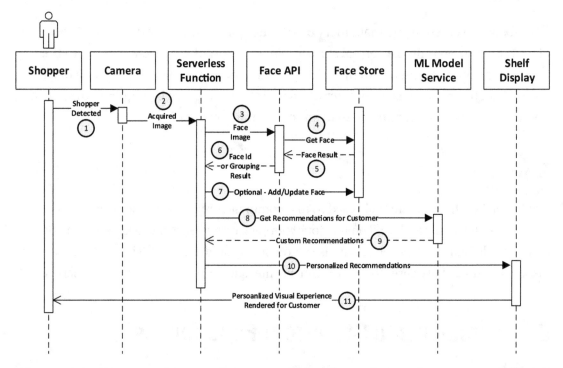

Figure 8-4. *Sequence diagram for a personalized storefront solution*

1. The shopper is detected when she approaches a certain aisle or section in the store, and a facial image is captured.

2. The acquired image is passed on to a serverless function.

3. The serverless function makes a call to the Face API with the acquired image.

4. The Face API queries the Face store behind the scenes to get the shopper profile.

5. The resulting shopper profile based on the facial image is returned from the Face store.

6. The facial identification or grouping result is returned by the Face API to the calling function.

7. If the profile does not exist, meaning the shopper is at the store or that section for the first time, the facial profile is stored or updated in the Face store.

8. Based on the face profile, a recommendation is requested from a machine-learning model or recommendation engine.

9. Custom recommendations are returned to the calling function.

10. The recommendation from the model are passed on to the shelf-mounted display for rendering to the shopper.

11. An animated graphical display for the recommendations is rendered and presented to the shopper.

8-8. Fast Food Drive-thru Automation Problem
Solution

Fast food restaurants have already introduced mobile apps for advance ordering and touch-based point-of-sale (POS) kiosks to enable an even faster serving of customers while driving more traffic to their more efficient locations because of the quality and speed of service. However, many fast food stores or branches struggle to efficiently serve their drive-thru customers, especially during peak breakfast and lunch hours where longer wait times just to order food drive customers away altogether.

Solution

To ensure the timely serving of drive-thru customers, AI can be applied to effectively speed up the traditional wait times in the drive-thru lanes by focusing on the time taken during the following three stages of the drive-thru ordering process:

a) Wait-to-order times: Time between the arrival of a customer in the drive-thru lane and the point at which she gets to the ordering microphone.

b) Time-to-order times: The time spent ordering the food at the microphone.

c) Order-serving times: The time it takes for the food to be served
    from the drive-thru window.

By reducing (b) and (c), (a) can be greatly reduced or eliminated. Let's look at the
sequence diagram in Figure 8-5 and its explanation to understand the solution. To
conserve real estate, I am using a single lane/lifeline for all cognitive services, i.e., Vision,
Face, Speech, etc., instead of creating a separate lifeline for each API.

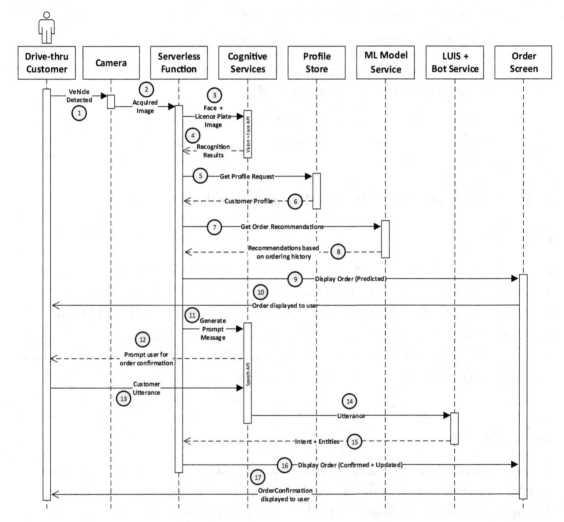

Figure 8-5. *Sequence diagram for a fast-food drive-thru automation solution*

1. The customer arrives at the fast food restaurant drive-thru, the vehicle is detected, and the images of the driver and the license plate are captured.

2. The acquired images are passed on to a serverless function.

3. The serverless function makes calls to the Vision and Face APIs with the acquired images.

4. The Vision and Face APIs return the recognition results back to the calling function.

5. Based on the recognition results, a profile request is made to a customer profile store or database.

6. The profile store returns the recognized customer's profile back to the calling function.

7. For the returned profile, a recommendation is requested from a machine-learning model or recommendation engine.

8. A predicted order based on the previous ordering history is returned to the calling function.

9. When the customer pulls up her car to the ordering display and microphone, the function makes a call to display the forecasted order on the display screen.

10. The forecasted order is presented to the drive-thru customer.

11. A request is also made by the function to the Speech API to play a custom message to the customer.

12. A voice message prompting order confirmation is played to the customer.

13. The customer communicates their intent to confirm the order verbally (using voice).

14. The utterance is passed on to a Bot Service LUIS endpoint.

15. The intent and entities extracted from the utterance are returned to the serverless function.

16.   If a confirmation intent is determined, the function makes a call to display the order confirmation to the user.

17.   The order confirmation is displayed (and possibly communicated through voice using the text-to-speech capability).

Concluding Remarks

We have attempted to demonstrate in the preceding chapters how to develop simple AI solutions to common business problems. The intent was to identify individual components and the general flow of the solution and outline steps to develop that solution on your own. We hope that once you understand the building blocks of a typical AI solution, applying that knowledge to another business use case will become easier.

In order for any enterprise technology solution to be successful, managing the three P's is of paramount importance: people, process, and platforms. A consistent or recurring theme you may have noticed in use cases discussed in this chapter was to treat machine learning and/or AI as simply a black box or swim lane, implying that beyond being just algorithms for building neural networks or machine-learning models, cognitive or intelligent applications are fairly similar to each other in terms of components and platforms. Where each use-case implementation differs is in the data collected for machine learning, the algorithms used to train the AI, and the user personas that derive value from the AI solution.

As you embark on developing your own intelligent applications, try not to get too bogged down by algorithms, frameworks, technical jargon, and a desire to know them all. AI is simple; putting all the solution components together and getting all the right data is the hard part.

I wish you the best of luck.

Public Datasets & Deep Learning Model Repositories

"Data is the new oil" is a quote whose attribution may require some research, but it is not far from truth. In today's world of AI and machine learning, researchers and practitioners in a variety of disciplines live and breathe data. The repositories across the web provide easy access to a multitude of datasets. The following is a brief list of the most popular datasets and search engines; far from being perfect, this list provides you with a glimpse of what data sources are available, and build your own.

Dataset Finders

Google Data Search

```
https://toolbox.google.com/datasetsearch
```

Recently released, Google Dataset Search lets a user find datasets wherever they're hosted, whether it's a publisher's site, a digital library, or an author's personal web page. Google Public Data Explorer provides public data and forecasts from a range of international organizations and academic institutions, including the World Bank, OECD, Eurostat, and the University of Denver.

Kaggle

https://www.kaggle.com/

Among the most popular data-science websites, Kaggle contains a variety of externally contributed interesting datasets.

UCI Machine Learning Repository

http://mlr.cs.umass.edu/ml/

Among the oldest sources of datasets on the web, and a great first stop when looking for interesting datasets from UC Irvine, it currently maintains 22 data sets as a service to the machine-learning community.

Popular Datasets

MNIST

http://yann.lecun.com/exdb/mnist/

MNIST is one of the most popular datasets put together by Yann LeCun and a Microsoft & Google Labs researcher. The MNIST database of handwritten digits has a training set of 60,000 examples and a test set of 10,000 examples.

Size: ~50 MB

Number of Records: 70,000 images in ten classes

MS-COCO

http://cocodataset.org/#home

COCO is a large-scale dataset and is rich for object detection, segmentation, and captioning. It has several features:

- Object segmentation

- Recognition in context

- Superpixel stuff segmentation

- 330K images (>200K labeled)

- 1.5 million object instances

- 80 object categories

- 91 stuff categories

- 5 captions per image

- 250,000 people with keypoints

Size: ~25 GB (Compressed)

ImageNet

http://image-net.org

ImageNet is a dataset of images that are organized according to the WordNet hierarchy. WordNet contains approximately 100,000 phrases, and ImageNet has provided around 1,000 images on average to illustrate each phrase.

Size: ~150 GB

Total number of images: ~1,500,000, each with multiple bounding boxes and respective class labels

Open Images Dataset

https://github.com/openimages/dataset

Open Images is a dataset of almost 9 million URLs for images. These images have been annotated with image-level labels and bounding boxes spanning thousands of classes. The dataset contains a training set of 9,011,219 images, a validation set of 41,260 images, and a test set of 125,436 images.

Size: 500 GB (compressed)

Number of Records: 9,011,219 images with more than 5k labels

VisualQA

http://visualqa.org

VQA is a dataset containing open-ended questions about images. These questions require an understanding of vision and language. Some of the interesting features of this dataset are as follows:

- 265,016 images (COCO and abstract scenes)

- At least 3 questions (5.4 questions on average) per image

- 10 ground truth answers per question

- 3 plausible (but likely incorrect) answers per question

- Automatic evaluation metric

Size: 25 GB (Compressed)

The Street View House Numbers (SVHN)

http://ufldl.stanford.edu/housenumbers/

This is a real-world image dataset for developing object-detection algorithms. This requires minimal data preprocessing. It is similar to the MNIST dataset mentioned in this list, but has more labeled data (over 600,000 images). The data has been collected from house numbers viewed in Google Street View.

Size: 2.5 GB

Number of Records: 6,30,420 images in ten classes

CIFAR-10

https://www.cs.toronto.edu/~kriz/cifar.html

This dataset is another one for image classification. It consists of 60,000 images of ten classes (each class is represented as a row in the above image). In total, there are 50,000 training images and 10,000 test images. The dataset is divided into six parts—five training batches and one test batch. Each batch has 10,000 images.

Size: 170 MB

Number of Records: 60,000 images in ten classes

Fashion-MNIST

`https://github.com/zalandoresearch/fashion-mnist`

Fashion-MNIST consists of 60,000 training images and 10,000 test images. It is a MNIST-like fashion product database. The developers believe MNIST has been overused so they created this as a direct replacement for that dataset. Each image is in greyscale and is associated with a label from ten classes.

Size: 30 MB

Number of Records: 70,000 images in ten classes

IMDB Reviews

`http://ai.stanford.edu/~amaas/data/sentiment/`

This is a dream dataset for movie lovers. It is meant for binary sentiment classification and has far more data than any previous datasets in this field. Apart from the training and test review examples, there is further unlabeled data for use as well. Raw text and preprocessed bag of words formats have also been included.

Size: 80 MB

Number of Records: 25,000 highly polar movie reviews for training and 25,000 for testing

Sentiment140

`http://help.sentiment140.com/for-students`

Sentiment140 is a dataset that can be used for sentiment analysis. A popular dataset, it is perfect to start off your NLP journey. Emotions have been pre-removed from the data. The final dataset has the following six features:

- polarity of the tweet
- ID of the tweet
- date of the tweet
- the query
- username of the tweeter
- text of the tweet

Size: 80 MB (Compressed)

Number of Records: 1,60,000 tweets

WordNet

https://wordnet.princeton.edu/

Mentioned in the ImageNet dataset, WordNet is a large database of English synsets. Synsets are groups of synonyms that each describe a different concept. WordNet's structure makes it a very useful tool for NLP.

Size: 10 MB

Number of Records: 117,000 synsets linked to other synsets by means of a small number of "conceptual relations."

Yelp Reviews

https://www.yelp.com/dataset

This is an open dataset released by Yelp for learning purposes. It consists of millions of user reviews, businesses attributes, and over 200,000 pictures from multiple metropolitan areas. This is a very commonly used dataset for NLP challenges globally.

Size: 2.66 GB JSON, 2.9 GB SQL, and 7.5 GB photos (all compressed)

Number of Records: 5,200,000 reviews, 174,000 business attributes, 200,000 pictures, and 11 metropolitan areas

The Wikipedia Corpus

http://nlp.cs.nyu.edu/wikipedia-data/

This dataset is a collection of the full text on Wikipedia. It contains almost 1.9 billion words from more than 4 million articles. What makes this a powerful NLP dataset is that you search by word, phrase, or part of a paragraph itself.

Size: 20 MB

Number of Records: 4,400,000 articles containing 1.9 billion words

EMNIST

https://www.westernsydney.edu.au/bens/home/reproducible_research/emnist

Extended MNIST (EMNIST) is a variant of the NSIT dataset, an extension of MNIST to handwritten letters. This dataset is designed as a more advanced replacement for existing neural networks and systems. There are different parts within the dataset that focus only on numbers, small, or capital English letters.

CLEVR

http://cs.stanford.edu/people/jcjohns/clevr/

This Diagnostic Dataset for Compositional Language and Elementary Visual Reasoning (http://vision.stanford.edu/pdf/johnson2017cvpr.pdf) is essentially a diagnostic dataset that tests a range of visual reasoning abilities. Led by Stanford's Fei Fei Li, this dataset was developed to enable research in developing machines that can sense and see about them.

Number of Records: Training set of 70,000 images and 699,989 questions, a validation set of 15,000 images and 149,991 questions, and a test set of 15,000 images and 14,988 questions

JFLEG

https://arxiv.org/pdf/1702.04066.pdf

This new corpus, "A Fluency Corpus and Benchmark for Grammatical Error Correction," is developed for evaluating grammatical error correction (GEC).

STL-10 dataset

http://cs.stanford.edu/~acoates/stl10/

This is an image-recognition dataset inspired by the CIFAR-10 dataset (https://www.cs.toronto.edu/~kriz/cifar.html) with some improvements. With a corpus of 100,000 unlabeled images and 500 training images, this dataset is best for developing unsupervised feature learning, deep learning, and self-taught learning algorithms.

Uber 2B Trip Dataset

https://www.kaggle.com/fivethirtyeight/uber-pickups-in-new-york-city
https://github.com/fivethirtyeight/uber-tlc-foil-response

This repository contains data from over 4.5 million Uber pickups in NYC, from April to September 2014, and 14.3 million more Uber pickups from January to June 2015.

Maluuba NewsQA Dataset

`https://github.com/Maluuba/newsqa`

Microsoft-owned AI research firm put together a crowd-sourced machine-reading dataset for developing algorithms capable of answering questions requiring human-level comprehension and reasoning skills. This dataset of CNN news articles has over 100,000 question–answer pairs.

YouTube 8M Dataset

`https://research.google.com/youtube8m/download.html`

The biggest dataset available for training with a whopping 8 million YouTube videos tagged with objects within them. Done in collaboration with Google, the YouTube 8M is a large-scale labeled video dataset developed to push research on video understanding, noise data modeling, transfer learning, and domain adaptation approaches for video.

SQuAD—The Stanford Question-Answering Dataset

`https://stanford-qa.com/`

The Stanford Question-Answering Dataset (SQuAD) is a new reading-comprehension dataset consisting of 100,000+ questions posed by crowdworkers on a set of Wikipedia articles where the answer to each question is a segment of text from the corresponding reading passage. We analyze the dataset to understand the types of reasoning required to answer the questions, leaning heavily on dependency and constituency trees. We build a strong logistic regression model, which achieves an F1 score of 51 percent, a significant improvement over a simple baseline (20 percent). However, human performance (86.8 percent) is much higher, indicating that the dataset presents a good challenge problem for future research.

CoQA—A Conversational Question-Answering Challenge

`https://stanfordnlp.github.io/coqa/`

CoQA is a large-scale dataset for building Conversational Answering systems. The goal of the CoQA challenge is to measure the ability of machines to understand a text passage and answer a series of interconnected questions that appear in a conversation.

CNN/Daily Mail Dataset—DeepMind Q&A Dataset

https://cs.nyu.edu/~kcho/DMQA/

CNN: This dataset contains the documents and accompanying questions from the news articles of CNN. There are approximately 90k documents and 380k questions.

DailyMail: This dataset contains the documents and accompanying questions from the news articles of *Daily Mail*. There are approximately 197k documents and 879k questions.

Code to obtain the CNN/Daily Mail dataset (non-anonymized) for summarization by Abigail See, Stanford University: https://github.com/abisee/cnn-dailymail.

Data.gov

https://www.data.gov/

Data from multiple U.S. government agencies and can range from government budgets to school performance scores.

Other Datasets

Food Environment Atlas: https://catalog.data.gov/dataset/food-environment-atlas-f4a22

School system finances: https://catalog.data.gov/dataset/annual-survey-of-school-system-finances

Chronic disease data: https://catalog.data.gov/dataset/u-s-chronic-disease-indicators-cdi-e50c9

The U.S. National Center for Education Statistics: https://nces.ed.gov/

The U.K. Data Centre: https://www.ukdataservice.ac.uk/

Data USA: http://datausa.io/

Quandl—Economic and financial data: https://www.quandl.com/

World Bank Open Data: https://data.worldbank.org/

International Monetary Fund data on international finances: https://www.imf.org/en/DataFinancial Times Market Data: https://markets.ft.com/data/

Google Trends: http://www.google.com/trends?q=google&ctab=0&geo=all&date=all&sort=0

Labelme: http://labelme.csail.mit.edu/Release3.0/browserTools/php/dataset.php

LSUN—Scene understanding with many ancillary tasks (room layout estimation, saliency prediction, etc.): `http://lsun.cs.princeton.edu/2016/`

COIL100 —100 different objects imaged at every angle in a 360 rotation: `http://www1.cs.columbia.edu/CAVE/software/softlib/coil-100.php`

Visual Genome—Visual knowledge base with captioning of ~100K images: `http://visualgenome.org/`

Labeled Faces in the Wild—13,000 labeled images of human faces: `http://vis-www.cs.umass.edu/lfw/`

Stanford Dogs Dataset—Contains 20,580 images and 120 different dog-breed categories: `http://vision.stanford.edu/aditya86/ImageNetDogs/`

Indoor Scene Recognition—67 indoor categories and a total of 15,620 images:`http://web.mit.edu/torralba/www/indoor.html`

Multi-domain sentiment analysis dataset—features product reviews from Amazon: `http://www.cs.jhu.edu/~mdredze/datasets/sentiment/`

Stanford Sentiment Treebank—Standard sentiment dataset with sentiment annotations: `http://nlp.stanford.edu/sentiment/code.html`

Twitter U.S. Airline Sentiment: `https://www.kaggle.com/crowdflower/twitter-airline-sentiment`

Amazon Reviews: !35 million reviews from Amazon spanning 18 years: `https://snap.stanford.edu/data/web-Amazon.html`

Google Books Ngrams—A collection of words from Google books: `https://aws.amazon.com/datasets/google-books-ngrams/`

Wikipedia Links data—The full text of Wikipedia. The dataset contains almost 1.9 billion words from more than 4 million articles. You can search by word, phrase, or part of a paragraph itself: `https://code.google.com/p/wiki-links/downloads/list`

Gutenberg eBooks List—Annotated list of ebooks from Project Gutenberg: `http://www.gutenberg.org/wiki/Gutenberg:Offline_Catalogs`

Jeopardy—Archive of more than 200,000 questions from the quiz show *Jeopardy*: `http://www.reddit.com/r/datasets/comments/1uyd0t/200000_jeopardy_questions_in_a_json_file/`

SMS Spam Collection in English—A dataset that consists of 5,574 English SMS spam messages: `http://www.dt.fee.unicamp.br/~tiago/smsspamcollection/`

Yelp Reviews—An open dataset released by Yelp, contains more than 5 million reviews: `https://www.yelp.com/dataset`

UCI's Spambase—A large spam email dataset, useful for spam filtering: `https://archive.ics.uci.edu/ml/datasets/Spambase`

Berkeley DeepDrive BDD100k—100,000 videos of 1,100-hour-plus driving experiences: `http://bdd-data.berkeley.edu/`

Baidu Apolloscapes—26 different semantic items, such as cars, bicycles, pedestrians, buildings, street lights, etc.: `http://apolloscape.auto/`

Comma.ai—More than seven hours of highway driving, including car's speed, acceleration, steering angle, and GPS: `https://archive.org/details/comma-dataset`

Oxford's Robotic Car—Over 100 repetitions of the same route through Oxford, U.K.: `http://robotcar-dataset.robots.ox.ac.uk/`

Deep-Learning Models

BVLC Model Zoo

`https://github.com/BVLC/caffe/wiki/Model-Zoo`

Model Depot—Open, Transparent Machine Learning for Engineers

Discover and share the right pre-trained machine learning model for every problem, project, or application: `https://modeldepot.io`.

Azure AI Gallery

`https://gallery.azure.ai`

Enables growing community of developers and data scientists to share their analytics solutions in Azure

Models and Examples Built with TensorFlow

`https://github.com/tensorflow/models`

Open ML

https://www.openml.org

An open, collaborative, frictionless, and automated machine-learning environment.

Datasets are automatically analyzed, annotated, and organized online; machine-learning pipelines are automatically shared from many libraries. Offers extensive APIs to integrate OpenML into your own tools and scripts; reproducible results (e.g., models and evaluations) for easy comparison and reuse; ability to collaborate in real-time, right from your existing tools; ability to make your work more visible, reusable, and easily citable; and open source tools to automate experimentation and model building.

Index

A

Printed in the United States
By Bookmasters